VERA
MILES

VERA
MILES

THE HITCHCOCK BLONDE WHO GOT AWAY

CHRISTOPHER McKITTRICK

UNIVERSITY PRESS OF KENTUCKY

Published by the University Press of Kentucky,
scholarly publisher for the Commonwealth,
serving Bellarmine University, Berea College, Centre
College of Kentucky, Eastern Kentucky University,
The Filson Historical Society, Georgetown College,
Kentucky Historical Society, Kentucky State University,
Morehead State University, Murray State University,
Northern Kentucky University, Spalding University,
Transylvania University, University of Kentucky,
University of Louisville, University of Pikeville, and
Western Kentucky University.
All rights reserved.

Editorial and Sales Offices: The University Press of Kentucky
663 South Limestone Street, Lexington, Kentucky 40508-4008
www.kentuckypress.com

Cataloging-in-Publication data is available from the Library of Congress.

ISBN 978-1-9859-0219-0 (hardcover : alk. paper)
ISBN 978-1-9859-0221-3 (pdf)
ISBN 978-1-9859-0222-0 (epub)

This book is printed on acid-free paper meeting
the requirements of the American National Standard
for Permanence in Paper for Printed Library Materials.

Manufactured in the United States of America.

Member of the Association
of University Presses

Cheers to Eric Roth and Nancy Ward
for getting me started in "Hollywood" (Sherman Oaks)

Contents

Preface
The (Other) Girl

"What in the world can you write about me?" actress Vera Miles asked the *Los Angeles Mirror* while doing a promotional interview for her 1958 film *The FBI Story* on the Warner Bros. studio lot in Burbank, Los Angeles, California. "I don't make any exciting headlines like Liz and Eddie. I'm just a happily married mother with three children who enjoys making pictures."[1]

Though her statement stems from Miles's long history of downplaying her stature in Hollywood, decades later, that remains a valid question. Miles is most remembered today for the movies she made with renowned filmmakers John Ford and Alfred Hitchcock, three of which—*The Searchers*, *Psycho*, and *The Man Who Shot Liberty Valance*—still frequently appear on greatest-movies lists and have all been selected for preservation in the US National Film Registry by the Library of Congress for their cultural significance. And while Miles's career is most often the focus of scholars of Ford and Hitchcock, those three films alone barely scratch the surface of her fifty-year career in Hollywood. Miles appeared in nearly two hundred television programs, including dozens of pilots, yet—mostly by choice—was never a regular on any series. She made six films for Walt Disney Studios, and Walt Disney himself referred to her as his "favorite" actress on more than one occasion. She starred in films opposite some of the biggest stars in Hollywood history, including John Wayne, James Stewart, Henry Fonda, Bob Hope, and Joan Crawford, and managed to do the once-thought impossible by starring in the box office hit sequel to *Psycho* twenty-three years after the original film. While it is also true that Miles never made headlines quite like "Liz and Eddie" (better known as Hollywood stars Elizabeth Taylor and Eddie Fisher, who famously were married after having an affair), the four-times married Miles still had her share of Hollywood sensationalism, including getting fired by eccentric billionaire Howard Hughes for marrying one of his favorite drivers and a short-lived marriage to one of the Tarzan stars—all while raising four children.

Despite Miles having such a successful career in the golden age of Hollywood through the 1990s, much of what has been written about her since her retirement from the screen focuses on the experiences of another actress entirely, all in the context of the two films she made with Alfred Hitchcock—*The Wrong Man* (1956) and *Psycho* (1960)—and one film that she ultimately didn't make with Hitchcock, *Vertigo* (1958). Miles's accomplishments as an actress and in her personal life have frequently been treated as footnotes to the story of other actresses and their associations with Hitchcock.

The public perception of Hitchcock and his methods as one of the premier filmmakers of the twentieth century can be divided into two distinct periods: before the publication of biographer Donald Spoto's 1983 book, *The Dark Side of Genius: The Life of Alfred Hitchcock*, and after the contents of the book had been digested by both film scholars and the general public. Published three years after the death of Hitchcock, the book details many aspects of his career that were hitherto unknown outside of his professional circle. The most sensational details in *The Dark Side of Genius*, which were naturally pounced on by the international press, are extensive interviews with actress Tippi Hedren, the star of Hitchcock's films *The Birds* (1963) and *Marnie* (1964), who for the first time spoke about the emotional and mental abuse that she said she endured while she was committed to a five-year exclusive contract with Hitchcock. Hedren's revelations sparked a critical revaluation of Hitchcock's oeuvre, and while he was generally no less acclaimed as an artist for creating some of the most celebrated films of the mid-twentieth century, his reputation suffered over the salacious details of his relationship with Hedren. Before the publication of Spoto's book, Hitchcock was simply the Master of Suspense, who perhaps had some odd foibles. Afterward, he was viewed as a much more controversial, more complex figure.

Since the publication of *The Dark Side of Genius*, Hedren has continued to speak about the period that she was under contract to Hitchcock and shared even more detailed experiences with Spoto for his 2008 book *Spellbound by Beauty: Alfred Hitchcock and His Leading Ladies*. This book served as the basis of the 2012 HBO television film *The Girl*, which depicted the relationship between Hitchcock (portrayed by Toby Jones) and Hedren (portrayed by Sienna Miller). Because the film brought Hedren's allegations into a new light, it also inspired significant backlash and accusations of treating Hitchcock unfairly, since biopics are so often subject to creative license. Ardent defenders of the director questioned why some details of Hedren's various accounts of her mistreatment by Hitchcock varied on different occasions, and crew members and other actresses who had worked with Hitchcock—most notably Kim Novak, who starred in his 1958 film *Vertigo* in place of Miles, and Eva Marie Saint, who starred in his 1959 film *North by Northwest*—spoke out to say that while they did not dispute Hedren's personal accounts, they did not have the same experience working with the man. *The Girl*, marred by controversy, received little critical acclaim, and its surrounding controversy overshadowed the film itself. By her account, Hedren's relationship with Hitchcock as his protégée—no matter how beneficial it was for her career—was riddled with abuse. So much so that it warrants comparison to how Hitchcock worked with Miles, another actress he had signed to an exclusive personal contract. Seven years before Hitchcock had first glimpsed Hedren in a soda commercial and brought her to Hollywood, he had signed Miles, who had recently wrapped production on a career-breakthrough role in *The Searchers*, to a five-year contract.

Unlike Hedren, who had appeared in just one film—an uncredited role in the 1950 Columbia musical *The Pretty Girl*—followed by a successful decade-long career as a model before she was discovered by Hitchcock, Miles had an established, though inconsistently successful, career as an actress before meeting the director. After strutting the stage as a beauty pageant contestant—Miles was crowned Miss Kansas in 1948 and later that year was third runner-up in the Miss America pageant—she did what many beauty queens did in those years and headed to Hollywood. In the aftermath of the pageant, Miles signed a contract with RKO Pictures after turning down smaller initial offers from RKO and two other studios. RKO certainly had the financial resources to increase its offer as the studio had recently been taken over by millionaire industrialist Howard Hughes. While attending voice lessons on Hughes's dime, the future Vera Miles began a relationship with one of Hughes's drivers, Bob Miles, whom she married in November 1948. Despite competing in pageants under her birth name, Vera Ralston, she would use the name Vera Miles professionally, because another actress, the Czech-born figure-skater-turned-actress Věra Helena Hrubá, used the name Vera Ralston professionally (like Miles, the Czech-born Ralston would also star in films with John Wayne, 1945's *Dakota* and 1949's *The Fighting Kentuckian*).

Hughes would sell Miles's contract to 20th Century Fox in early 1949, though that studio would also have little use for her. But even away from Hughes's handlers, Miles's Hollywood career had a very slow start. During her first six years in Hollywood, Miles had few substantial film roles. As famed *Los Angeles Times* gossip columnist Hedda Hopper would later write about Miles, "One Hollywood studio after another put her under contract. She collected her salary, but was given nothing to do." She had her most notable early part in the 1955 adventure film *Tarzan's Hidden Jungle*, the twelfth (and final) Tarzan movie released by RKO Studios and the first to star Gordon Scott, a muscular newcomer who had been recruited by a talent agent who had been impressed by his physique while Scott was working as a lifeguard at the pool at the Sahara Hotel and Casino in Las Vegas. Scott would continue as Tarzan in four other films and would go on to portray other heroic characters like Samson and Zorro and became a star of

Italian sword-and-sandal epics. Significantly, Miles and Scott married in April 1956, just over a year after the release of *Tarzan's Hidden Jungle* (Vera and Bob Miles had divorced in 1954, though she retained his last name professionally for the rest of her career).[2]

Because the studios were underusing her in film, Miles would have her breakthrough on television. Between her film roles, Miles regularly appeared on the small screen in popular programs like *Crown Theatre, Medic, Four Star Playhouse, The Pepsi-Cola Playhouse, Science Fiction Theatre*, and *The Ford Television Theatre* (she would frankly tell the *Los Angeles Times* in May 1956 that she took the television roles "when I couldn't get any movie parts"). In fact, that is how she was discovered by Hitchcock when he spotted Miles in one of her television episodes as a rerun ("Many fans write that they have cursed reruns of popular shows but you can't get pretty Vera Miles to say a word against them because it was a rerun of her first *Medic* show that started her toward the top of the acting ladder," wrote the *Los Angeles Times* in October 1956).[3]

Hitchcock cast Miles in an episode of his new foray into television, the anthology series *Alfred Hitchcock Presents* on CBS. He was so taken by her performance, talent, and screen presence that he selected the episode as the season premiere and signed Miles to an exclusive five-year contract that called for three films a year. Before the end of the month, Hitchcock was already touting to the press that he had cast Miles in *The Wrong Man*, a Warner Bros. drama based on a true story about a New York City musician who was charged with committing robberies that he could not have possibly committed. Henry Fonda would star as the wrongfully accused man and Miles as his wife. Hitchcock also revealed at the time that he would be filming an adaptation of the recently released French novel *D'entre les morts (From among the dead)* by Boileau-Narcejac, a project that eventually became his 1958 film *Vertigo*. Hitchcock was positioning Miles as his favored leading lady, a role that had been abandoned by Grace Kelly—an Oscar-winning actress and previous star of three Hitchcock films who had recently left Hollywood to marry into European royalty.

Hopper would write much more about Miles in her column over the next several months, and, if taken at face value, her reporting detailed the strict terms of her contractual arrangement with Hitchcock. In her September 10, 1956, column, Hopper wrote that Hitchcock "refuses to allow his star, Vera Miles, to pose for cheesecake." Five days later, Hopper's column headline read "Vera Miles' Screen Career Skyrockets," with the copy calling the actress "the hottest player on the Paramount lot these days with producers bidding for her the way they're fighting for Tony Perkins" (the same Anthony Perkins whom she would costar with four years later in Hitchcock's *Psycho*). But it would be Hopper's colleague at the *Los Angeles Times*, Walter Ames, who began to publicly reveal the more complicated aspects of Miles's contract with Hitchcock in his reporting on October 25, 1956. "He has some unusual rules for her," Ames wrote. "She must wear either black, gray, or white and her only jewelry is to be pearls. It has something to do with bringing out her personality, according to the ace producer-director." Hitchcock worked with an eight-time Academy Award–winning costume designer, the famed Edith Head, to design a complete wardrobe for Miles to wear off-screen in addition to her wardrobe for their film and television projects together.[4]

However, as far as the press was concerned, this arrangement was not onerous to Miles. Hopper interviewed Miles for her November 11, 1956, column, with Miles calling Hitchcock "so wonderful" and thanking him for loaning her out to make films like *23 Paces to Baker Street* (a 20th Century Fox mystery film that is reminiscent of Hitchcock's *Rear Window*) and *Beau James* (a Bob Hope–starring Paramount Pictures biopic of New York City mayor Jimmy Walker).[5]

Production on *From among the Dead* was set to start in November 1956 with James Stewart and Miles, but Hitchcock was unhappy with the first version of the script by Maxwell Anderson, who had cowritten the screenplay for *The Wrong Man*, and production was delayed. But even the new March 1957 start date became questionable when Hitchcock experienced several medical problems in early 1957, including having to be hospitalized and then homebound because of a navel hernia and colitis and then rehospitalized because of gallstones in March.

In November 1956, Miles completed makeup and hairstyle tests for *Vertigo*, while Head had completed Miles's wardrobe by mid-February 1957. But then Miles further disrupted the lengthy prepro-duction period by telling Hitchcock in March while he was recovering that she was pregnant with her third child and would be unable to film the movie until later in the year. Even though filming on *Vertigo* would not start until September 30—the day before Miles gave birth—because Hitchcock was dissatisfied with the screenplay, Hitchcock cast actress Kim Novak, who was recommended to him by MCA president Lew Wasserman, to replace Miles.

On its May 1958 release, *Vertigo* received mixed reviews from crit-ics and performed poorly commercially, which severely disappointed Hitchcock. He never made a film with Stewart again, and Novak became one of the many prominent actresses who only appeared in a major role in one Hitchcock film, including Carole Lombard, Marlene Dietrich, Doris Day, Eva Marie Saint, and Janet Leigh.

Hitchcock appeared to never forgive Miles for leaving the project and ultimately lost interest in making her his next star. For her part, Miles never felt like she owed Hitchcock an apology for choosing motherhood over the movie. Hitchcock and Miles renegotiated their contract to allow her to now accept film roles without his approval and only owe him one film year—a scenario that also did not come to pass. Her role as Lila Crane in 1960's *Psycho* would be the most prominent work she did with Hitchcock before Miles's agent negotiated an end to her contract with Hitchcock at the end of that year.

Less than two weeks after Miles initially renegotiated her contract with Hitchcock, she signed a contract with Warner Bros. that gave her the first chance to work with her would-be *Vertigo* costar James Stew-art. She starred opposite Stewart in 1959's *The FBI Story* and again (much more memorably) in John Ford's 1962 Western *The Man Who Shot Liberty Valance*. In both films, Miles plays Stewart's wife, and the pair demonstrates strong on-screen chemistry that might have translated to the more complicated relationship between the two leads in *Vertigo*.

Much has been written about Hitchcock and Miles's largely unsuccessful partnership, but it has often been viewed through the lens of Hitchcock's later relationship with Hedren. The prevailing narrative has been that Hitchcock, hurt both professionally and personally by Grace Kelly's decision to remove her radiant presence from the screen after making three films with Hitchcock by marrying Prince Rainier III of Monaco, endeavored to never let another one of his preferred lead actresses slip from his grasp again (incidentally, Miles and Gordon Scott married the same week that Kelly married Prince Rainier III). Much of that narrative appears accurate, though it lacks the complexities of working in Hollywood in the 1950s and 1960s and also robs Miles of her own agency in her career with Hitchcock. In its simplest form, this narrative casts Kelly, Miles, and Hedren as a mere collective of objects of the director's obsession rather than considering each actress as an established professional with their own career paths in show business before working with Hitchcock.

Miles entered her contract with Hitchcock as an eight-year veteran of Hollywood, spending most of those years struggling to get by with whatever work she could get. On the other hand, Kelly was already well on her way to stardom when she began working with Hitchcock, while Miles was keeping her head above water with her television work to sustain her inconsistent film career. Coincidentally, both actresses appeared in acclaimed John Ford films shortly before they worked with Hitchcock—Kelly in 1953's *Mogambo*, for which she was nominated for an Academy Award for Best Supporting Actress, and Miles in *The Searchers*. But in Miles's case, her professional relationship with Hitchcock was intended to make her one of Hollywood's biggest stars of the late 1950s through the 1960s.

"In terms of perception, between the two of them, it was a very uneven relationship in terms of the power dynamic as director and actress," explains Rebecca McCallum, writer, speaker, editor, and creator/host of the *Talking Hitchcock* podcast. "But from what I've read she was very tenacious and very strong-willed and would not put up with that kind of behavior. I don't think she was someone who could have been molded, though that's obviously what Hitchcock was attempting to do."[6]

Meanwhile, too often, Hitchcock's behavior toward Hedren in the early 1960s has been conflated by commentators with his treatment of Miles in the mid- to late 1950s, portraying them both as victims in his impossible attempts to replicate Kelly. But despite some similarities between their careers with Hitchcock, Miles's and Hedren's experiences as his protégées were radically different. For example, while Miles, like Hedren, only made two films with Hitchcock, Miles's contract with Hitchcock (unlike Hedren's) allowed her to freely work on television—and in between the film roles that Hitchcock would allow her to take, she appeared on television in episodes of *Lux Video Theatre, Studio 57, Schlitz Playhouse, Climax!,* and *Colgate Theatre*. That is why when Miles received one of the initial stars on the Hollywood Walk of Fame in 1960, it was awarded for her television work, despite her ultimately being much more remembered today for her film performances. Miles's continuation of her television work during her contracted period with Hitchcock was an opportunity that Hedren refused to pursue. Hitchcock was also far more willing to loan Miles out for other films—she appeared in five films that were released between *The Wrong Man* and *Psycho* that were not directed by Hitchcock—than he was with Hedren, who would only agree to do two television episodes released in 1965 after their difficulties working together on *Marnie*. Kelly, of course, had none of these restrictions imposed on her by Hitchcock because she was a contracted MGM performer who had to be loaned to other studios for the three films she did with Hitchcock (Warner Bros. for *Dial M for Murder*, Paramount Pictures for both *Rear Window* and *To Catch a Thief*).

Miles did not speak with Spoto for *The Dark Side of Genius*, nor did she participate in Janet Leigh's 1995 book, *Psycho: Behind the Scenes of the Classic Thriller*, or various other retrospectives about Hitchcock's work. But most significantly, Miles disputed the prevailing narrative about Hitchcock's behavior toward her and was very critical of his portrayal in *The Dark Side of Genius*. But the fact that she has been less outspoken about her relationship with Hitchcock in the decades since has led to speculation and conjecture by commentators and critics. Miles largely withdrew from the public eye after starring in the 1989 television movie *The Hijacking of the Achille Lauro*, only appearing afterward as a guest star in two episodes of the mystery television series *Murder, She Wrote* in 1990 and 1991 and a small role in her final film, *Separate Lives*, released in 1995.

Despite ample interest in her work with Hitchcock, Ford, and Disney, Miles has remained silent. Yet her silence, which she has every right to maintain, should not obscure her underappreciated career in Hollywood. Unlike Kelly or even Hedren, Miles was never nominated for any significant awards, and her most famous films—two directed by Hitchcock and two directed by Ford—feature her in supporting roles. Yet after *Psycho*, Miles had a substantial career in television, appearing on some of the most popular television series of the 1960s through the 1980s, including *The Twilight Zone*, *Wagon Train*, *Route 66*, *The Fugitive*, *The Virginian*, *The Outer Limits*, *My Three Sons*, *I Spy*, *The Man from U.N.C.L.E.*, *Bonanza*, *Ironside*, *Gunsmoke*, *Hawaii Five-O*, *Cannon*, *Columbo*, *Fantasy Island*, *Mangum P.I.*, *The Love Boat*, *Little House on the Prairie*, and *Murder, She Wrote*. Even today, Miles remains a constant presence in classic television reruns, bolstered by many of these programs being available for new audiences on streaming services.

"What first comes to mind about Miles is how overlooked she is," says McCallum. "I think there is an earthiness and a relatability in Miles—I love the performances given by Grace Kelly and Ingrid Bergman, but there is something so grounded about Miles, in both *The Wrong Man* and *Psycho*. She feels like a woman I would be familiar with and who I recognize from my own life and that really helps facilitate a strong connection."[7]

Miles may not have had the superstar career that Hitchcock envisioned for her, but she remained a commanding presence in film and television for thirty-five years after the release of *Psycho*. Her fascinating history as a young working mother in Hollywood during a period that was not frequently kind to actresses over the age of twenty-five makes Vera Miles not just an anecdote of the history of the production of *Vertigo* but rather a gifted actor who deserved the spotlight as much as Kelly, Hedren, or any other of her contemporary actresses did.

1

From Boise City to Atlantic City

In a 1989 interview, Vera Miles was asked if she was aware of the critical consensus that she did not attain the level of stardom expected of an actress who appeared in multiple films by Hollywood masters John Ford and Alfred Hitchcock early in her career.

"Yes, I've heard all that before, that I didn't fulfill my potential," she responded. "What in hell do they think was my potential? Who sets potential anyway? As far as I'm concerned, I fulfilled my potential. I had four children. I supported them well and didn't leave them to be raised by anyone. That's all I set out to do, and I did it."[1]

Reviewing Miles's nearly fifty-year career in Hollywood, it's clear that she often chose to put her family first—in fact, Miles was unable to appear in what would have perhaps been the most significant role of her career in the 1958 Alfred Hitchcock film *Vertigo* because she was pregnant. On the other hand, few working mothers in Hollywood worked as rigorously as Miles did from the 1950s through the 1970s, when barely a month went by that she wasn't featured on television, even while she was pregnant. Her dedication to her career resulted in Miles appearing in hundreds of hours of television content by the end of her career in 1995. And yet, despite never fulfilling her "potential," Miles became a success in Hollywood by becoming an incredibly prolific actress, so much so that she became a "type" all unto herself. A feature on her best television work in *Films in Review* described Miles as "[having] a beautiful face, a good figure, and a genteel bearing. The adjective 'lady-like' is often applied to her. The American public reacts favorably to her almost unanimously. Fundamental reason: she projects *both* sexuality and integrity (even when she's 'a heavy')."[2]

If Miles truly just set out to have children and support them, she could have found much easier paths to that than in Hollywood. She could have accomplished that by staying in Wichita, Kansas.

Miles, like every other film star, is granted a bit of creative license by Hollywood to tell her backstory in whatever way she chooses. Even as late as the 1950s, Hollywood remained firmly committed to star mythmaking. After all, this was the industry that rebranded the former University of Southern California football player Marion Morrison with the more masculine moniker John Wayne and even shaved a year off the age of child star Shirley Temple to make her seem even more precocious and talented than she already was at her young age.

When Miss Vera Ralston—soon to become Mrs. Vera Miles—began her career in Hollywood, she had less opportunity to cultivate such an image makeover. She had already been on the national stage, literally, as an eighteen-year-old contestant in the 1948 Miss America pageant, and unless she wanted to pretend that she flouted the rule of the competition at the time that said contestants were required to be eighteen years old, studios would not be able to declare she was younger if they wanted to keep that famous competition as part of her official backstory. Likewise, her married name proved convenient in avoiding confusion with Czech Olympic figure-skater-turned-actress Věra Helena Hrubá, who began using the stage name Vera Hruba Ralston in 1944, though it did take several years for Miles's hometown newspaper, the *Wichita Eagle*, to finally refer to her by her married name (and, by that time, she had been divorced from her first husband, Bob Miles, for several years). The professional confusion between the stars continued, however. Even as late as 1956, famed gossip columnist Sheilah Graham was conflating the two Veras as a single, extremely multitalented starlet, and in June 1956, a Wichita television station aired a film that was promoted as starring hometown star Vera Miles but actually starred Vera Hruba Ralston (the host of the program apologized during the first commercial break).

But where Miles could do some mythmaking of her own was in her history before she walked the Miss America stage in Atlantic City, New Jersey, though her youth was already full of hardship before any embellishment took place. Miles was born August 23, 1930, in Boise City, Oklahoma, to Thomas A. Ralston, an ordained minister in the Church of Christ who alternately worked as a farmer and a laborer, and Bernice Wyrick. Many sources give her birth year as 1929, but the family's entry in the 1930 US Federal Census does not list Vera Ralston (the 1950 US Federal Census also gives Miles's age as nineteen years old, meaning she would have been turning twenty in August of that year, and other government sources put her year of birth as 1930). The family normally resided on a farm in Pratt, Kansas, more than two hundred miles northeast of Boise City. Thomas had been born in Woodward County, Oklahoma Territory, on May 23, 1902 (five years before Oklahoma would become the forty-sixth state), while Bernice was a native of Missouri born in 1905. Thomas served in the navy for a short period from October 1920 to February 1921 (Thomas's headstone in the Nashville National Cemetery indicates that he served in World War I, though his military records show that he did not enlist until nearly two years after Armistice Day).

Miles was the fifth and youngest of Thomas and Bernice's children after Thelma (born 1923), Thomas Jr. (born 1924), Elmer (born 1926), and Wanda (born 1928). Miles was born in tragic circumstances. Her sister Wanda (known as Wana), died at just one year old after ingesting several sleeping pills that had been prescribed to their father (Wana, like Vera, is not listed in the family's 1930 Federal Census). Miles has rarely spoken about the older sister she had never known, but it appears that Miles's birth brought little comfort to a family that was facing such grief. Just ten months before Miles's birth, the Wall Street Crash of October 24 plunged much of the world into the Great Depression, though the ensuing economic crisis did not seem to change the circumstances of the already strapped family much.

Later profiles of Miles would say that Thomas would abandon the family and move to Alaska (some even say he was doing missionary work in the Last Frontier), but that truncates the events that followed. Thomas and Bernice divorced in the early 1930s, and while Thomas would end up in Alaska sometime later, he remained in Pratt, Kansas, for several years. He married Edna Madeline Houghtaling, over a dozen years his junior, in 1935. Thomas ran for Congress as a Democrat in the now nonexistent 7th District of Kansas in 1936 on a platform of primarily supporting the old-age pension plan proposed by California doctor and political activist Francis Townsend that would eventually influence the establishment of Social Security. Thomas won the Democratic primary and would subsequently run against incumbent Republican Clifford R. Hope in the general election. Though Thomas won the primary, he failed to unseat Hope, who held the seat from 1927 to 1943—the entire lifespan of the district. Shortly after the election loss, Thomas and Edna and their first child, a daughter named Martha, moved to Washington State. In 1939, the family was living outside of Mineral, Washington, where they had two more children (both boys) and ran a camera shop, though Thomas also briefly lived in Luna, New Mexico (his draft card, dated October 1940, indicates he was working for the Atchison, Topeka & Santa Fe Railway in Belen, New Mexico, at the time). During World War II, he worked as an engineer on army transport ships. After the war, the Ralston family split their time between Seattle and Alaska by living on a forty-foot fishing boat named the *Lo-Rayne* as Thomas worked as a chief engineer for tugboats in both states. He and his wife later retired to Southern California.

What relationship Miles had with her father during these years is not clear, though it was unlikely to be close because of the considerable distance between them once he left their family and then later when he moved away from Kansas with his new family. She would tell *Los Angeles Times* beauty columnist Lydia Lane in January 1970 that because her father was a minister, he had taught her the importance of character by telling her, "Once you know what is right, stubbornly adhere to it." They had a relationship later in her life, with Thomas serving as the minister for Miles's daughter Kelley's first marriage in 1968.[3]

Miles would recall the years following her parents' divorce as difficult ones. "I remember that there wasn't enough food in the house to feed us," she recalled to *Parade* in January 1957. "We never had enough money." Her older siblings did what they could to escape the difficult family situation. In Miles's earliest years, her older sister, Thelma, helped raise her, but Thelma married at age fifteen in 1938 and moved in with her spouse's family. Older brothers Thomas Jr. and Elmer joined the Civilian Conservation Corps, and then Thomas enlisted in the army and Elmer enlisted in the navy during World War II.[4]

Miles would later speak of having no social life because of her shyness and an inferiority complex. With her mother earning only about twelve dollars per week, Miles spoke about busing tables with her mother at age eleven and said that she took a job in a pasteboard factory at age twelve. She also claimed that she didn't last in the latter position after smashing both of her fingers (in the September 1957 issue of *Photoplay*, Miles would instead claim she worked nine hours a day in a paper box factory at age fourteen and nearly lost both her hands in a machinery accident). When Miles was a teenager, she and her mother moved to Wichita to live with her grandmother, though Miles would later claim that arrangement was hardly any better. "We were two generations apart," Miles told *Screenland* about her grandmother. "We were like strangers, and we couldn't live together." Shortly afterward, Bernice moved to Colorado for a job at a hotel, leaving Miles with her grandmother. Decades later, Miles would tell conflicting stories about the jobs she had and the places she lived as a teenager. Typically, she claimed that at age fourteen she moved to a room at the YWCA in Wichita, and in addition to working in the cafeteria at the YWCA in the mornings, she began working at Western Union after lying to the company about her age. "Everywhere I worked I lied about my age," she told *Parade*. "I had no close girls friends [*sic*], no companionship—nothing except the terrible knowledge that I was really poor and alone in the world." She recounted that her arduous daily routine consisted of waitressing in the morning, going to school, and working at Western Union from 4 p.m. to midnight; in her downtime, she studied to be a teacher, having no interest in acting at the time.[5]

In a somewhat surprising amount of actual investigative journalism in what otherwise reads as a puff piece promoting Miles as Hitchcock's next big star, the January 3, 1957, issue of *Parade* featured a profile of Miles titled "Vera Miles: She's Hitchcock's Newest Acting Find" that questioned the veracity of Miles's origin story, claiming it could find no one it could contact who could remember "Vera going hungry in Kansas or slaving in a pasteboard factory or living at the YWCA for more than a month or so." Western Union's employment records indicated that she only worked there for a few weeks, and she didn't get a job with Western Union until April 1948, when Miles was seventeen. Miles's maternal grandmother, Frances Walker, told *Parade* that Vera lived in her nine-room house and that Miles's mother earned a living managing coffee shops, not waiting tables. "I don't know how those stories started that Vera almost starved as a child," said Walker. "That girl never worked in a pasteboard factory, not to my knowledge. She never worked in any factory. She won a beauty contest after graduating from high school and went right off to Atlantic City with her mother." Bernice Ralston was still managing a coffee shop in Colorado Springs, Colorado, when the *Parade* article was published. Bernice also supported her mother's version of Miles's past and also claimed that contrary to Miles's version of her childhood, the future star had an interest in becoming an actress at a very early age. "It's true we never had much money," she told *Parade*.

> Who did in Kansas during the depression? But Vera never had to work very hard. The war broke out in 1941, and my two sons signed up. That meant I got allotment checks when Vera was only 11. Naturally we didn't have many luxuries. I can't remember Vera's father ever sending any support money. But the child never went hungry. I'd say she had a fairly happy youth. She was always a sweet, good-looking child who wanted to dress up in my clothes. "Mommy,"

she used to say when she was little, "I wanna grow up and become a famous movie star."

Miles herself would seemingly confirm her early acting ambitions in a June 1958 newspaper column that she guest wrote, writing, "I've wanted to be an actress since I was big enough to recite Tennyson's 'The Brook.'" Regardless of when she was bitten by the acting bug, Miles did not act in high school—she would later confess that she tried out for a play, didn't get the part, and was too deflated from the rejection to try acting again.[6]

Other aspects of her origin story would change later in Miles's life. She spoke far more warmly about her "stranger" grandmother in a 1974 *Los Angeles Times* interview, casting Frances as a pillar of her family's strength in a story straight out of a Hollywood production. "When I see these spoiled and neurotic people around me, I am so grateful that I was brought up close to the soil," explained Miles. "It taught me to be self-reliant and to be in tune with nature. I had an inspiring example in my grandmother, who possessed the true pioneer spirit. I will never forget a big cyclone that sent us all to the cellar to huddle together. When we came out, our house and barn—everything—had been demolished. My grandmother never shed a tear, but turned to the group and said, 'Well, if we want to have supper tonight, we had better start gathering firewood.' She never uttered a word of complaint."[7]

Despite later claiming she was nearly friendless, isolated, miserable, and alone as a teenager, Miles was popular enough to be occasionally named in the society pages of the *Wichita Eagle* and was also a candidate for the queen of the Wichita North High School junior-senior prom, held on February 7, 1948. She was photographed among the other candidates for prom king and queen in the February 1, 1948, edition of the *Wichita Eagle*. Miles was elected prom queen and was pictured again in the *Wichita Eagle* on February 9, alongside prom king Bob Shank. She would also reveal later that she had an on-again, off-again romance with another Wichita North student who was a year older than she was, Kent Frizzell. The following month, Miles was selected as the "Girl of the Month" of March 1948 by the Wichita Transportation Company to appear in advertisements on city buses. She didn't intend to enter the competition; while working for the school newspaper and trying to secure an advertisement from Estelle Compton School for Models, a small chain of charm schools, she was asked by the agency to enter the contest. She was offered the opportunity to attend the modeling school for a sixteen-week course. She didn't have to wait very long to start along her stated career path of becoming a professional model—the Compton School secured her an appearance in the *Wichita Eagle*'s fashion column on April 4, modeling clothes alongside two other Compton students. She also posed for "Swing Girl" photos for *Swing*, the quarterly magazine for the Kansas City–based AM radio station. The April 25, 1948, edition of the *Wichita Eagle* announced that Miles was hired as the "new teletype operator for Western Union" while she was also attending the Estelle Compton School, which appears to be the origin of her stories about working there at a much younger age. But it's surprising that she even had time to work at Western Union with how quickly her career as a model picked up (in a 1997 article, the *Wichita Eagle* claimed that Miles had even modeled nude for a painting class at the local art association). In an interview with the *Atlantic City Press* during the Miss America pageant, Miles said she was "on furlough" from her telephone operator job at Western Union but didn't plan to return to it since she was named head instructor of the Wichita Estelle Compton School for Models before the pageant. Ultimately, Miles only worked at Western Union for about four months.[8]

Miles's Hollywood version of her formative years depicts her as a lost, lonely little girl who, after barely being able to scrape by to survive by doing whatever odd jobs she could, stumbled into a successful modeling career that was followed by Hollywood stardom by her sheer force of professional drive. That story is certainly more compelling than the accounts of Miles's youth being fairly typical of a pretty teenager growing up in the 1940s. While the truth likely lies somewhere in the middle, Miles would be a rare breed in Hollywood if she hadn't embellished her backstory. More significantly, it was her drive to succeed that played an essential role in her success, which is apparent no matter which narrative you accept about her youth.

It was at that time that Miles's modeling career led to beauty pageants, and her social calendar filled up very quickly. On August 11, Miles was selected as Miss Kansas in a Kansas City pageant and thus would represent the state the following month in Atlantic City at the national Miss America pageant. She was also selected as the National Baseball Queen and presented the Coca-Cola trophy to the winners of the 1948 National Baseball Congress World Series held in Wichita. The baseball tournament brought teams from all over the United States and thousands of spectators to Lawrence Stadium in Wichita, where Miles was featured in the tournament's opening ceremonies parade. During the tournament, the main headquarters of Estelle Compton, Inc. in Chicago whisked her away to train her under the titular Compton herself to become the head instructor of the Wichita school after the Miss America pageant. On August 18, 1948, Miles left for Chicago. While in Chicago, Miles was scheduled for a screen test for Metro-Goldwyn-Mayer on August 22. What became of that screen test isn't clear, but it may have resulted in one of several initial offers that Miles turned down before she accepted a contract with RKO. She returned to Wichita to present the Coca-Cola trophy to the winners of the baseball tournament, the Fort Wayne General Electrics from Indiana, on August 31.

After a short stay in Kansas City, Miles arrived with her mother in Atlantic City on September 6, 1948, for the Miss America pageant. The New Jersey coastal resort city, dubbed "the world's playground" for its famous pier, boardwalk, beaches, and nightlife, had established the pageant in 1921 as an annual early fall event to help extend its summer season. The formative years of the pageant faced controversy from various religious groups who believed it promoted lasciviousness, and by the mid-1930s, the pageant made efforts to reform itself as a showcase for beautiful and talented young women who would be awarded college scholarships for placing in the finals.

Miles certainly fit the definition of *beautiful*. When she entered the pageant, her measurements were given as five-foot-five, 115 pounds, 37-inch bust, 24-inch waist, and 19-inch thighs. The pageant proceedings began on the day after Labor Day, Tuesday, September 7, launching with the annual parade of the contestants along the famed Atlantic City boardwalk. The following day, Miles won the swimsuit portion of the competition. She did not fare as well in the talent competition later that week—Miles would later claim that her "talent" presentation simply consisted of her telling the judges that she didn't have any talent. In reality, Miles's talent routine consisted of her giving a three-minute speech entitled "Modeling as a Career," which included her explaining that she intended to use any scholarship money that she might win for voice and music training because she didn't have any other talents. Her bio in the 1948 Miss America Pageant's Yearbook supports that, as it lists voice and music training as her ambition along with photography as her favorite hobby. "I don't know how those fools back in Kansas ever picked me," Miles told the *Atlantic City Press* before the talent competition. "But I'm going to talk my heart out out there tonight. I'm just fool enough to want to be something." Entertainment columnist Earl Wilson was one of the judges of Miss America 1948, and he would later recall Miles's "no talent" speech in several of his columns over the years after Miles became famous.[9]

Despite her lack of "talent," Miles was chosen by the judges as one of the six finalists for the competition's grand finale on September 11. The crown was awarded to Miss Minnesota, BeBe Shopp, and Miles placed fourth in the competition and was named third runner-up. As her prize, Miles received a $2,000 scholarship, which she intended to use to attend Wichita University to study acting after she returned home to Kansas.

Hollywood talent scouts had become standard attendees of the Miss America competition since even before the film *The American Venus* was partially shot at the 1925 Miss America pageant and brought the pageant increased national attention. Studio executives and other Hollywood professionals were regularly part of the judging panels. After the pageant, Miles returned to Wichita on September 20 with two offers from Hollywood studios—20th Century Fox and RKO Pictures—to come to Los Angeles. Before Miles, other Miss America contestants-turned-actresses included Miss America 1939 Patricia Donnelly, Miss America 1941 Rosemary LaPlanche, Miss America 1942 Jo-Carroll Dennison, Miss America 1946 Marilyn Buferd, and 1946 contestant and future Oscar and Emmy Award winner Cloris Leachman. Another contestant and semifinalist in 1948, Lois Nettleton (Miss Chicago), would also become an actress and would eventually win two Emmy Awards. If Miles wanted a career in Hollywood after the Miss America pageant, it was hers for the taking.

Fox offered her a seven-year contract at $300 a week, while RKO—which had recently been purchased by millionaire industrialist Howard Hughes in May 1948—initially offered her $250 a week. However, despite the Hollywood offers, Miles told the *Wichita Eagle* on her return home that she had no plans to leave the city because her boyfriend, Kent Frizzell, a student studying prelaw at Northwestern University, did not want her to leave Wichita and that she planned to marry him when he graduated. But Miles's plans to become the future Mrs. Frizzell changed when RKO Pictures doubled its offer to $500 a week and Miles agreed to move to Hollywood. By the time the Wichita Transportation Company declared her its first-ever "Girl of the Year" on October 1, Miles was already in Hollywood.

While her plans obviously changed, when Miles returned to Wichita in March 1964 to promote the film *A Tiger Walks*, she learned that Frizzell was president of the school board. Later that year, he would be elected a state senator for a single term and serve as the attorney general of Kansas from 1969 to 1971 and then the US under secretary of the Interior from 1975 to 1977.

Miles arrived at RKO at the beginning of a tumultuous period in the history of the studio, after Hughes gained control of the studio in 1948. Hughes had experience in film production after producing several films over the previous two decades, beginning with the unreleased 1926 silent short film *Swell Hogan*, which Hughes deemed so bad after its completion that he refused to release it. He had bigger success producing films like 1930's *Hell's Angels*, 1931's *The Front Page*, 1932's *Scarface*, and, after nearly a ten-year break from Hollywood, 1943's *The Outlaw*. Hughes's productions were often controversial—the gangster film *Scarface* was censored because of its violence, while the Western *The Outlaw* (one of two films that Hughes directed himself) seemed to be made for the sole reason of showing off actress Jane Russell's ample bust. Other Hughes productions, like the 1932 films *Sky Devils* and *Cock of the Air*, focused on airplane action (Hughes established his airplane company, Hughes Aircraft, in 1932). Though Hughes's films of the 1920s and 1930s were distributed by United Artists, when he returned to the industry in the early 1940s to produce *The Outlaw*, he began a new partnership with RKO Pictures, a major studio that had released classic films like 1933's *King Kong*, 1939's *Gunga Din*, 1941's *Citizen Kane*, and 1948's *Fort Apache* and was the primary distributor of films and shorts created by Walt Disney Studios. However, the studio's fortunes had declined by the time Hughes gained control of RKO in May 1948. Hughes bought his ownership stake in the business from fellow millionaire Floyd Odlum, who decided to leave the entertainment industry to focus on his other ventures.

By the time Hughes purchased his stake in RKO, he had already developed a reputation for being an eccentric playboy. He flight-tested many of his experimental aircraft himself, leading to two significant crashes in the 1940s—the fatal 1943 crash of the Sikorsky S-43 that killed a Civil Aviation Authority inspector on board and the 1946 crash of the XF-11 that damaged a neighborhood in Beverly Hills. Hughes sustained injuries in both crashes. He was also known for his high-profile romances with some of the most famous screen actresses in Hollywood, including Joan Crawford, Ava Gardner, Joan Fontaine, Jean Harlow, Katharine Hepburn, and Terry Moore, among several others.

Hughes's acquisition of a controlling interest in RKO proved to be disastrous for the studio. He insisted on being a hands-on owner and oversaw many aspects of productions that other studio executives would leave to production experts. Perhaps one of the worst examples of Hughes's interference with the studio's operations is the film *Jet Pilot*, starring John Wayne and Miles's future *Psycho* costar Janet Leigh. *Jet Pilot* went through several directors as the film's footage was shot over four years, 1949–53, though the primary actors had finished filming their parts by early 1950, and much of the later years were concentrated on location shooting of then-advanced aircraft that Hughes wanted to feature in the film. He made seemingly endless editing changes to the film, and it was not released in theaters until October 1957, which was after Hughes had sold the studio. The new owners of RKO finally pried *Jet Pilot* out of Hughes's control and ultimately sold it to Universal for release. By that time, much of the "advanced" aircraft featured in the film had become outdated.

While RKO still had a few hits under Hughes's tenure, such as the 1951 science fiction film *The Thing from Another World*, by the time Hughes sold his interest in the studio in 1955, the company had suffered crippling financial losses and closed its doors by the end of the decade.

When Miles was signed with the studio at the beginning of Hughes's ownership, the millionaire was in the process of grooming young women whom he intended to be future starlets and, in some cases, his lovers. He insisted on keeping tight control on all aspects of the training of his young actresses, who were expected to adhere to a regime of acting classes to prepare them for RKO films that many would never appear in.

One way that Hughes kept tabs on his actresses was by assigning each of them a driver. For Vera Ralston, he chose one of his personal drivers, Robert "Bobby" Jennings Miles Jr., known professionally as Bob Miles, to serve as her chauffeur. Bob Miles was born in Hollywood in 1927, the son of two stunt performers, Robert Jennings Miles Sr. and Mary Frances (Martinson) Miles. In their marriage announcement, which was reported by the Associated Press, Frances was also described as a boxer of some renown under the name Frances Marton in the women's circuit. According to *Hollywood Stunt Performers,*

1910s–1970s: A Biographical Dictionary (2nd edition), by Gene Scott Freese, the young Bob Miles worked as a child stunt performer. When he was two years old, his parents divorced, and by the late 1930s, Miles settled with his mother in Utah. But by the mid-1940s, Bob Miles had returned to Hollywood (his draft card, dated September 17, 1945, lists his employment location as "Various Studios" and his employer as "Central Casting," the agency responsible for hiring extras and stand-ins for productions), where his father was still working. After briefly serving in the military, Bob Miles returned to Hollywood and began working for RKO Pictures. When Hughes purchased the studio, he selected the tall, well-built Miles to serve as one of his drivers after Miles was asked to deliver an important message to him and he accidentally encountered Hughes while Hughes was sitting on the toilet.

When Vera Ralston arrived in Hollywood, the first person she met was Bob Miles, who picked her up from the airport. Though she had left Kent Frizzell back in Wichita, marriage was still in the immediate plans for the woman who almost became Mrs. Frizzell. An article about Vera's life in the September 1957 issue of *Photoplay* described Bob Miles as "a well-dressed, nice looking, popular young man . . . the personification of Big City" and cast Vera as "lonely, frightened, and young" as an explanation for why she fell for him so quickly. It did not take long for Bob to ask Vera out on a date, and the two began a quick courtship that led to a November 1948 wedding. A June 1957 feature in *Photoplay* would describe the courtship as Vera jumping "headlong into an early marriage at eighteen, after knowing the boy a month" and explain that she was ill-prepared for being a housewife. News of the marriage appeared back home four months later in the March 2, 1949, edition of the *Wichita Eagle*.[10]

Of course, Hughes eventually learned that one of his drivers married one of his beautiful starlets. "That just insulted the hell out of Howard Hughes," says David Boushey, a close friend of Bob Miles in his later life. "Here Miles was seeing one of Hughes' top girls, and of course, Hughes wanted to play a bit with Miss Ralston. But she wasn't into that." Hughes, who made his whims of firing employees of RKO a seemingly daily occurrence, saw the marriage as a severe breach of loyalty, and he fired Bob Miles for his "transgression" of marrying Vera. "Hughes said to Bobby, 'I thought you were kind of dumb, but I never thought you were *that* dumb,' and fired him on the spot," says Boushey.[11]

Nearly seven decades later, a similar situation to the real-life one involving Bob and Vera Miles and Howard Hughes played out on screens in a 2016 film titled *Rules Don't Apply*. Academy Award–winning actor and filmmaker Warren Beatty made the film based on Hughes's later life, with Beatty himself starring as Hughes. It was Beatty's first film in fifteen years and came after Beatty had wanted to make a film about Hughes for nearly forty years, after he had a chance encounter with the reclusive tycoon. The film's setup—that one of Hughes's ambitious drivers begins dating one of his newest starlets whom he is assigned to drive—either intentionally or coincidentally is similar to how Bob and Vera Miles met. Of course, Beatty's film takes the scenario in a wildly different direction (the young starlet, played by Lily Collins, becomes pregnant by Hughes and has his secret, but entirely fictional, lovechild). Reporting about the film, which was a box office bomb and quickly disappeared from theaters, did not acknowledge any connection between the film's fictitious story and the real-life relationship between Bob and Vera Miles. Nor has either of the film's screenwriters, Beatty and Academy Award–winning screenwriter Bo Goldman, acknowledged any debt to the courtship of Bob and Vera Miles as an inspiration for the screenplay.

Three months after the marriage, RKO sold Miles's contract to Fox. Though Hughes and RKO had hired her because she was a beauty queen, Miles would eventually say that her pageant poise did very little to prepare her for acting. In fact, Miles would try to hide the fact she was a former Miss America contestant because she was concerned that it would present a preconceived notion of her as simply a pretty face that could be easily replaced by the next year's crop of beauty pageant contestants. In June 1958, Miles served as a guest columnist for vacationing entertainment columnist Vernon Scott, and she utilized the column to give free advice to aspiring actresses: stay away from beauty pageants. Although Miles noted that this was how she got her start in the industry, she explained that if young girls "really believe that being a beauty contest winner is the shortest way to a movie contract, then their bustlines must be bigger than their I.Q." and that "in my entire career, there's only one thing that I regret doing and that was to enter that beauty contest," explaining that in her early career as an actress, she was stigmatized by the "beauty contest winner" label.[12]

Years later, Miles told Don Alpert of the *Los Angeles Times* in 1964, "I don't think looks can help you in anything. I had to learn a trade that was foreign to me. I had never seen a play. I had seen very few movies. I had to learn show biz lingo." Later in the article, she added, "People will say actors are crazy or showoffs but in my case my inhibited nature was improved by acting simply because I had to explore myself and other people. My beginning years as an actress was my psychotherapy—only I didn't have to pay for a psychiatrist." In hindsight, Miles was lucky to be released from her RKO contract. Though Miles did not learn much about acting in her brief time at RKO, she did credit the tutelage of acting coach Florence Enright for helping her get rid of her Kansas accent. But because of Hughes's strict control of the studio and the other younger actresses under contract to him whom he favored, it was unlikely she would have developed much of a career there.[13]

2

Vera Miles on TV and in 3D

20th Century Fox may not have been run by the mercurial Howard Hughes, but Vera Miles was far from an immediate sensation at Fox either. On June 22, 1949, *Variety* reported the RKO castoff as one of Fox's contract player "newcomers" who were hired because of a survey of the National Theatres chain. A decade later, Miles reflected on going from doing very little at RKO to being offered a contract by Fox, where she also expected to do very little. "I wasn't a bit excited when they did. The money was useful but I had no high hopes."[1]

At Fox, Miles participated in several of the requisite activities that came along with being a young Hollywood starlet—that is, except for actually making movies. For example, the *Oceanside Daily Blade-Tribune*, a northern San Diego newspaper, reported on June 27, 1949, that Miles was one of the judges of the Fairest of the Fair beauty pageant at the San Diego County Fair. On September 12, 1949, the nineteen-year-old was featured as the intermission guest on the *Lux Radio Theatre* production of *Deep Waters*, a sixty-minute radio adaptation of the 1948 Fox drama movie. Miles was billed as an "eighteen-year-old charmer" who was discovered by one of Fox's talent scouts (there was no mention of her stint at RKO or even her Miss America experience). Unsurprisingly, the "interview" with Miles with series host and producer William Keighley is framed as a promo for Lux soap, the sponsor of the program, including how well it washes her husband's college varsity sweatshirts. Bob Miles did go to UCLA to study law after the pair were fired from RKO, but the soon-to-be father was far from being a young freshman on the sidelines of Bruins games.

Vera's short time at Fox was only marginally more productive than her time at RKO. She appeared in a small, uncredited part as a soldier's date in Fox's World War II comedy *When Willie Comes Marching Home*, directed by prestige filmmaker John Ford. It was the first time that she worked with the acclaimed director, though it was in a very limited capacity. That was believed to be the only Fox film Miles appeared in while under contract to the studio, though the *Wichita Eagle* reported that she had "minor roles" in the Fox family comedy movie *Cheaper by the Dozen*, starring Clifton Webb and Myrna Loy and released in March 1950, and the Fox Western movie *A Ticket to Tomahawk*, starring Dan Dailey and Anne Baxter and released in April 1950. However, no other sources give Miles credit for appearing in these films, and if she did work on them, she was either cut from the films or regulated to an indistinguishable background role. Of course, another, more likely explanation is that she or a Fox representative simply padded her then-thin résumé to look good for her hometown paper.[2]

Vera and Bob Miles's first daughter, Debra, was born in April 1950, and Miles took some time away from her fledgling acting career for her first months of motherhood. With few movie opportunities being offered to her, she returned to modeling. In addition to various ads and magazine covers, Miles was featured in ads in August 1951 for Ivory soap in magazines and on the cover of the August issue of *U.S. Camera* (in January 1952, *U.S. Camera* named her the most popular cover girl of 1951), which helped support the family while Bob was attending school.

Curiously, it was Vera Miles's modeling career that led to her first television appearance. Over a dozen years before she would make three films produced by Walt Disney, Miles made her first television appearance on Christmas Day 1950 in the opening minutes of Disney's *One Hour in Wonderland* television special to promote the release of its animated film *Alice in Wonderland* in July 1951. As the announcer promotes the show's sponsor, Coca-Cola, Miles emerges from a Christmas box dressed in a formfitting Santa Claus outfit while carrying a tray of Coca-Cola bottles and offers it to the camera. While Miles was just a pretty face in the part, her pageant poise is obvious as she maintains an ear-to-ear smile over the few seconds that she appears.

It was not glamorous work but exciting enough that Miles's modeling and acting career was reported in the August 26, 1951, edition of the *Wichita Eagle* along with the note that Miles would embark on "an extensive modeling tour which will take her from Cincinnati, O., to Bermuda," noting that she would be visiting her sister Thelma McDowell in Wichita in mid-December. However, it does not appear that the trip occurred as scheduled, as Miles would not return to Wichita for many more years and might have been yet another example of padding her still-thin résumé.[3]

Despite being released from her contract with RKO, she shot a film for Howard Hughes and RKO in late 1950. This film, *Two Tickets to Broadway*, is a textbook example of how Hughes's heavy hand on the studio's output was ruinous. During the production of the film, Hughes made several costly production decisions, delaying the film for months. The musical film stars Miles's future *Psycho* costar Janet Leigh as a member of a trio of singers looking for its first big break on a television show hosted by Bob Crosby (Bob was the younger brother of the better-known entertainer Bing Crosby). Miles has an uncredited role in the movie as a showgirl, along with several actresses from Hughes's stable of starlets. *Two Tickets to Broadway* was finally released in November 1951 after being in production for over a year and was a financial flop. The film's director, James V. Kern, would later become a go-to television director and directed Miles in three 1965 episodes of *My Three Sons* nearly fifteen years later.

In the meantime, Miles made her television debut as an actress on November 13, 1951, in "The Seven Graces" on NBC's *Fireside Theater*, a filmed anthology series. The program was based on a story by nineteenth-century American writer H. C. Bunner. Playing one of seven sisters in a half-hour program, Miles had limited screen time—but it was on-screen work nonetheless. Though Miles would later be able to credit her future stardom to her constant work on television in the mid- to late 1950s, "The Seven Graces," which was shot in June 1951, would be her only television role for nearly two years.

Bob Miles told *Parade* in January 1957 that his and Vera's split from RKO put their new marriage in a rough spot. "After that things got tough. I lost my job. Debts started to mount up. For a while I went back to college, hoping to become a lawyer. Vera went to school with me for one semester [using the scholarship money from the pageant]. But it was no soap."[4]

In articles about Vera that mentioned Bob, he was variously described as a law student, a photographer, an actor, or a casting director, having worked at Universal in that last role for some time. Bob Miles seemed to be trying whatever was available to him within the fringes of the entertainment industry to provide for his young family. By 1953, he returned to stunt work, appearing on television shows like *Gunsmoke* and a few low-budget Western films from independent producer Nat Holt. Miles continued modeling and had some excellent opportunities—such as being featured in *U.S. Camera* magazine in both August 1951 and January 1952—but she seemed to be running out of opportunities in her once-promising career in acting.

Finally, Miles's modeling led her to get acting representation, and she was offered a billed role in a film directed by Paul Henreid. Though Henreid is best known today for his role as Victor Laszlo in *Casablanca*, he spent much of his later career directing films for smaller studios after being blacklisted in the late 1940s for publicly protesting the House Committee on Un-American Activities. Miles was hired to appear in his official directorial debut, the 1952 film *For Men Only*, which he directed for the small studio Lippert Pictures. The studio was established by San Francisco–based movie theater tycoon Robert L. Lippert, who entered the production side of the business when he figured he could produce low-budget films himself for his theaters to avoid paying major studio rental fees to screen their films. Henreid was an example of an actor who wanted to direct but was unlikely to have gotten the opportunity from a major studio. As such, Henreid was a perfect fit to direct a low-budget film for Lippert. Previously, Henreid had mostly directed the 1948 film noir *Hollow Triumph* after an on-set dispute with original director Steve Sekely; Henreid, as producer and star, stepped in to finish the film, though Sekely retained directorial credit.

For Men Only stars Henreid as a college professor who is investigating the death of a student rushing for a fraternity. The subject manner, as well as the title, was fully intended to be provocative. The Motion Picture Producers and Distributors of America initially objected to the title because it could potentially be mistaken for that of a pornographic film, but Henreid insisted that the title referred to the men-only nature of fraternities (anyone confusing the movie with a stag film because of its title would have been sorely disappointed). The female stars, including Miles, disliked the title as well, with the opposite belief that nobody would know there were women in the film. Henreid used this in a tongue-in-cheek ad for the film featuring the three female stars, who expressed their dissatisfaction with the title and declared the movie "every woman's picture!" Likely because of the confusion generated by the title—though it was also standard practice for low-budget films to attract new audiences—the movie was rereleased in April 1952 as *Time for Men Only* and again in May 1953 as *The Tall Lie*.

Miles was cast in the film as a college student's girlfriend after Henreid's original choice for the role, an actress named Bambi Linn, pulled out of the production because she had another commitment (Linn would have a short career in Hollywood mostly in dancing roles, with her most notable credit being her appearance in the 1955 film adaptation of the musical *Oklahoma!*). Columnist Sidney Skolsky claimed in the *Los Angeles Evening Citizen News* that Henreid hired Miles after running into her and her husband, who were both working at a gas station, though that story seems more likely a planted item to promote the novice actress. Still, the production of *For Men Only* was far from glamorous—Henreid shot the film in September 1951 in just sixteen days, two days under schedule, at the independent General Service

Studios in Hollywood (known today as Sunset Las Palmas Studios). Despite the compact schedule, years later Miles would recall to *Photoplay* in its September 1957 issue that working on the film was a good learning experience, remembering, "I was reading for the ingenue lead. [Henreid] gave me mounds of time—and the part. I did exactly what he told me. I was a kind of a puppet. I felt my only talent was having the sense to do what I was told."[5]

Nonetheless, it amounted to Miles's first credited film role, and she at least got some worthwhile press for the film—no doubt because Henreid, acting as his own press agent for the film and the cast, sent out promotional packages to over one hundred publications, pitching the film and its cast to anyone willing to give them attention. On January 12, 1952, Miles made her first live radio appearance to promote the film as a guest on the CBS radio program *Meet the Missus*, hosted by Harry Koplan (her 1949 appearance on *Lux Radio Theatre* was prerecorded).

Five years after the release of *For Men Only*, Henreid began a very fruitful collaboration with Alfred Hitchcock by directing his first of nearly thirty episodes of Hitchcock's television series through 1962. Henreid's daughter, Monika Henreid, credits *For Men Only* as what brought her father's directorial talents to Hitchcock's attention, though it was after Hitchcock had already started working with Miles.

On the original theatrical release of *For Men Only* on January 15, 1952, Miles received her first critical reviews from the press. The *New York Times* review named Miles as one of the film's "earnest supporting players," while the *Los Angeles Daily News* review said that Miles "acted just like the girl friend of a college student," which, of course, meant she fulfilled the job that she was hired to do. The *Hollywood Reporter* review said that Miles "plays her role with restrained poignancy." The *Los Angeles Times* called her performance one of several "highly convincing" performances in the film, though the March 1952 issue of *Modern Screen* simply called her "cute."[6]

Whatever the reviews said, Miles's performance in the film must have been sufficiently impressive within Hollywood that just two months after *For Men Only* opened, she was cast in another college-themed film, *The Rose Bowl Story*, which started shooting on March 31, 1952, for Monogram Pictures, a more prominent small studio than Lippert Pictures. A March 22 article in the *Los Angeles Times* that announced the cast noted that Miles "is known from her work on TV." Of course, by the time of that publication, Miles had only been on television in her brief appearance in *One Hour in Wonderland* and as an actress in "The Seven Graces."[7]

The plot of *The Rose Bowl Story* is constructed around the titular annual New Year's Day football game held at the Rose Bowl Stadium in Pasadena, California, and Miles starred as one of the princesses attending the Queen of the Rose Parade, an honor bestowed annually on a college-aged woman living in Pasadena. The film was shot on location in Pasadena in the spring of 1952, and the cast included the real-life 1952 Queen of the Tournament of Roses and five of her six real-life "princesses," with Miles putting on the sixth princess crown for the film. The film was Miles's first movie in color and costarred her future third husband, Keith Larsen, as a supporting player on the Midwest football team that is selected to play in the Rose Bowl game. Larsen would later tell *Radio and TV Mirror* after meeting her on set, "I knew then that she was the woman for me. But though I was always fond of her, whenever I wanted to date her, she was married."[8]

Miles was in her first trimester with her second daughter, Kelley (born in early November 1952) during the production of *The Rose Bowl Story*. The movie was released on August 24, 1952, a month before the start of the college football season. The review in the industry trade magazine *Exhibitor* singled Miles out for praise, though the praise only amounted to "Miles, a newcomer, is attractive." However, the *Hollywood Reporter* review noted that "Miles makes an appealing and capable female lead." The film did well enough at the box office that it would later be reissued; on September 6, 1953, Allied Artists Productions, which owned Monogram Pictures, rereleased *The Rose Bowl Story* in advance of the 1953 college football season.[9]

A week before shooting began on *The Rose Bowl Story*, famed Hollywood gossip columnist Hedda Hopper, who would later develop a friendly relationship with Miles, reported in her March 25 column that Miles had been signed by Warner Bros., hence becoming the third major studio to put the now twenty-one-year-old actress under contract in her so-far short career. As luck would have it, a casting agent from Warner Bros. had spotted Miles on television in "The Seven Graces" and offered her a contract. Still, Miles remained on shaky ground as her career began. Several months later, the August 1952 issue of *Photoplay* downplayed her growing career, calling Miles "awfully sweet and appealing" but noting that "her debut [in *For Men Only*] didn't cause any great commotion. Maybe next time."[10]

Miles's second pregnancy delayed the beginning of her contract with Warner Bros., which formally began in the new year, 1953. Unlike her time at RKO and Fox, Miles's new studio initially did not hesitate to cast her in her first role for the studio, announcing that she would costar with Vincent Price in *The Wax Works*, which would be the first 3D film produced by one of the major studios. However, the film, re-titled *House of Wax*, went into production in mid-January—earlier than anticipated—to rush to an April 23, 1953, release date to get the jump on other studios' attempts to release 3D films (on its release, it was the first color 3D feature from a major studio; Columbia's *Man in the Dark*, a black-and-white 3D feature, premiered two days earlier than *House of Wax*). Fellow Warner Bros. contract player Phyllis Kirk was cast in the film instead of Miles, and, unfortunately for Miles's career, the movie became one of the biggest hits of the year, helped kick-start the initial 3D movie craze, and launched Price as an icon of horror films.

But Warner Bros. didn't keep the photogenic Miles away from the cinematic third dimension for long. She was cast in the studio's sec-ond 3D film, *The Charge at Feather River*, which began shooting in late February 1953 at the Warner Bros. Calabasas movie ranch under the title *The Burning Arrow*. The 3D Western features Miles as Jennie McKeever, one of two white women captured by the Cheyenne and forced to live among them. Against the acceptable mores of the time, Jennie grows accustomed to the ways of the Cheyenne and accepts her new life with them. Of course, this makes Jennie a villain in the context of 1950s Hollywood Westerns, and she is doomed to die late in the film for her transgressions of her betrayal of her race. The complex issue of a captured white girl becoming assimilated to the tribe of her captors was more maturely examined in Miles's 1956 film *The Searchers*, but the main purpose of Miles's life among the Cheyenne in *The Charge at Feather River* is that the fair-skinned, blue-eyed beauty could wear a formfitting buckskin costume throughout the film.

The Charge at Feather River missed out on being the first 3D Western by a little over a week. MGM's *Arena*, starring later Academy Award winner Gig Young, was released on June 24 (*Arena* was also MGM's first 3D feature—the stalwart studio, typically historically hesitant to jump on trends or new technological advances in cinema, only released one other feature in 3D, 1953's *Kiss Me Kate*). Miles's costar Frank Lovejoy, who was cited by the *Los Angeles Times* as an expert in three-dimensional filmmaking because he starred in both *House of Wax* and *The Charge of Feather River*, said to the newspaper that curvy actresses like Miles should not be concerned about the way they looked in 3D films. *Los Angeles Daily News* columnist Howard McClay went further to assuage this concern, noting in his April 13 column that "Miles' Miss America dimensions are soon to be put on public view in third-dimension—a fact that should bring a gleam to the eyes of the anatomy-fanciers of America" and that "it isn't unlikely that Vera will turn out to be one of the most whistled-at actresses since [Marilyn] Monroe."[11] McClay's suggestive comments, while virtually unthinkable for a columnist to print today, are simply a slight rewrite of the suggested copy that Warner Bros. put in *The Charge at Feather River* exhibitor manual about Miles's figure, which went along with dozens of publicity photos that Warner released of Miles in her Cheyenne outfit.

The world premiere of *The Charge at Feather River* was held on June 30 in Vernon, Texas, to open the brand-new 1,450-seat Plaza Theatre, the first movie house in the United States that was built specifically to exhibit 3D movies. The premiere was followed by several other special screenings throughout Texas: Houston (July 1), San Antonio (July 2),

Dallas (July 3), and Fort Worth (July 4), before opening nationwide on July 11. Miles was scheduled to appear at all the Texas screenings alongside costars Guy Madison, Helen Westcott, Ron Hagerthy, and James Brown, even though Miles had appeared in publicity pinup photos to hype the American Legion's July 4 fireworks show at the Los Angeles Coliseum. Despite those promo photos, Miles was not in Los Angeles for Independence Day and returned home on July 6, after the brief Texas tour, in time for the film's July 16 Los Angeles premieres at the Paramount Theater and Hollywood Theater, both of which were reported as Hollywood's first-ever "Buckskin Premiere," featuring attendees appearing in Western garb. Miles, Madison, Lovejoy, Westcott, Wesson, and Hagerthy appeared at both premieres—with the stars arriving in a stagecoach—and Warner Bros. studio head Jack L. Warner himself attended the premiere, also in Western wear. KECA (later KABC-TV) broadcast the offbeat premiere with popular local broadcaster Larry Finley hosting.

Seventy years after its release, *The Charge at Feather River*, a pedestrian Western otherwise most notable for its early 3D effects, would likely be virtually forgotten by the public if not for featuring and giving the name to one of the most famous sound effects in film history, the Wilhelm Scream. The notorious effect is a recording of a man screaming in pain that was first used in the 1951 Western *Distant Drums* but was dubbed the "Wilhelm Scream" decades later by famed sound designer Ben Burtt after a character in *The Charge of Feather River* named Private Wilhelm emits the same scream (the scream is actually used three times in the film). Burtt would use the scream in several films for which he recorded sound, including the original *Star Wars* trilogy and the *Indiana Jones* film series. Many other sound designers have used the effect in dozens of other films, television shows, and video games, making the Wilhelm Scream perhaps the most popular and recognizable vocal sound effect in the history of film.

While the film's legacy is tied closely with the popularity of the Wilhelm Scream, luckily for Warner Bros., *The Charge at Feather River* turned out to be an early 3D craze hit. *Motion Picture Daily* praised

The Charge at Feather River and its use of 3D, noting, "Hard to see how a showman could keep people away from this one if he tried." *Variety* called it "topnotch" and said it was "slated for strong b.o." Edwin Schallert's review in the *Los Angeles Times* said that Miles "registered in as a nasty vindictive little minx" but noted that she was "killed to[o] early for my personal satisfaction."[12]

Modern sources note that *The Charge at Feather River* was the highest-grossing Western of 1953, and its success was a much-needed boost to Miles's career. In an interview with columnist Vernon Scott, Miles noted that *The Charge at Feather River* generated so much fan mail for her that she had to hire an answering service. Referring to her earlier films, Miles said, "Those pictures pulled in some fan mail, but it was mostly from little girls. Their big brothers just weren't interested. . . . Ever since *Feather River* my mail has been so heavy I've had to hire a fan mail answering service to handle it. And this time most of the letters are from men. They complain about my buckskin outfit and ask for more revealing pictures." (Of course, by this time in her modeling career, Miles had posed for, as Scott noted, "several hundred photographs undressed to reveal as much as the law allows.")[13]

Despite the box office success of *The Charge at Feather River*, producers at Warner Bros. did not immediately cast Miles in another one of their projects except for including her in a small, uncredited role as a schoolgirl in the drama *So Big* (shot at the same time as *The Charge at Feather River*) and featuring her in the trailer for a movie that she did not actually appear in, the stop-motion monster film *The Beast from 20,000 Fathoms*. Warner Bros. acquired the B-movie—which directly inspired the later Japanese film *Godzilla*—from the independent production company Jack Dietz Productions. In an attempt to increase the film's commercial prospects, the studio decided to include one of its lesser-known pretty faces, Miles, in the trailer to deliver an absurd piece of exposition ("Who knows what waits for us in nature's no man's land?"). *The Beast from 20,000 Fathoms* was a hit (particularly considering its low budget), though how much of that can be attributed to Miles's face is anyone's guess.

Her lack of work from Warner Bros. was not a result of a lack of trying. In the fall of 1953, Miles screen-tested for a role in an independent film that was distributed by Warner Bros., *Ring of Fear*, though she did not appear in the film. Miles also angled for a role in the 1954 Fritz Lang Columbia film *Human Desire*, but that also did not pan out. Instead, Warner Bros. began regularly loaning Miles out for television broadcasts. On October 30, 1953, Miles appeared on the *Schlitz Playhouse of the Stars* episode "The Soil" from Meridian Productions. The *Los Angeles Daily News* said of the arrangement that it was "the first time a major studio entered into a loan-out deal with television." It would mark Miles's first of four appearances on *Schlitz Playhouse of the Stars* through 1958. Her appearance in "The Soil" resulted in a booming interest in her services. "Suddenly I began getting offers from nearly every TV producer in town," she would tell *Parade* in January 1957. She also signed a contract with the Helen Ainsworth Agency for representation. By August 1954, Warner Bros. had dropped Miles from her contract (though a few weeks later she was considered by the studio for a role in the 1956 film *Giant*), and a screen test with MGM that month and Fox in January 1955 did not result in a new studio contract for her. But virtually nothing had changed in Miles's career—she continued to appear regularly on television and in films for smaller studios and could do so more frequently without the restrictions of a studio contract.[14]

The day after the buckskin premiere for *The Charge at Feather River* (July 17), Miles began shooting her next film, *Pride of the Blue Grass*, at Hollywood Park for Allied Artists Pictures (although Warner Bros. had released a movie with the same title in 1939, this was an entirely different project and not a remake). Allied Artists was a production studio in Hollywood and was the successor of Monogram Pictures, which had released Miles's *The Rose Bowl Story* two years earlier. While the studio aspired to grow and signed many top-named filmmakers for various projects, B-films like *Pride of the Blue Grass* are more representative of the studio's standard output. The horseracing drama, costarring Lloyd Bridges and Margaret Sheridan, offered

Miles a leading romantic role as the owner of a racing horse that she believes has the potential to be a champion, though its trainer (played by Bridges) believes the horse is a fruitless pursuit (naturally, the horse proves to be a winner). After wrapping production, director William Beaudine told Mike Connolly of the *Hollywood Reporter* that Miles "will be a top star in two years."[15]

Beaudine was right in his assessment, but Miles's success would be built not on the movie screen but on television. After five years of piecing together a career in acting and modeling as a young wife and later as a mother, Miles now found herself in a near-constant stream of television acting work. On January 14 and February 11, Miles appeared as the intermission guest on *Lux Video Theatre*, and between that, Miles appeared in "Walking John Stopped Here" on *General Electric Theater* (January 1954) and also made an appearance on the CBS music panel show *Juke Box Jury* (the *Hollywood Reporter* noted that the network received twenty-eight phone calls about the amount of cleavage displayed by Miles and another guest, actress Joan Weldon, on the program). For the rest of 1954, she was regularly featured on various network anthology series: "The Great Lady" on *Schlitz Playhouse of the Stars* (March 5), her first live broadcast in "The Exposure of Michael O'Reilly" on *Lux Video Theatre* (March 18), "The Grey and Gold Dress" on *Pepsi-Cola Playhouse* (April 2), "The Tryst" on *Ford Theatre* (June 17), "This Day Is Yours" on *Crown Theatre* (September 9), "The Immortal Oath" on *Hallmark Hall of Fame* (October 10), "Such a Nice Little Girl" on *Pepsi-Cola Playhouse* (October 31, though it would be rebroadcast in syndication in July 1955 and then again in April 1956, this time as part of the anthology series *Strange Stories*), "My Own Dear Dragon" on *Four Star Playhouse* (November 18, which received overwhelmingly positive reviews in both *Variety* and the *Hollywood Reporter*), and "A Championship Affair" on *Four Star Playhouse* (December 16, which was another program under consideration for a series). She also did several lucrative commercial spots—Mike Connolly wrote in his column in the *Hollywood Reporter* that Miles "made more moo reading a three-minute Hazel Bishop TV commercial than for a two-week stint under her Warner pact." Six months later, Connolly again wrote about Miles's constant work in television by quipping, "Every time we turn on TV we see Vera Miles and we like it."[16]

Most of these programs cast Miles in mostly forgettable ingenue supporting or lead roles, including some in which the mother of two played a teenager. Two years later, Miles would admit to *Los Angeles Times* columnist Hedda Hopper that her repeated appearances on television were simply a matter of survival when she could not land film roles under her Warner Bros. contract. "I had no choice when I went into [television]," she explained. "I'd been in a few pictures but parts were getting increasingly difficult to find. I did about 30 TV shows in one year—took everything they offered so long as they were leading roles. I had only about a week off that entire year because I refused few jobs. It was more or less a matter of making a living. . . . I'd been paid a salary as an actress for a year and a half, and I still knew nothing about acting. So I started freelancing." With many film actors unable to do television roles because of their studio contracts, Miles was able to have her pick of television projects while also being an emerging film star.[17]

She also had the opportunity of landing a regular role in two different series. First, in May 1954, Miles filmed the pilot of *Mr. Tutt*, starring Walter Brennan in the title role. However, the pilot was not picked up, and the program was not even broadcast until four years later, when it aired as an episode of *Colgate Theatre* on September 9, 1958. Then the May 29, 1954, issue of *Billboard* said that Miles was one of several actresses who auditioned for the role of Lorelai in the drama series *Big Town*, which NBC was picking up for the 1955 season after it aired on CBS from 1950 to 1954 (the screen tests were completed on May 22 in Hollywood). The role was previously played on the CBS series by Mary K. Wells (1950–51), Julie Stevens (1951–52), and Jane Nigh (1952–54). Trudy Wroe was cast in the part on the NBC version, which only aired for two more seasons. Though Miles appeared in more than a dozen pilot episodes during her career—including so many that were picked up without her as a regular that the press kit for

1983's *Psycho II* referred to her as "pilot insurance"—she never was a star of a television series. In 1962, she told Hedda Hopper that it was a deliberate choice. "I think the worst thing that can happen to you is a successful TV series," Miles said and, reflecting on her career at the time as both a film actress and one of the television industry's most preeminent guest stars, "I'm happy and I'm having fun."[18]

Miles would later credit her steady television work as the training in acting that she had never received while under contract to RKO, Fox, and Warner Bros. She recalled to *Photoplay*,

> About that time television really started taking hold, especially the thirty-minute dramas. I began to work hard again. It was about halfway through my TV period that I really started reading my scripts. I'd be working on one when I'd think, "This girl is mixed-up, unhappy—so I'll be angry in this scene." I was thinking for myself what she might be. It opened up a whole new world. It whetted my highly active imagination carried over from childhood. I transplanted my daydreams—but without me in them. While the camera was rolling, I could lose myself in another character. And off-camera, having found an outlet for my introverted dream world, I was thinking and living more like a normal human being. My career was zooming.[19]

3

Up the Tree with Tarzan

While Miles's career on television was far outpacing her career in films in 1954, she made the effort to keep pace on the silver screen. *Pride of the Blue Grass* was released in April, and advance reviews were generally positive (though largely calling the film unoriginal), with the *Variety* review noting that in the movie, Miles is "registering strongly with a marked ability and pert attractiveness." The *Hollywood Reporter* review had even stronger praise for her, noting that Miles is "a very pretty young lady who shows promise of becoming a top acting ingenue." However, the film failed to register at the box office.[1]

Miles would then be cast in a film that would have far more impact on her personal life than it would on her career. In August, producer Sol Lesser announced that he had cast Miles in the RKO production of the next Tarzan movie, *Tarzan's Hidden Jungle*, opposite the screen's newest version of Edgar Rice Burroughs's hero, Gordon Scott, who was making his screen debut in the film. Mike Connolly reported that Miles was getting paid $1,250 per week for the role but also noted that each chimpanzee in the film was getting $1,500 per week.

Gordon Scott was born Gordon M. Werschkul in Portland, Oregon, in 1926 into a large family—he was the youngest of nine siblings. When he was a teenager, his father passed away, and he became interested in bodybuilding as an opportunity to stand out. He put on a substantial amount of muscle—so much, in fact, that when he was drafted in 1944 by the US Army, his standard-issue uniform did not fit him, and he had to have one custom made. After working as a drill instructor and in the military police without being deployed overseas, Scott was honorably discharged in 1947. While spending time in California, he became familiar with other renowned men in the then-burgeoning bodybuilding scene including future actor (and Scott's future costar in the 1961 Italian film *Duel of the Titans*) Steve Reeves and fitness icon Jack LaLanne. Shortly afterward, he married his first wife, Janice Mae Wynkoop, in Reno, Nevada; their brief marriage produced a daughter.

After a series of working-class jobs, including working as a ranch hand and driving a soda delivery truck for one of his older brothers, the athletic Scott eventually ended up in Las Vegas, where he got a job lifeguarding at the pool at the Sahara Hotel. During his time in Las Vegas, Scott married Leah Duarte, who worked as a telephone operator at the Sahara, in Tijuana, Mexico, in March 1954. Duarte and Scott reportedly had a son together in December 1954. After a short time of lifeguarding (anywhere from two weeks to a year, depending on how Scott was telling the story), he was spotted poolside by Walter Meyers, a talent agent who was aware that Tarzan film series producer Sol Lesser was looking for a new actor to star as the loincloth-clad hero. Lesser, who had first bought the rights to make Tarzan films in 1933 and had become the sole guiding hand behind the series in 1943, was searching for a replacement for departing Tarzan actor Lex Barker, who had played the character in five movies from 1949 to 1953. After putting Scott through a six-hour audition that was more of a physical obstacle course than a traditional screen test, Lesser signed Werschkul, who was rebranded "Gordon Scott" in part to distance his surname from that of the most well-known actor to play Tarzan, Johnny Weissmuller, to a seven-year contract. Meyers also became Scott's agent.

Scott was cast as the eleventh actor to play the Lord of the Jungle in the nearly forty years since Elmo Lincoln first swung across screens in 1918's *Tarzan of the Apes*, which was released just six years after Burroughs had published his first Tarzan story. Scott, however, would be only the fourth actor to play Tarzan in multiple feature films after Lincoln, Olympic champion swimmer Johnny Weissmuller (the most famous and prolific actor to play the character), and Lex Barker, whom Scott was succeeding in the role. At the time, Tarzan was by far Hollywood's most successful film franchise, having produced twenty-one features and seven serials since Lincoln's 1918 debut. Getting cast as the Ape Man immediately vaulted the unknown Scott into Hollywood royalty.

As a physical specimen, Scott certainly looked every inch the part. *Variety* columnist Frank Scully essentially salivated over Scott's physical appearance in his October 6, 1954, column, calling him "the handsomest giant" who has ever played Tarzan and claiming that "he is six feet three, [and] weighs 215 of the tightest pounds you ever saw," with "magnificent teeth in ideal alignment."[2]

Tarzan's Hidden Jungle started shooting in late August at RKO-Pathé Studios and lasted a little over two weeks. Though the film's leading lady, Miles does not portray Tarzan's typical love interest, Jane, in the film. Instead, she plays Jill, an animal nurse who meets Tarzan when he brings an injured baby elephant to the doctor. Later in the film, Tarzan rescues her when she is trapped in quicksand and, in the film's climax, rescues her again when she is thrown into a lion pit. Though Jill spends a lot of time in Tarzan's arms, the two characters do not have the romantic relationship typical of Tarzan and Jane in the other films of the series (indeed, the film concludes with a kiss between two chimpanzees, not the leading male and female stars). For two actors who would eventually become romantically involved off-screen, the pair demonstrates little emotional connection on screen that would suggest their real-life romance.

The role in *Tarzan's Hidden Jungle* led to Miles's first lengthy profile piece in the *Los Angeles Times* on September 19, 1954, in an article by John L. Scott titled "Vera Leaps to Jungle," featuring a large photo of Miles holding one of her costars, Zippy the chimpanzee. When asked why she was starring in a Tarzan movie after spending much of the previous year starring in more down-to-earth television dramas, Miles answered, "Experience is priceless in the entertainment business. Nature provides the frame but an actress must get the experience herself to get anywhere in Hollywood" and noting that "TV is today's version of theatrical stock. It's a fine training ground because TV producers aren't afraid of off-beat casting, which gives players opportunity for a variety of roles—something film producers shy away from." She also credited the quick demands of her television work for making her better at learning her lines and experiencing different emotional ranges of characters. In short, *Tarzan's Hidden Jungle* offered Miles yet another paying job that helped her build her career, and starring in the latest film of Hollywood's most successful franchise, no matter how cliché the part was, was a major step in her career.[3]

Vera and Bob Miles decided to separate in December 1954 and began divorce proceedings in March 1955. At that time, Vera was already dating Scott, though Scott spent most of February on a promotional tour for *Tarzan's Hidden Jungle*, which was released on February 15. Scott himself also filed for divorce in March 1955, as he was still legally married to his second wife, Leah Duarte. Richard Lamparski, the author of the long-running Hollywood profile book series *Whatever Became Of?*, profiled Scott in his tenth volume in 1986 and noted that Miles was unaware that Scott was previously twice married and had other children until after they were married, which was repeated in several of Scott's obituaries. However, Scott's divorce from Duarte was noted in the trade newspapers and gossip columns at the time, so it's unlikely Miles would have been unaware of at least some of his history (for example, in April 1956, gossip columnist Harrison Carroll reported in his syndicated column that Scott and Duarte had settled their divorce). Speaking with *Photoplay* in September 1957, Miles confessed that she wasn't particularly fond of Scott's rookie exuberance when they started shooting the film, but she warmed to him as production went on. "But it wasn't until we returned to the studio two weeks after the picture was finished, that he saw any warmth in me," she told *Photoplay*. "We were back for retakes and it was like coming home. I had liked the people and I was warmer and more open that I'd ever been, and he suddenly decided to take me to dinner." She also noted that Scott—whom she referred to by his nickname,

Pete—was great with her two daughters, and shortly afterward, the now-separated Miles was regularly dating Scott. In her July 20, 1955, column, Sheilah Graham reported that Miles said that "talk of marriage to Gordon Scott is not only premature but impossible" because her divorce from Bob Miles would not be finalized until April 1956. Of course, the pair would ultimately marry that month; Ed Sullivan even announced the impending nuptials in his January 24, 1956, column, though *Photoplay* later stated that Scott proposed to her on March 2, 1956, over a long-distance phone call while he was in London filming *Tarzan and the Lost Safari*, several weeks after Sullivan reported that the pair would be married.[4]

Bob remarried before Vera did; gossip columnist Harrison Carroll reported in December 1955 that Bob finalized the divorce in Mexico on October 2 and was married again on October 5 in Las Vegas to Andrea Cleall, a woman noted to be outside of the entertainment industry (however, there was a model with the same name who worked for local television station KTTV at the time as Miss Top of the Morning, named after the channel's daily morning show). After the divorce from Vera, Bob Miles continued working in Hollywood primarily in stunt work, including in films like *Spartacus* (1960) and *Dirty Harry* (1971) but more prominently on television. He was a regular as both a stuntman and background actor (in roles like "townsman" and "barfly") on the Western series *Bonanza* from 1959 to 1969, frequently working as the stunt double for star Michael Landon, with whom he became friends. Miles would eventually work as the stunt coordinator of the series. He also worked on other popular television Westerns like *Gunsmoke* and *The Wild Wild West*. Incidentally, Vera would guest star on an episode of *Bonanza* in 1966 titled "Four Sisters from Boston," though it does not appear that Bob worked on that episode. In December 1961, Vera filed a petition asking for $300 a month of child support from Bob Miles for their two daughters, perhaps because of his increased success as a stuntman.

Bob Miles also served as a mentor to younger stunt professionals. David Boushey met Miles in 1984 at the Utah Shakespeare Festival when Boushey was choreographing stage fights for the festival. At the time, Boushey—the founder of the Society of American Fight Directors, after becoming the first American to be inducted into the Society of British Fight Directors—was considered one of the top theatrical fight coordinators in theater. While Boushey had a few brushes with film productions, he had yet to break into Hollywood. During a rehearsal at the festival, Boushey heard a voice shouting, "Hey kid! You're pretty damn good!" Boushey had no idea that the voice belonged to Miles, whose career in Hollywood by that time had suffered a downturn, and he was living back in Utah, where he had been raised. The two met and struck a friendship that was very beneficial for both men; Boushey encouraged Miles to get back into the stunt industry ("he was pretty well finished when he met me . . . he had kissed it all off," says Boushey), and Miles helped Boushey break into Hollywood and work on films like *Blue Velvet* (1986), *Drugstore Cowboy* (1989), and *Sudden Death* (1995). By the late 1980s, Miles was back to working regularly in the industry as a stuntman and stunt coordinator, mostly for low-budget productions and most notably for 1988's *Halloween 4: The Return of Michael Myers*. In recognition of their work, both Miles and Boushey were inducted into the Hollywood Stuntman Hall of Fame in 1992.[5]

Boushey says that even when he met Bob decades after the divorce from Vera, Bob still felt stung about Vera divorcing him and marrying Gordon Scott. "Bobby sure was hurt when Vera threw him over for Gordon Scott," Boushey recalls from his conversations with Bob Miles. "He'd never admit it, but he was heartbroken by that. Bobby had an ego, especially after he was in the business for a while because he was well regarded in the business. By the time I met him, he had already done *Bonanza*, which was his big break. But he knew he was a stuntman, not a famous actor. He was bitter about it, and Bobby could definitely hold a grudge."[6]

After wrapping up his career in stunt work in the 1990s, Bob Miles passed away in April 2007 at the age of seventy-nine in Utah, just eighteen days before the death of Vera's second husband, Gordon Scott.

After filming *Tarzan's Hidden Jungle*, Miles continued her prolific television work, though she also had an unsuccessful screen test with legendary director William Wyler on October 6, 1954, for his 1955 film *The Desperate Hours*. On December 6, 1954, Miles had her highest-profile television role to date with her appearance as a patient with breast cancer on *Medic*, an NBC medical drama series, in an episode titled "The Wild Intruder." To ensure that the production accurately portrayed the diagnosis, operation, and post-op psychological read-justment, physicians from the American Cancer Society served as consultants for the program. Miles would later credit her *Medic* performance, which received a superb review in the *Hollywood Reporter*, as the one that caught the eye of Alfred Hitchcock, although he did not reach out to her until he saw a rerun of the episode about six months after it initially aired.

Miles wrapped up her television-heavy year with her appearance on *Four Star Playhouse* on December 16 in an episode titled "A Championship Affair" and then joined the comedy team of Dean Martin and Jerry Lewis for *Colgate Comedy Hour* on December 19 (she told the *Los Angeles Times* before the show, about the intimidation of acting opposite the madcap duo, "One friend frankly told me to have last rites said for myself before I ventured onto the stage with them"). Miles holds her own in the episode, including a memorable skit in which Martin and Miles play husband and wife and "adopt" Lewis, playing a rambunctious child, from an orphanage. As if that wasn't enough programming featuring Miles, she made her final television appearance of 1954 on December 30 on the CBS anthology series *Climax!* in an episode titled "Adventure in Copenhagen" opposite her *The Charge at Feather River* costar Frank Lovejoy. She started the New Year on television as well when she returned to *Pepsi-Cola Playhouse* for the January 9, 1955, episode "The Golden Flower."[7]

Miles celebrated the New Year by being cast as the female lead in another Allied Artists Pictures movie, a Western film about notorious lawman Wyatt Earp titled *Wichita*. Indeed, 1955 was intended to be a banner year for Allied Artists Pictures, one in which the company was scheduled to produce thirty-two films, more than Allied Artists had produced in any previous year as the studio was in the beginning stages of an, ultimately, largely fruitless play for expansion; the studio would return to B-movie production after struggling to expand its position in the industry in the mid-1950s.

Wichita reunited Miles with her *Pride of the Blue Grass* costar Lloyd Bridges, who played one of the film's outlaw antagonists, and her *The Rose Bowl Story* costar (and future third husband) Keith Larsen, who played a young Bat Masterson, the renowned Western lawman and journalist. Leading man Joel McCrea starred as Earp. McCrea had become a bankable star in Westerns after a more diverse earlier career (two of his most acclaimed films before becoming a nearly exclusive Western actor were Alfred Hitchcock's 1940 film *Foreign Correspondent* and Preston Sturges's 1941 film *Sullivan's Travels*). *Wichita* marked the third Western that McCrea starred in that was directed by French-born filmmaker Jacques Tourneur, who had been working in Hollywood since the mid-1930s. The film was a particularly appropriate title for Miles, who (after all) was once Miss Wichita and depicts a brief period of Earp's life when he served as the marshal in the bustling cow town of Wichita, Kansas. In the film, Earp bans guns in the city after the city's wild cattlemen accidentally shoot and kill a young boy during drunken revelry ("If men aren't carrying guns, they can't shoot each other," declares Earp in the film. "It's as simple as that"). As was standard in Hollywood Western biopics, *Wichita* played extremely loosely with the facts of Earp's life—for example, McCrea was over twenty years older than Earp actually was during the events depicted in the film, and the real-life Earp may have actually had a common-law wife who ran a brothel in Wichita at the time. Of course, this film depicts Earp as an upstanding lawman who abhors violence except for the need to keep peace and protect the innocent. Miles stars as Laurie McCoy, the daughter of a local businessman who had been instrumental in bringing the railroad to the growing city, and is Earp's love interest. Miles's character and her relationship with Earp is a wholly fictional creation—Earp and

Laurie get married at the film's conclusion, a development with no historical basis.

Wichita started filming on January 3 in Hollywood, with filming completing on January 29. During production, Miles had to be temporarily hospitalized because of a virus, but she recovered and completed the film. Unsurprisingly, the production of *Wichita*—and Miles's participation—was extensively covered in the *Wichita Eagle*, even though the film was entirely shot in California and Arizona (shots of distant mountain ranges, typical of California but not Wichita, appear in the film). In fact, the start of production of the film was announced on the front page of the newspaper with a headshot of Miles. The article included the announcement that the production invited Wichita mayor L. A. Donnell to the location shooting in Modesto, California, as a guest of the studio and Harry Marks, mayor of Modesto (who symbolically temporarily renamed Modesto "Wichita, California" for the duration of filming). The article noted that Allied Artists planned to hold the film's world premiere in Wichita in the summer. The Modesto shoot was to begin on January 18, with Donnell scheduled to visit Modesto that day by way of Los Angeles and San Francisco (where he also visited with that city's mayor, Elmer E. Robinson). However, persistent rain in Modesto led the production to reschedule the exterior scenes as soundstage shooting at the Allied Artists studios in Los Angeles for January 18. Donnell returned to Los Angeles to observe production there, where he met the cast and crew (including Miles). While on set, Donnell extended an official invitation to host the premiere of the movie in its namesake city. On April 1, 1955, the *Wichita Eagle* reported that the premiere was indeed tentatively set for Wichita in July. By the end of the month, the premiere was confirmed to be held in Wichita on July 13, though ultimately the film would unofficially premiere several days earlier in Reno, Nevada. The film's stars, including Miles, were expected to attend the Wichita premiere.

The coverage of *Wichita* in the *Wichita Eagle* included a profile of Miles published on January 23 as production was close to the end. The article noted that Miles's salary "comes to close to $1,500 a week" and that because she sensed that she was a star on the rise, "Miss Miles refuses to sign a contract which might be a drawback as her popularity increases" (the article also noted that she was separated from her husband).[8]

Production on *Wichita* wrapped at the end of January. Miles obviously impressed in the film as Allied Artists Pictures executive Walter Mirisch afterward signed her to a two-film contract with her script approval. According to actress Dana Wynter, Allied Artists Pictures had attached Miles for the role of Becky Driscoll in the studio's science fiction film *Invasion of the Body Snatchers*, which was to begin shooting in April, though Miles was ultimately unavailable (Wynter was cast in the role). It marked an unfortunate turn of events for Miles, since not only was *Invasion of the Body Snatchers* one of Allied Artists Pictures' biggest hits, but it was also a lasting cult classic. It was added to the National Film Registry in 1994 and would have been yet another film starring Miles in that exclusive company.

On February 16, *Tarzan's Hidden Jungle* premiered in Los Angeles. The initial reviews evaluating Gordon Scott's debut as Tarzan were not strong. The *Variety* review called it a "stock entry" in the long-running Tarzan series (it was the twelfth produced by Sol Lesser) and said that acting neophyte Scott was "a well-muscled man but seldom convincing in the part." The review's only mention of Miles is to describe her as "the pretty nurse." The review in *Harrison's Reports* was even harsher, calling the film one of the "weakest" of the Tarzan series, adding that Scott's acting "lacks conviction," and only mentioning Miles in the context of the plot summary.[9]

The trade journal *Film Bulletin* was perhaps the harshest of all, calling the film "strictly class D stuf [*sic*]" that is "better suited to TV playing time than theatre dates." The *Motion Picture Exhibitor* review simply referred to Miles as "shapely." The *Independent Film Journal* review was one of the few to actually comment on Miles's performance, though it simply noted that she "is attractive and plays her part well." Nonetheless, while *Tarzan's Hidden Jungle* failed to make the *Variety* list of 1955 films that grossed at least $1 million at the US box office, the worldwide box office appeal of the Tarzan character and the continuation of Scott in the role for several more movies, as well as the general popularity of the series, indicate that the movie was profitable because of its low costs.[10]

By the time *Tarzan's Hidden Jungle* was released to theaters on February 16, 1955, *Wichita* was in postproduction. Miles promptly returned to her busy television schedule, appearing on the April 17 episode of *The Pepsi-Cola Playhouse* on ABC titled "The House Where Time Stopped," in which she plays a character claiming to be the daughter of a woman who had mysteriously disappeared twenty years before, and the April 22 episode of *Science Fiction Theatre*, a syndicated series that debuted earlier that month (some markets played the episode later in the season). In the episode, titled "No Food for Thought," she portrays a woman whose scientist father dies after ingesting an experimental artificial nutrient, though a cure is developed before she succumbs to the same fate.

While shooting "The Merle Roberts Story" episode of *The Millionaire* (aired May 18, 1955, on CBS)—a series about characters who receive a million dollars from a mysterious benefactor—Miles dyed her hair brown to play the title character. Shortly afterward, she appeared on an episode of *The Ford Television Theatre* titled "P.J. and the Lady," which aired on June 2. But Miles wasn't just appearing on television in new material; her old programs were beginning to be rerun. For example, on July 16, 1955, NBC reran "The Grey and Gold Dress," which had aired the previous year on *The Pepsi-Cola Playhouse*, and then NBC reran "The House Where Time Stopped" on August 26, 1955, as part of its *The Best in Mystery* "summer series" on Friday nights—in other words, a series of rebroadcast programs, some of which even originally aired on other networks ("The House Where Time Stopped" originally aired on ABC). Just weeks away from shooting the biggest film of her career so far, Miles received praise for her television work from the most important consumer magazine devoted to the small screen: *TV Guide*. The issue dated July 9 featured an article titled "Desi Arnaz Chooses This Year's TOPS (Television's Own Promising Starlets)," naming Miles as one of the six TOP starlets of 1955. The famed star of *I Love Lucy*—or, more likely, the article's ghostwriter—praised Miles as "a hard-core dramatic actress, a thoroughgoing young professional well on her way up the ladder" and a "genuinely fine talent, combined with the delicate features of fine breeding."[11]

In fact, it was directly because of Miles's frequent appearances on television that she got her next big film role, the most prestigious of her career at that time.

4

Tea in Monument Valley

Cornelius Vanderbilt Whitney was a scion of both the wealthy Vanderbilt and Whitney families and built on his family's already monumental fortunes through business enterprises in several industries, including mining. Another industry that Whitney tried his hand at was film production, having put up some of the financing to produce *Gone with the Wind*. After Whitney served in several roles in the Truman administration, he returned to film by establishing his own production company in the early 1950s, C. V. Whitney Pictures, and set out to make a prestige film as his company's first production. Whitney hired famed producer Merian C. Cooper, the driving force behind the iconic film *King Kong*, to run his production company. In his role as vice president in charge of production at C. V. Whitney Pictures, Cooper purchased the film rights to Alan Le May's bestselling 1954 Western novel, *The Searchers*, and offered the project to his longtime collaborator and close friend John Ford, with whom Cooper was a partner in his production company, Argosy Pictures Corporation. Argosy had previously released five John Ford films starring Hollywood superstar John Wayne, beginning with 1948's *Fort Apache*.

It's no surprise that to make the biggest splash in the industry possible, Whitney sought out Ford to direct his company's first project. By then Ford had become the most acclaimed director in Hollywood history, the only person to receive four Academy Awards for directing. Working with Ford meant the production would have access to a qualified roster of talent both in front of and behind the camera, the so-called John Ford Stock Company, a menagerie of frequent collaborators who often starred in or worked on his films, including the industry's biggest star, John Wayne, and actors like Ward Bond, Olive Carey, and Harry Carey Jr. Though Ford was well known for directing Westerns, *The Searchers* would be his first Western since 1950's *Rio Grande* and his first film with Wayne since 1952's *The Quiet Man* (also starring Bond), which were both Argosy Pictures Corporation releases. However, Ford had shot some scenes (uncredited) for the 1953 Western *Hondo*, which also starred Wayne and Bond, as a favor to Wayne when the film's original director, John Farrow, had to leave the film to begin work on another project.

During preproduction, Ford cast *The Searchers* with a host of his frequent collaborators in roles both big and small, including Harry Carey Jr., Ken Curtis, Jack Pennick, John Qualen, and Wayne's son, Patrick. In addition, much of the talent behind the camera included longtime Ford collaborators. The screenplay was written by Frank S. Nugent, who had written six previous films directed by Ford, including the Ford–Wayne collaborations (and Argosy releases) *Fort Apache* (1948), *3 Godfathers* (1948), *She Wore a Yellow Ribbon* (1949), and *The Quiet Man* (1952). Like with many of Ford's recent films, Cooper served as producer of *The Searchers*. Other previous Ford collaborators who were brought into the production included Wingate Smith (assistant director), Max Steiner (music), Winton C. Hoch (cinematography), and James Basevi and Frank Hotaling (art direction). In addition, Warner Bros. agreed to distribute *The Searchers*.

Ford was coming off the success of the 1955 hit *The Long Gray Line*, released in February, and during the production of *The Searchers* he would have an even bigger hit with *Mister Roberts*, released in July (*Mister Roberts* would be nominated for three Academy Awards the following year, resulting in a Best Supporting Actor win for Jack Lemmon). However, the production of *Mister Roberts* was difficult for nearly everyone involved. Ford was removed from the film as director by Warner Bros. after he came into conflict with the stars of the film, Henry Fonda and James Cagney, and because Ford needed emergency surgery on his gallbladder. Though many of Ford's regulars were also in *Mister Roberts*—including Ward Bond, Harry Carey Jr., Patrick Wayne, Jack Pennick, and Ken Curtis—it was likely a relief for Ford after that experience to be working with even more members of his "team" on *The Searchers*, a film he had much more control over.

By the time production started on *The Searchers*, Ford was now in his sixties, and his health had started to decline after his gallbladder surgery (after directing over one hundred films before 1956 since his 1917 debut, Ford would only direct eleven more features after *The Searchers*). But Ford's well-known temperament endured. Patrick Wayne, who began appearing in films in Ford's 1950 film *Rio Grande*, appears in *The Searchers* as Lieutenant Greenhill, a young cavalry soldier, and remembers that Ford kept him on his toes when they worked together. "One of the characteristics of working with Ford that separated me from everybody else is that he was my godfather, so I got treated specially," he shares. "I did not realize it at the time—I was always expecting that I would be the beneficiary of his acerbic wit because he really got everybody at one time or another. But I was always prepared for it. I had the same anxiety as every other person working on the film."[1]

Similarly, John Wayne was coming off a difficult shoot for the RKO Pictures film *The Conqueror*, a much-maligned movie in which he was horrendously miscast in "yellowface" as Genghis Khan (before production started on *Tarzan's Hidden Jungle*, Gordon Scott visited the set of *The Conqueror* and was photographed with John Wayne in his Genghis Khan costume; both *The Conqueror* and *Tarzan's Hidden Jungle* were RKO Radio Pictures). Though *The Conqueror* would not be released until after *The Searchers* wrapped production, the shoot was difficult for Wayne and had gone significantly over budget, so much so that the film's producer, millionaire Howard Hughes, would exit the film business in part over his frustration with the doomed project. While *The Conqueror* would ultimately do well on release— according to *Variety*, *The Conqueror* was the eleventh highest-grossing film at the US box office in 1956, with an estimated $4.5 million take (ranked right above it was *The Searchers*, with an estimated gross of

$4.8 million)—the expensive production would end up in the red and received largely negative reviews. Though the much more negative reception of the film would come later, Wayne was likely also relieved to again be working with Ford and so many familiar faces after that challenging experience.

Ford, Wayne, and the rest of the stock company would also be returning to familiar territory to shoot the film—Monument Valley, an expansive landscape on the Utah-Arizona border with towering sandstone buttes that have been featured in dozens of films set in the American West. Ford first shot a Western in Monument Valley for 1939's *Stagecoach*—his first film with Wayne in a starring role and the role that launched Wayne into stardom—and the pair returned to shoot *Ford Apache* (1948) and *She Wore a Yellow Ribbon* (1949) in Monument Valley. *The Searchers* was the fifth film that John Ford shot in Monument Valley and the first of his Monument Valley films to be shot in widescreen (VistaVision). To shoot with such a large crew in the remote location, the production built infrastructure like roads and utilized a tent city for its cast and crew, which numbered three hundred, including some local Navajo who were hired as extras. Most of the cast was on location for all five weeks of the production, and the location shoot alone cost C. V. Whitney Pictures $500,000.

The Searchers features Wayne in what many historians consider one of his most complex roles. After spending a quarter of a century portraying mostly altruistic cowboys and soldiers in dozens of films, in *The Searchers*, Wayne plays Ethan Edwards, an imposing former Confederate soldier with a questionable background. In 1868, he arrives unannounced at the home of his brother in West Texas. While his brother's family is happy to see him, Ethan does not explain his whereabouts since the Civil War ended three years earlier. Shortly after Ethan arrives, the Comanche steal cattle belonging to the Edwardses' neighbors, Lars Jorgensen and his family. When Ethan and other men of the area set out to recover the cattle, the Comanche raid the Edwardses' homestead; murder Ethan's brother, sister-in-law, and nephew; and abduct Ethan's two nieces. The elder of the two girls is soon discovered dead by Ethan's hunting posse (the film implies that she may have been raped before her murder), and a grief-stricken Ethan sets off on a multiyear search to find his youngest niece, Debbie (played as an adult by Natalie Wood). It quickly becomes clear that Ethan may be less interested in rescuing her than he is in potentially killing her for being "soiled" by her life among the "savages." Wayne's riveting performance as Ethan is among the Duke's greatest performances and is arguably the one for which he is most remembered. "It was one of my dad's best roles," says Patrick Wayne. "It was a different role for my dad, certainly at the time for him. He was really a nasty character that was not typical of the John Wayne character."[2]

Though *The Searchers* cast and crew were filled with Ford's usual collaborators, there was room in the picture for new faces. While Miles had appeared in an uncredited role in Ford's 1950 comedy movie *When Willie Comes Marching Home*, she would be among the few actors on set in *The Searchers* who hadn't previously appeared in a half-dozen or more Ford films. Miles's casting in *The Searchers* resulted from the filmmaker seeing her on television. She told *Parade* in January 1957 that when her agent told her that Ford wanted to see her for a part in *The Searchers*, "I didn't think I had a chance. Later, I found out that he had seen me on TV and already made up his mind." It had been Ford's wife, Mary, who spotted her in "The Tryst" on *The Ford Television Theatre* in June 1954 and pointed her out to her husband. Miles claimed her interview with Ford lasted three minutes and would recall to *Screenland* that the "meeting" simply consisted of Ford asking her, "Would you like to do a picture for me?"[3]

Miles was cast in *The Searchers* as Laurie Jorgensen, the love interest of a young cowboy, Martin Pawley, Wayne's character's searching companion. Pawley is played by Jeffrey Hunter, a handsome actor with leading-man potential who, like Miles, had yet to have a true breakout film role. Though Pawley rides with Wayne's Edwards, the former Confederate soldier holds the younger man in contempt for being a "half-native" who was adopted by his brother's family. Laurie, in love with Pawley, waits for years at home for him to end his search for his adopted sister's whereabouts and settle down with her. At one point, she even tells Pawley to give up, siding with Ethan's point of view that Debbie has been tainted by the Comanche and saying that Debbie has likely become the "leavings of a Comanche buck, sold time and again to the highest bidder, with savage brats of her own." She tells Pawley that his adoptive mother would have rather seen Debbie dead than a bride of a Comanche.

Throughout the film, Laurie tempts Pawley to quit his search and settle down so he does not end up a cold, ruthless man like Ethan. Though Ford presents and photographs Laurie as an extremely appealing beauty as a representation of a settled-down life in opposition to life on the trail, Pawley rejects that life because of his mission with Ethan. Laurie nearly marries another man (played by later star of *Gunsmoke*, Ken Curtis, who at the time was Ford's son-in-law) before Pawley interrupts the wedding when he and Ethan come to the Jorgensen ranch for a brief respite from their search. Ultimately, after Ethan and Pawley find Debbie (and Ethan opts not to kill her), the pair bring her to the Jorgensen ranch. Laurie runs out to greet their arrival and is last seen in the film entering the Jorgensen ranch with Pawley, symbolic of Pawley finally coming off the trail. As a counterpoint, Ethan, a cynical eternal rambler, never enters the Jorgensen ranch in this final scene, and the film concludes with Ethan walking away toward the horizon. As such, Laurie—hopeful, enthusiastic, and beautiful—represents the comforts of a domesticated life, one that Pawley can finally engage in now that the search for his adopted sister is over, but it is a life that is no place for a man like Ethan.

The casting of both Miles and Hunter was announced in the June 15, 1955, edition of the *Los Angeles Times* with the film only days away from production. According to the film's production reports, Miles and Olive Carey (who played the mother of Miles's character, Mrs. Jorgensen, and would be Miles's roommate during the on-location production) traveled from Los Angeles to Flagstaff, Arizona, overnight from June 29 to 30, then arrived at the production base camp at 10:45 a.m. on June 30. The three-hundred-person production crew camped out in a tent city for five weeks, meaning that Miles was shooting on location in Monument Valley through July 10. The production then moved to RKO Studios in Los Angeles, with Miles working in the studio from July 18 through August 3. Finally, the primary cast, including Miles, was called to RKO Gower Studios on August 15 and 16 for publicity portrait sessions. Patrick Wayne was on location for the entire shoot and, after the production moved to Hollywood, was on set nearly every day even when he wasn't in a scene. "When you're in a remote area—like 350 miles to the nearest post office—the only place you're going to have a conversation or any contact with anyone is on the set," he recalls. "I got to know Vera Miles very well because you get to know everyone very well because you become a close-knit family. One of Ford's techniques was taking meals together. In the afternoon at four o'clock, he would break and have a table set up. All of the principals would sit down and have a formal tea."[4]

On set, Patrick Wayne spent a lot of time, and developed a friendship, with Natalie Wood (who was only a year older than he was). He recalled that they were often teased on set as the youngest cast members, but Miles did not join in on the teasing. "She was very sweet to us and very sympathetic," he remembers. "I got along with her great."[5]

While Miles had appeared in more than a half-dozen films before *The Searchers*, it was by far the most prestigious and expensive project of her burgeoning career. Reflecting on being dropped from three contracts with three major studios in the preceding few years in an interview for Dorothy Manners's gossip column, Miles remarked, "I didn't let it get me down. I just squared my shoulders and determined to learn to act. I received my reward making *The Searchers* when John Ford told me after my big scene, 'Kid, you're okay.'"[6]

For her part, Miles said she had a positive experience working alongside Ford, Wayne, and the other luminaries involved in *The Searchers*. She told the *New Orleans Times-Picayune* in 1981, "*The Searchers* really was terribly exciting. My first big film, a big, well-done western directed by one of the best-known directors in the world. It was a wonderful initiation. . . . Those two powerful men (Ford and Wayne) were terribly in love with each other, such great friends. They acted very gruff, but there was so much kindness and sensitivity in them. There was a great feeling of family, of being in a very close-knit group on that movie. It was such a mass of wonderfully talented people." In the press kit for 1983's *Psycho II*, Miles pointed to working with Ford on *The Searchers* as the first moment she saw being a film actress as a career versus a temporary excursion. She remarked, "It was the first time that I'd worked with anyone so intensely interested in and so serious about filmmaking. His passion inspired and even intrigued me; and I began to understand what it was that happened up on the screen."[7]

At the same time, she also recognized decades later that her role in *The Searchers* cemented the perception people had of her as a character and set her as the "domestic" type: "John Ford set my image, and in those days, what you looked like was more or less what you got stuck with as far as image went. I played some heavies later on, but you couldn't fight your physical appearance, and when I came out from Kansas, I still had the hay in my hair. I looked straight, and I looked Midwest, and those were the roles I got. Things are more flexible for actresses now, but then it was a bitch to break type."[8]

Ford and Wayne worked with Miles several more times over the next dozen years, obviously impressed by the performance and professionalism of the twenty-six-year-old actress, who portrayed Laurie with both youthful exuberance and domestic maturity. That was no easy feat, especially for Ford, who, even on his most agreeable days, could treat his actors, even the ones he considered close friends, harshly. Patrick Wayne recalls that Miles quickly exceeded Ford's strict expectations for actors. "I was crazy about her," he says. "First of all, she was very beautiful and extremely talented. She was always engaged when she was performing. I thought she was great. She had the right disposition to work with Ford. You had to be flexible, and you had to be ready for anything because he had in his mind the way he wanted a scene to go and how he wanted his actors to perform, even to the point of giving line readings. So, you better be prepared because he would hold on like a wolverine until he got it the way he wanted it."[9]

Miles's experience working with Bond, another longtime friend and collaborator of Ford, was allegedly far less respectful. Decades after the production of *The Searchers*, Carey Jr., who played Brad Jorgensen in the film and was the son of Ford favorites Harry Carey Sr. and Olive Carey, wrote in his autobiography *Company of Heroes: My Life as an Actor in the John Ford Stock Company* that Bond, who was his roommate for the shoot, was determined to seduce Miles during production. Attempts by Bond, nearly thirty years Miles's senior, to attract her by walking around naked or trying to catch her naked were futile. Bond's behavior—coming from a man just recently married to his second wife, Mary—would clearly be understood today as the type of sexual harassment that was rife in the entertainment industry for decades. As far back as her experience working for Howard Hughes, Miles had regularly rejected the advances of older, established men, and Bond would have been no exception to that because Carey said that Miles never even noticed Bond's nudity. However, Miles never publicly addressed Bond's alleged on-set behavior toward her, and she went on to work with him on two television projects before he died in 1960.

By mid-August, Miles had sufficiently impressed C. V. Whitney Pictures with her performance in *The Searchers* that the company signed her for a three-year, three-picture nonexclusive contract, making Miles the new company's first contracted star. Nonetheless, months would pass without any announcement regarding Miles appearing in any C. V. Whitney Pictures films. In her May 19, 1956, column, Sheilah Graham reported that Miles was "postponing" her next Ford / C. V. Whitney film because she was "torn between so many picture assignments, and marriage with 'Tarzan' Gordon Scott." Even as late as May 1957, the *Los Angeles Times* reported that C. V. Whitney Pictures was "busy seeking new story properties" for the films left on Miles's contract with the production company. However, the production company would only make two additional films, 1958's *The Missouri Traveler* and 1959's *The Young Land*, before folding, and Miles appeared in neither film (John Ford also was not involved in either movie, though his son, Patrick Ford, produced both). Some reports say that Miles was initially supposed to star in *The Missouri Traveler*, but she ultimately did not make the film (perhaps she was pulled by Hitchcock after signing her contract with him).[10]

Even shortly after *The Searchers* entered postproduction, the film gave a significant boost to Miles by pushing her name more regularly into the gossip columns. In the aftermath of Jeffrey Hunter's divorce from actress Barbara Rush (with whom Miles would star in a memorable episode of *The Outer Limits* in 1964), Sheilah Graham reported in her August 13, 1955, column that "press agents are trying to stir up a romance between Jeff Hunter and Vera Miles," despite Miles's by now well-documented relationship with Gordon Scott. Two weeks later, Graham reported that Ford gifted Miles a pair of the tight-fitting pants that she wore in one scene of *The Searchers* with a cheeky note saying, "Wear these more often, and I can guarantee you will receive better parts." In one of his February 1956 columns, Hollywood columnist Mike Connolly remarked, "Give her two years and I'll bet almost anything I own that there'll be no bigger name among Hollywood's leading ladies than Vera Miles, John Wayne's leading lady in *The Searchers*." While Miles has the most substantial female speaking role in the film, it was a big stretch to refer to her as "Wayne's leading lady" in the movie, as she is the love interest of Hunter's character. However, the association with the screen's biggest star certainly wouldn't have hurt Miles any.[11]

The Searchers truly was a star-making performance for Miles, who manages to make a memorable impression as the only prominent female character in the film (Wood's Debbie, while visually striking, is more of a plot point than a full character). Miles portrays Laurie as a determined, graceful young woman who is as headstrong as she is beautiful. Audiences instantly recognized her character's promise—*The Searchers* had an extremely successful preview screening on December 3, 1955, at the Paramount Theatre in San Francisco. Walter MacEwen, an executive at Warner Bros., wrote a memo to Jack L. Warner that praised the film and the audience's response to it (the memo was reproduced as an insert of the fiftieth anniversary Ultimate Collector's Edition DVD release of *The Searchers*). Of Miles, MacEwen wrote, "Vera Miles is lovely, with lots of spirit."

While *Psycho* may be Miles's most-watched film, *The Searchers* is almost inarguably the best film she made in her career, and her spirited performance is the reason so many critics thought that she would be one of the industry's top stars by the end of the decade. It remains one of the most highly regarded American films of the studio era and is thought by many critics, scholars, and fans to be Ford and Wayne's greatest collaboration. The film's esteem has grown substantially in the years since its release. When the American Film Institute (AFI) created a list of the one hundred greatest American films in 1998 by polling fifteen hundred principals in the film industry, *The Searchers* ranked at number ninety-six. When AFI revised the poll nine years later, *The Searchers* jumped an astounding eighty-four spots to number twelve, by far the largest gain of any film on the list. Likewise, the British Film Institute's once-a-decade *Sight and Sound* critics' poll has ranked *The Searchers* as one of the top films ever made since 1982, with the film ranking at number seven in 2012 and number fifteen in 2022.

Following production of *The Searchers*, Ford carried over four of the film's principal actors—Miles, Bond, and John and Patrick Wayne—and assistant director Wingate Smith for one of his first television productions, which started shooting on October 10, 1955, two months after production wrapped on *The Searchers*. The NBC anthology series *Screen Directors Playhouse* launched in 1949 as a radio program that adapted popular films for radio broadcasts. In 1955, NBC revived the series for television. Through its sponsorship by Eastman Kodak and because its productions were shot at Hal Roach Studios, *Screen Directors Playhouse* had access to high-caliber talent from the Screen Directors Guild, like Ford. Ford's production, titled "Rookie of the Year" from a script by Frank S. Nugent (who had also written the screenplay for *The Searchers*), was the tenth program broadcast in the series.

In the program, Patrick Wayne stars as a promising rookie baseball player, Lyn Goodhue, who plays for the New York Yankees. Goodhue's father is Buck Garrison, played by Bond, who was (unbeknownst to the rookie and the public) a member of the notorious Black Sox who threw the 1919 World Series. The elder Wayne plays Mike Cronin, a small-town sportswriter who has been itching to get out of his dead-end job in Emeryville, Pennsylvania. Cronin discovers the truth about Goodhue's disgraced father, and he sees the scandal as the breakthrough story he's been waiting to write for his entire career. Miles portrays the girlfriend of Goodhue, Ruth Dahlberg, who threatens Cronin by gunpoint not to expose the story when she discovers his snooping and learns the truth about Buck herself. After talking it over with Ruth, Cronin accepts that the story would ruin the promising career of a rookie who could end up an all-time great and agrees to not publish it—only to discover that Goodhue's parentage is common knowledge among his sportswriter acquaintances in New York, and they've all also agreed not to write about it to protect Goodhue's reputation. However, Cronin is offered the opportunity by one of his acquaintances in New York to travel to Japan to cover a baseball tour there in exchange for keeping the story quiet so he can escape his small-town paper regardless.

Though Miles plays Patrick Wayne's girlfriend in the program, the pair do not appear on screen together, as much of her screen time is opposite John Wayne. "We were never in a scene together," recalls Patrick Wayne. "We were never even on the set together. I think I saw her once during the production. Our scenes were completely different."[12]

The half-hour program aired on NBC on December 7, 1955 (six months before *The Searchers* would premiere in theaters), and amounted to one of Miles's strongest and most visible supporting television roles in a year that was already full of them for her. NBC reaired the episode on April 18, 1956, a month before the release of *The Searchers*. Luckily for Miles, it would not be the last time she would work with either Ford or Wayne.

Unfortunately for Miles, the production of *The Searchers* meant she had to miss an important homecoming event. The July 13, 1955, premiere of *Wichita* was heralded with pomp and circumstance of all kinds in its namesake city, including a multiday celebration dubbed

"Pioneer Days" to highlight the history of Wichita. It even included a wedding on the day of the premiere, which stars from the film were expected to attend. As late as the day before the premiere, the *Wichita Eagle* was still reporting that Miles was hoping to be in attendance, with ads for the film running "Wichita's Own" above Miles's name in ads for the film (meanwhile, the *Hollywood Reporter* had already noted the previous month that Miles wouldn't be able to attend). Miles was shooting on location on *The Searchers* through July 10 and would be on set in Hollywood for interior shooting starting July 18 so was unable to attend the premiere in Wichita (the studio supplied a thousand photos of Miles to be distributed at the premiere as a substitute). Nevertheless, several of Miles's relatives, including her mother, Bernice Ralston, did attend the premiere, and afterward, Miles's sister Thelma flew to Los Angeles to visit Miles for a vacation.

Though Miles was deeply involved in the production of *The Searchers*, she likely was happy to hear that *Wichita* was receiving strong reviews. The *Independent Film Journal* predicted that the "well-mounted western" would "do good business," and the *Motion Picture Daily* review was equally complimentary, calling Miles a "fast-rising" name. Most beneficial to Miles was the review in *Variety*, which said that she "makes much more of her Western heroine role than is usual in this type of filmfare." According to *Variety*, *Wichita* was the forty-seventh highest-grossing film of 1955 with a box office take of $2.25 million. More importantly for Allied Artists, it was the studio's highest-grossing film of the year and a strong success for the smaller studio that was a bright spot in its otherwise mostly unsuccessful attempt to grow into a more prominent studio.[13]

Yet Miles hardly gave herself time to bask in the good reviews. Starting September 6, 1955, she was shooting the melodrama *Autumn Leaves* for director Robert Aldrich and Columbia Pictures under the title *The Way We Are* (the title was later changed to match the credit song, Nat King Cole's recording of the standard "Autumn Leaves"). Miles would later tell *Parade* in January 1957 that she was hired for *Autumn Leaves* after Columbia heard that John Ford had cast her in

The Searchers and figured that Ford would not be casting an actress in one of his prestige pictures simply because of her good looks. Indeed, at the beginning of the shoot, columnist Louella Parsons wasn't alone in heaping praise on Miles as she noted, "And when a girl as new as Vera gets star billing you know she must be good. Of course, her name won't be in as large letters as Joan's in *The Way We Are*, but her credit will say 'co-starring.'"[14]

The "Joan" in question was the film's star, Joan Crawford, one of the biggest stars of the 1930s, who had seemingly become a Hollywood star through the sheer force of her personality. Like Miles, Crawford made a name for herself through constantly working (she made more than two dozen films in the 1930s), even after a notorious advertisement from the Independent Theatre Owners Association in the *Hollywood Reporter* in May 1938 listed Crawford among the actors "whose dramatic ability is unquestioned, but whose box office draw is nil." Though it wasn't a completely fair assertion at the time, Crawford's career suffered for several years because of the accusation in that advertisement, until she had a major comeback with 1945's *Mildred Pierce*, which earned her the Academy Award for Best Actress. By 1955, Crawford had settled into middle-aged roles, though she was still seven years away from the role that would define her later career in 1962's *What Ever Happened to Baby Jane?*, also directed by *Autumn Leaves* director Robert Aldrich.

Crawford had been a pioneer in roles for older actresses who were considered by Hollywood too old to play a standard leading lady yet too popular and glamorous to be relegated to grandmotherly roles. In *Autumn Leaves*, Crawford plays Millie Wetherby, an unmarried middle-aged woman who works as a typist in Hollywood and secludes herself in her apartment. However, she meets and later marries a younger army veteran, Burt (later Academy Award winner Cliff Robertson), after meeting him in a diner and lowering her guard. Unfortunately for Millie, she soon learns that Burt is a serial liar, and the situation becomes worse when his ex-wife, Virginia (Miles), shows up after Burt claims he had never been previously married. Virginia tells Millie that

Burt is lying to her about his past and that he is a weak but danger-ous man. Millie discovers that Burt is suffering from mental anguish stemming from discovering an affair between Virginia and his father, and he begins to suffer a mental breakdown after Virginia reemerges in his life. However, after treatment in a mental hospital, Burt emerges with a clearer mind, and he and Millie reunite. The film's relatively simplistic depiction of mental illness is absurd under a modern lens, but it is certainly not uncharacteristic of depictions of mental illness in Hollywood films at the time.

This "competition" between lead actresses of *Autumn Leaves* in the screenplay was highlighted in the *New York Times* review of the movie, with writer Bosley Crowther calling *Autumn Leaves* a "dismal tale." Among numerous shots at Crawford's performance in the film, Crowther remarked that "Vera Miles looks a lot more fetching than Miss Crawford," which was certainly not a fair comparison as Craw-ford was about twenty-five years older than Miles, and her character was clearly supposed to feel self-conscious in the film in comparison to Miles's character's youth and beauty, though Miles's Virginia is depicted as a "tramp" and a "slut," as Crawford's Millie calls her. The review in *Picturegoer* even complimented Miles for being "excellent in the role of [Burt's] sluttish first wife." Unsurprisingly, Miles was ulti-mately unsatisfied with her performance in the film as a rather one-note character, telling Mike Connolly, "That wasn't Vera Miles in that picture—that was a girl named Verna Mills." Nonetheless, the film did win over some critics, and Aldrich was awarded the inaugural Silver Bear for Best Director for the film at the 1956 Berlin International Film Festival.[15]

As important as starring in a Columbia film alongside Hollywood royalty like Joan Crawford, Miles remained committed to her televi-sion career, which had been sustaining her between her infrequent film roles. Her hard work on the small screen was paying off for her big time—the September 28 edition of *Variety* reported that Miles's increasing stardom led to her television salary increase from $500 an episode to $2,000 an episode. In his March 2, 1956, column, Mike

Connolly revealed that Miles's television salary now started at $3,500 an episode. Connolly updated the number in February 1958 to $5,000 an episode.

Even more important for Miles than the money was the exposure. Much like how one of her television roles caught the eye of John Ford's wife, another one of Miles's roles caught the attention of another prestigious filmmaker—one whose mentorship of her would, for better and worse—go on to define the rest of her career.

5

The New Grace Kelly

By the mid-1950s, English-born filmmaker Alfred Hitchcock was arguably the most recognized name in filmmaking on both sides of the Atlantic. After beginning his career in film in England as a title card designer in 1919 for Famous Players–Lasky (later Paramount Pictures), Hitchcock delved into nearly every aspect of film production, and by the mid-1920s, he was directing films. His most notable early production, 1927's *The Lodger: A Story of the London Fog*, a thriller about a serial killer, marked the type of film that Hitchcock would become best known for—suspenseful dramas that thrilled audiences, often with beautiful women in prominent roles as victims in distress. *The Lodger* was a significant hit, and its success would lead Hitchcock to direct 1929's *Blackmail*, which is generally considered by historians to be the first British sound film (it began production as a silent film, and both silent and talkie versions were released to theaters). *Blackmail*, about a woman who is blackmailed after killing a man in self-defense for trying to rape her, was another major hit for Hitchcock. Behind the scenes, the filmmaker married Alma Reville in 1926, and she would become a key collaborator on many of his films as a screenwriter, editor, and confidant, among other roles.

Over the next ten years, Hitchcock directed several hit films in England, with many also released to great acclaim and box office success in the United States, including 1935's *The 39 Steps* and 1938's *The Lady Vanishes*. The former marked the first film Hitchcock made with actress Madeleine Carroll, who established the mold for the character archetype that would become so associated with the filmmaker's movies, the "Hitchcock blonde"—an icy, mesmerizing, and nearly ethereal beauty whose allure is virtually impossible to ignore by Hitchcock's male protagonists. Though Hitchcock and Carroll only made two films together—their second film was 1936's spy thriller *Secret Agent*—her character left a significant impression on Hitchcock, and he would continue to cast Hitchcock blondes in many of his films throughout his career.

After the box office success of *The Lady Vanishes*, a mystery thriller about a woman who disappears while traveling by train, Hitchcock agreed to a substantial contract with Hollywood producer David O. Selznick—at the time working on the historical epic *Gone with the Wind*—to create films in Hollywood. His first American film, *Rebecca*, marked a stylistic change for the director under Selznick's control but resulted in a hit that was awarded Best Picture at the following year's Academy Awards ceremony. Through World War II, Hitchcock directed several films for various studios, and his now-standard cameo appearances in his films made him one of the most recognizable filmmakers in the world. Hitchcock's popularity and success continued to grow postwar, and his 1946 spy film, *Notorious*, marked his first collaboration with favorite stars Cary Grant and Ingrid Bergman, with the latter as the latest Hitchcock blonde to grace his films. However, after Bergman became involved in a sex scandal with Italian filmmaker Roberto Rossellini, she did not work in the United States for several years. Hitchcock, who arguably reached his peak as a filmmaker in the 1950s, moved on to his latest Hitchcock blonde with star Grace Kelly in his 1954 films *Dial M for Murder* and *Rear Window* and the 1955 film *To Catch a Thief.* Kelly, an elegant figure who was adept at portraying both vulnerability and sexiness in her performances, had recently become a star after her roles in 1952's *High Noon* and John Ford's 1953 hit *Mogambo* and won the Academy Award for Best Actress for 1954's *The Country Girl.* Refined, beautiful, and radiant, Kelly became the quintessential example of the Hitchcock blonde archetype.

Though Miles was also working in Hollywood, her experience in the industry might as well have been on a completely different planet from Kelly's success. Regardless of Miles's frequent work on television throughout 1955, few of the programs offered her substantial opportunities to act. Her most promising television role at that time in her career so far remained her December 1954 starring role on *Medic* as a breast cancer patient. Though Hitchcock saw the program in its initial airing and attempted to reach out to Miles, their attempts at contact fell through. Miles would later tell columnist James Bacon, "He called me and said he would like to talk to me but he left the next day for France to make a picture with Grace Kelly. I was forgotten again—and discouraged." Miles's timing is incorrect here, perhaps for dramatic effect; the *Medic* episode premiered on December 6, 1954, and Hitchcock had filmed the French sequences (featuring Kelly) in *To Catch a Thief* months earlier, in May and June. In actuality, Hitchcock was on his way to his regular holiday in St. Moritz, Switzerland, after completing reshoots on both *To Catch a Thief* and *The Trouble with Harry*, and that was what got in the way of his attempted contact with Miles.[1]

Luckily for Miles, Hitchcock saw a repeat of the episode several months later and again sought her out, this time not neglecting to follow up with her. This time around, Hitchcock had a greater need for Miles than he had at the end of 1954 as he was now seeking a replacement for his preferred leading lady, Grace Kelly.

Though Kelly had quickly become Hitchcock's favorite actress, and he envisioned creating many projects starring her and shaping her career as a star, his three films with Kelly represented some of her final on-screen appearances. In April 1955, Kelly attended the Cannes Film Festival, where she met Prince Rainier III of Monaco. Within weeks, the two began a relationship that increasingly kept Kelly away from Hollywood (she would make just two more films after *To Catch a Thief*: *The Swan*, in which Kelly incidentally played a princess, and *High Society*, both released in 1956). Hitchcock had already been unable to acquire Kelly for his 1955 film *The Trouble with Harry* from her contracted studio, Metro-Goldwyn-Mayer, as he had been able to do for his previous films starring her. Rainier proposed to Kelly in December 1955, and by the fall of that year, it had become clear to Hitchcock that he ought to be on the hunt for a new leading lady who was not bound to start life as a princess across the globe.

Hitchcock was not the only person to see similarities between Kelly and Miles. Comparisons between the two had started before Hitchcock showed any interest in Miles. In his July 1, 1954, column in the *Hollywood Reporter*, Mike Connolly remarked, "Keep Vera Miles in focus for a sudden rise, a la Grace Kelly." Connolly also remarked that "Miles comes across like 'a young Grace Kelly' in *Tarzan's Hidden Jungle*," in his March 28, 1955, column, despite Miles being less than a year younger than Kelly.[2]

Despite their similarities in age and appearance, the trajectories of Miles's and Kelly's careers had been vastly different up to that point. Whereas Miles had grown up in Kansas, came into acting via her beauty pageant experience, and was now a working mother who had appeared on dozens of television programs by the mid-1950s to sustain her career, Kelly was the daughter of a prominent and affluent Philadelphia family—her father, John B. Kelly, was a three-time Olympic gold medalist in rowing and would later lose a close election in his effort to become mayor of Philadelphia. Two of Kelly's uncles were involved in the entertainment industry, and Kelly attended the prestigious American Academy of Dramatic Arts in New York City, which quickly led her to high-paying modeling work and starring on Broadway before she was out of her teenage years. Like Miles, Kelly honed her screen acting in various television programs but made her film debut in 1951's 20th Century Fox film *Fourteen Hours*. Though Kelly kept acting on television, she continued to be cast in film roles, including the 1952 Western *High Noon* opposite Gary Cooper. Like Miles, she would catch the eye of John Ford, who persuaded Metro-Goldwyn-Mayer to sign her to a contract and cast her in his 1953 film *Mogambo*, an adventure film shot on location in Africa. Kelly's performance in *Mogambo* resulted in several accolades, including a Golden Globe Award for Best Supporting Actress and an Academy Award nomination for Best Supporting Actress. By that point, Kelly had arrived as a film star and starred in eight films, including her three films with Hitchcock, before retiring for her life as a princess. Because of Kelly's upbringing and acting education, society roles that Hitchcock and other directors selected her for came naturally to her. As prolific as Miles was, her star had yet to rise to the heights of Kelly's.

Kelly was seemingly born to be, and wanted to be, a respected actress and a star. Miles, on the other hand, wanted primarily to make a living for herself and her children. Professional respect and stardom would be welcome benefits to that end goal but not her motivating factors.

At the time Hitchcock contacted Miles, he was in the process of developing a new anthology television series for CBS, *Alfred Hitchcock Presents*. The series would feature Hitchcock himself as an on-screen presenter of a half-hour thriller or mystery story. Though his name was in the title, Hitchcock would not direct most of the episodes of the series (of the 361 episodes of *Alfred Hitchcock Presents* and its subsequent series, *The Alfred Hitchcock Hour*, Hitchcock directed just 17 episodes). However, Hitchcock directed 4 of the 39 episodes in the program's first season, including the episode that would become the series premiere, a thrilling psychological drama simply titled "Revenge" that starred Miles after Hitchcock was able to get back in contact with her and cast her in the episode.

Miles would not have been able to shoot the episode of *Alfred Hitchcock Presents* if not for Joan Crawford's willingness to accommodate her during the production of *Autumn Leaves*. At this point in her career, Crawford served as de facto producer of several of her projects, such as her 1954 Western *Johnny Guitar*. During the production of *Autumn Leaves*, Crawford and Aldrich approved a rearrangement of the shooting schedule so that Miles could have four days off in mid-September to shoot the episode of *Alfred Hitchcock Presents*, an opportunity she did not want to pass on. Miles later referred to herself as the "president of the Joan Crawford Fan Club" in gratitude for the elder actress's support.

In "Revenge," Miles portrays Elsa, a former dancer who is suffering from mental distress and tells her husband, Carl (portrayed by Ralph

Meeker), that she was attacked by an assailant (the nature of the attack is not clear, though rape is implied), leading the husband to murder the man she claims attacked her when they encounter him later. However, as they drive away from the scene of the crime, she points out another man and claims that he was the one who assaulted her. In the aftermath, her husband realizes that Elsa has lost her senses and that he has killed an innocent man. Miles's portrayal of Elsa—ranging from hysterics to a cold demeanor, along with a sunbathing scene in a bikini—left an impression on Hitchcock, who selected the episode to serve as the series premiere of *Alfred Hitchcock Presents*, airing on October 2, 1955.

"Revenge" marked the first appearance of the type of character that Miles would portray many times in film and television over the rest of her career—a beautiful woman unbalanced by psychological trauma, often revealed in a slow burn from levelheaded to manic throughout the film or episode. Miles was ideally suited for the role, and even if Kelly had been available (she was no longer doing television at that point), it is unlikely that she would have been able to play such a vulnerable character as well as Miles could.

Regarding Hitchcock's interest in her career, Miles told Bob Thomas that it was because Hitchcock felt she radiated something the director called "quiet sex"—a preferred attribute for his leading ladies. "I guess you would call it quiet sex," said Miles. "It appears that nearly all of his leading ladies have had it. This goes back to his earlier days in England when he directed Madeline Carroll. He continued in Hollywood with stars like Ingrid Bergman and Joan Fontaine." Miles cited the kissing scene between Cary Grant and Bergman in Hitchcock's 1946 film *Notorious* and the visit by Grace Kelly to James Stewart's apartment in his 1954 film *Rear Window* as examples of "quiet sex" on screen—scenes marked by their sexual energy that do not rely on revealing the actresses' skin. She continued, "I think there is a misconception in Hollywood. Some people think sex is a matter of measurements. I don't think that is the case."[3] Many may have taken this as odd words coming from a former Miss America contestant whose measurements were routinely touted early in her career, but at this point in Miles's career, she was ready to make a conscious effort to be taken more seriously as an actress.

To keep Miles available for his projects (and to avoid another situation where he was forced to borrow his preferred leading lady from a studio), Hitchcock decided to offer Miles a personal film contract. Herbert Coleman, a longtime collaborator of Hitchcock who worked as associate producer and second unit director on films like *The Trouble with Harry*, *The Man Who Knew Too Much*, *The Wrong Man*, *Vertigo*, *North by Northwest*, and *Topaz* and as a producer for seasons two and three of *The Alfred Hitchcock Hour*, wrote in his memoir *The Man Who Knew Hitchcock: A Hollywood Memoir* about meeting Miles on set at Revue Studios at Universal during the production of "Revenge." According to Coleman's account, Miles said to him that her agent was meeting with Fox about a contract, and if Hitchcock planned on signing her to a contract, he better do it quickly ("By lunchtime, the deal was signed," noted Coleman). Coleman's memory appears to have been off—according to *The Hollywood Reporter*, Hitchcock had initially offered Miles a seven-year deal in late August, three weeks before "Revenge" began filming, and the ultimate five-year deal was not finalized until October. Furthermore, in a 1956 interview with the UK celebrity magazine *Picturegoer*, Miles said that she signed the contract before even meeting Hitchcock.[4]

Miles's agent at the time was Milt Rosner, a veteran agent who had left the well-established Nat C. Goldstone agency in 1954 to open his own agency. Rosner matched Miles's aggressiveness in seeking television roles, and because of that, the deal he negotiated with Hitchcock was only for Miles's film appearances, which, outside of the as-yet-unreleased *The Searchers*, had not been in the same league as Hitchcock's productions. Rosner and Miles had turned down contract offers from Columbia and RKO earlier in the year, likely because they would not allow her to do her own television projects, which had previously sustained her career. New to television, Hitchcock had little interest in Miles's television pursuits and only intended to guide her career in movies.

Miles's role in "Revenge" served as a screen test of sorts, and after Hitchcock filmed the episode, the parties finalized the deal that signed Miles to a five-year, fifteen-film personal contract with Hitchcock, the first American actor Hitchcock had ever signed to such a deal. Of course, Hitchcock did not intend to direct Miles in three films per year and anticipated "loaning" the actress to other studios for projects subject to his approval that would not taint the image he intended to create of her. Hitchcock agreed to delay the start of the contract to January 1956 because of Miles's commitment to the 20th Century Fox film *23 Paces to Baker Street*, itself a Hitchcockian thriller, which was set to film in London.

Though "Revenge" was the second episode of *Alfred Hitchcock Presents* that Hitchcock directed (the first episode he shot, "Breakdown," which starred *Citizen Kane* actor Joseph Cotten, aired as the seventh episode on November 13, 1955), Hitchcock chose the episode starring Miles as the series premiere, partially to introduce his latest "discovery" to the television audience, though nearly every television viewer had likely seen Miles a half-dozen or more times before because of her prolific television work.

"On paper, that made perfect sense," notes Joel Gunz, president of HitchCon International Alfred Hitchcock Conference and editor of *Hitchcockian Quarterly*.

As a Hollywood A-lister and the villain of *Shadow of a Doubt* (1943), Joseph Cotten would have brought plenty of eyeballs to the new show and established its Hitchcockian bona fides. But then he worked with Vera Miles for the first time on "Revenge." Immediately, he knew he had something special. He loved her performance and her work so much that he decided to flip the order around and "Revenge" became the inaugural episode of the series. "Breakdown" is great, but it's very experimental—really an art film—something that would have been better tucked into the midseason. And with beautiful Vera Miles spending the first half of the episode in her bikini—well, that's another way to get your ratings up. But her performance, too, was so powerful. While working with her, Hitchcock discovered that she had it all—beauty, brains, and talent. A line from the episode sticks out in my mind, where her husband, Carl, describes her as "a woman of hidden talents, and some not so hidden." I can hear Hitchcock himself applying that to Miles.[5]

The *Variety* review of "Revenge" spent a good deal of its content questioning whether or not Hitchcock's "brand" could sustain a television series (of course, the series aired for ten seasons, not including a 1985 revival several years after Hitchcock's death) and questioned the absurdity of the episode's premise (particularly regarding how quickly Meeker's character turned to murder while knowing his wife's mental issues). In fact, the review gives more praise to Hitchcock for his bookending segments than to Miles or Meeker for their lead performances (similarly, the *Motion Picture Daily* review called Hitchcock "priceless, and the best introducer of a commercial yet seen"). *Hollywood Reporter* called the premiere episode "a brilliantly acted, neatly directed drama," though criticized the ending for being inconclusive. Regardless, the show turned out to be a hit, and the series was a significant reason Hitchcock sustained his reputation as one of the most well-known filmmakers in the world for the rest of his career.[6]

Miles's contract with Hitchcock was reported widely on October 12, 1955, just ten days after "Revenge" aired. In January 1957, Hitchcock justified signing Miles to his first-ever personal contract to *Parade* by claiming there was a "terrible shortage of leading ladies in the film industry," adding a not subtly aggressive shot at his previous protégé in his well-known droll manner, "I built up Grace Kelly in *Dial M for Murder, Rear Window*, and *To Catch a Thief* and I expected that she would stay around for a while. But no. She falls in love and calls it quits." Hitchcock noted that he found himself impressed by Miles's "quality of restraint plus her potential of sex appeal. This was the same combination Grace Kelly had. When Grace first began, you know, she was shy, lacked confidence. Once success touched her, she gained authority. She began to radiate. I thought there was a chance of this happening to Vera. . . . The great actress is someone who can do nothing well, but who tries," said Hitchcock. "Vera Miles tries very hard. She's a glutton for work. I'm sure she'll be great. There's always a market for quiet sex."[7]

The constant Grace Kelly comparisons by Hitchcock and the Hollywood press would become something of an image issue for Miles over the next several years. "I know Hitchcock said in interviews that he felt the same way directing Vera that he did with Grace, and he spoke about her style and intelligence as well as her quality of understatement," explains Rebecca McCallum, writer, speaker, editor, and creator/host of the *Talking Hitchcock* podcast. "I think very early on he's identifying or perhaps over-identifying or misidentifying her as being a kind of Grace Kelly template."[8]

Just days after the contract was announced, Hitchcock revealed to the press that Miles would star in his next film, *The Wrong Man* (his seventh and final film to be released by Warner Bros.), which would begin shooting in February 1956, and also said that his following film, titled *From among the Dead*, would shoot in Louisiana and would be based on the 1954 novel *D'entre les morts* by the French crime novelist team Boileau-Narcejac. Hitchcock also spoke about his intention to adapt the African-set novel *Flamingo Feather* by Laurens van der Post into a film. Though Hitchcock had originally hoped to reunite James Stewart and Grace Kelly as the leads of that film, he also briefly considered casting Miles when it became clear that Kelly would not be returning to Hollywood to make films. Ultimately, Hitchcock abandoned the project after visiting South Africa and determining that it would be too daunting with the country's limited production resources, and it's unlikely that Miles was in the mix for the role for very long before he dropped the film from his schedule. Hitchcock seemed to have already given up on *Flamingo Feather* by the time of his press conference on July 23, 1956, in Rome on the way back from his African scouting trip. At the press conference, Hitchcock announced Miles would star with Stewart in his next film, now reported as titled *Among the Dead* (though that may have been misheard or a mistranslation, as the title would later switch back to *From among the Dead*).

Because Miles retained her ability to do television work in her contract with Hitchcock, she was already back on television by the end of the month in the October 30 episode of *Schlitz Playhouse* on CBS titled "The Soil." In mid-November, Miles filmed an episode of *The 20th Century-Fox Hour* titled "Man on the Ledge," which was adapted from the 20th Century Fox 1951 film *Fourteen Hours*—incidentally, Kelly's first film—which aired on December 28.

In his November 12 column, Mike Connolly claimed that Warner Bros. wanted Miles to play the female lead opposite William Holden in the air force film *Toward the Unknown*, though it didn't happen because shooting would've overlapped with the filming of Hitchcock's *The Wrong Man* (the part was played by Virginia Leith instead). On November 26, Miles traveled to London to shoot the drama *23 Paces to Baker Street* for 20th Century Fox, her last film before the start of her contract with Hitchcock and her first trip outside of the United States. The role in that film was important to Miles for three reasons. "I took it because the role was a good one, I had never been abroad, and I needed the money," she told *Films in Review*.[9]

Production on the film carried over to the new year, though Miles returned to the United States in mid-December, and production picked up in Hollywood in January. At the same time, Gordon Scott was shooting *Tarzan and the Lost Safari* in London (Scott first shot the film in Africa, and before he left for the continent, Miles threw a going-away party for him at her home). RKO had released the previous film, *Tarzan's Hidden Jungle*, and though the Tarzan films were always reliable money makers, the studio canceled the Tarzan contract due to RKO's ongoing financial issues (RKO would release its final film, *Verboten!*, in March 1959). Lesser struck a deal with MGM (which had previously released the Tarzan films from 1932 to 1942), which meant two major improvements for *Tarzan and the Lost Safari*: a bigger budget and, for the first time for the long-running Tarzan series, a color feature in CinemaScope.

Erskine Johnson reported in his column on January 10, 1956, that Miles and Scott "lived it up in London nightclubs" while they were both in England. In her January 21 column, Sheilah Graham reported that after Miles returned to California, Scott called her every day, causing Miles to quip that the telephone bill would end up costing so many pounds that "it's going to be hard for Tarzan to pick up!" It seemed that Tarzan's loincloth was wearing well on Scott, because as early as January 1956, Sol Lesser was talking to the press about a Tarzan television series starring Scott, though the idea would not gain traction until 1958, after Lesser resolved a dispute over ownership of the Tarzan television rights with Commodore Productions, the company that produced the Tarzan radio serial and claimed to also hold the character's television rights.[10]

The mystery film *23 Paces to Baker Street* was a good primer for Miles to prepare for what was supposed to be a long association with Hitchcock. In the film, Miles assists a blind playwright (played by fellow American actor Van Johnson, whom Miles would work with again in 1959's *Web of Evidence*) in investigating a possible crime that Johnson's character overheard talk about at his local pub. While not a box office success, the film allowed Miles to shoot a movie in London, which was an experience she very much enjoyed. The production was not without its issues; to give the London scenes the "proper" foggy atmosphere befitting its reputation, the crew heated mineral oil until it evaporated and then ran it through cooling pipes. Miles would tell Sheilah Graham that the fog was so thick that "the pigeons aren't flying, they're walking." On its release in the United States in May 1956, shortly before the wide release of *The Searchers*, Miles received some positive reviews for her performance. The *Variety* review noted that Miles "adds a refreshing charm as well as some sound histrionics." The *Harrison's Reports* review called Miles "charming and sympathetic," though the review in the *Independent Film Journal* simply referred to her as a "comely brunette." Nonetheless, though Miles enjoyed working on the 20th Century Fox film and shooting in London, greater things for her career were yet to come.[11]

On March 12, 1956, Warner Bros. previewed *The Searchers* across the United States at thirty-two theaters. Approximately twelve thousand industry, exhibitor, and press representatives attended the screening, which was over eight weeks in advance of the film's May 26 general release. The glowing *Motion Picture Daily* review of *The Searchers*, which was published two days after the March 12 preview, said that Miles and costar Hunter "both play with a surprising humor and charm." *The Searchers* had its world premiere in Chicago on May 16, with both Wayne and Bond in attendance (Wayne received a special citation declaring him the leading motion picture star of Illinois by Governor William G. Stratton). It opened in Los Angeles on May 30 at thirteen theaters. After its release, the *Los Angeles Times* review called Miles's character "a very clever and appealing spitfire."[12]

By that time, Miles had already shot her scenes for *The Wrong Man*, which was intended to be a career-making film performance for her. Hitchcock first became interested in making *The Wrong Man* after his agent, Herman Citron, showed him an article in *Life* magazine about the true story of Christopher Emmanuel "Manny" Balestrero, a New York City musician who was wrongfully accused of committing several robberies in the vicinity of his home in Jackson Heights, Queens, New York City. When he attempted to borrow money from his wife's insurance plan in January 1953, he was identified by two employees of the insurance office as the man who had robbed the office twice the previous year. After a mistrial, Manny Balestrero was acquitted of the robberies during a second trial when police apprehended the true culprit, a man who looked uncannily like Balestrero. Unfortunately, during the proceedings, Balestrero's wife, Rose, suffered a nervous breakdown—blaming herself for the whole ordeal since Manny had been at the insurance office in the first place because they needed money for a dental operation for her—and had to be institutionalized. After the acquittal, the Balestrero family moved to Florida to seek help for Rose's mental health. Balestrero ended up receiving a small settlement after suing both New York City and the insurance company.

The material was very different from Hitchcock's other American films so far. Not only was it based on true events, but because the story was a matter of public record, the outcome of the film would not be in doubt. The real-life Balestrero, as a working musician, was far from the well-off society types often depicted in Hitchcock's films. Hitchcock instructed cinematographer Robert Burks to film *The Wrong Man* in black and white to add to its documentary-style authenticity. It also would be shot largely on location in New York City, including at Vitagraph Studios, located in Flatbush, Brooklyn. As one of the oldest production facilities in the United States, Vitagraph was established as a silent movie studio and was acquired by Warner Bros. in 1925. *The Wrong Man* would be Hitchcock's last film for Warner Bros., after which he began a long-term deal that he had already signed with Paramount Pictures.

Hitchcock intended to use the film to launch what he anticipated to be a long association with Miles, who he cast as Rose, and he asked the screenwriter of *The Wrong Man*, Maxwell Anderson, to expand her role in the screenplay. Hitchcock cast Henry Fonda as Manny. Fonda had been a Hollywood star even before his Academy Award–nominated performance in the 1940 film adaptation of John Steinbeck's novel *The Grapes of Wrath*, directed by John Ford. After that, he appeared in several hit movies, including *The Lady Eve* (1941), *The Ox-Bow Incident* (1943), *My Darling Clementine* (1946), and *Fort Apache* (1948). However, following *Fort Apache*, Fonda took a break from Hollywood and returned to Broadway, where he had started his career. On stage, he originated the title role in the play *Mister Roberts*. He reprised the role in the 1955 film adaptation codirected by John Ford, which led to a major falling-out between former frequent collaborators Fonda and Ford, though it marked Fonda's return to film after a seven-year absence from the screen. Now back to making films, Fonda, along with Hitchcock and Miles, traveled to Florida in January 1956 to visit with the Balestrero family to learn about the people they would be portraying on screen.

Miles's casting opposite Fonda, twenty-four years her senior, in *The Wrong Man* continued a pattern established in *Wichita* of Miles playing the spouse or love interest of much older men in her films (Fonda, who turned fifty-one years old during filming, plays a thirty-eight-year-old man in the film). This was not uncommon in Hollywood in that era, but for Miles, it was a regular occurrence—most of her leading men, including Joel McCrea, Bob Hope, James Stewart, John Wayne, and Fred MacMurray, were more than two decades older than she was (Lloyd Bridges, her love interest in *Pride of the Blue Grass*, seems like a youngster at only a mere sixteen years older than her). It wasn't until Miles starred opposite Sam Elliott in 1972's *Molly and Lawless John* that she was finally on the other side of the age equation (Miles is fifteen years older than Elliott).

Though Hitchcock had every intention of building Miles up as his next glamorous leading lady, there was one significant concern with her role in *The Wrong Man* in building that image—she would be playing a Queens housewife, a character far removed from the society women played by Grace Kelly or Ingrid Bergman in Hitchcock's earlier films. In an attempt at authenticity, Hitchcock intended that Miles would wear clothes purchased from the same Queens basement store where Rose purchased her clothes (Hitchcock and his wife, Alma, personally selected the wardrobe from the Queens store). The housewife wardrobe even took Fonda by surprise, and he admitted he didn't realize she was his costar at first, telling Miles on set, "I've been watching you from a distance for five minutes, wondering who the very pretty girl was. Honestly, I didn't recognize you until I came closer," to which Miles replied, "Henry, that's very complimentary—or else you need glasses."[13]

However, to get a more glamorous image of Miles out to the public before the release of the film, Hitchcock asked Herbert Coleman to accompany her on a ten-day press tour in New York City in clothing designed by Paramount Studios' famed costume designer Edith Head, who had already won six Academy Awards for costuming (she would receive a total of eight in her career, making her the most-awarded woman in Academy history in any category). Miles's new wardrobe cost Warner Bros. $5,000. The publicity tour involved Miles attending a meeting for the Variety Club Tent No. 35, a community service organization that included the New York Film Critics organization at Toots Shor's Restaurant, a popular New York City hot spot for celebrities. Humorously, according to Coleman, Warner Bros. wanted to present the $5,000 wardrobe to Miles as a gift on behalf of the studio after filming. However, Hitchcock had already gone ahead and gifted Miles the wardrobe himself before production wrapped. Miles charmed the New York press with her public appearances, speaking at length about her excitement for her new phase in her career with Hitchcock and her desire for more serious, substantial roles.

In another attempt at authenticity, the film had two technical advisers—Frank D. O'Connor, the Queens County district attorney, and George Groves, a retired sergeant of the New York City Police Department. O'Connor was the lawyer who defended Manny (he is played in the film by Anthony Quayle) and later served as the district attorney of the county from 1956 to 1965. Hitchcock and his production team also met with as many people as possible who were involved in the real-life case, including Judge William B. Groat, who presided over Manny's trials.

The film would also shoot at the real-life Stork Club, the famed Manhattan nightclub known as one of the pinnacles of New York City nightlife, where Manny played bass as part of the house band. Established in 1929 by Sherman Billingsley, the Stork Club was world-renowned and added the otherwise missing element of glamour to the film. A celebrity interview television series titled *The Stork Club* and hosted by Billingsley had recently wrapped up a five-year run, which further spotlighted the nightclub in popular culture. The film's title sequence depicts a typical night at the Stork Club. The production shot two nights at the Stork Club, including many of Billingsley's regular guests in the crowd (the film ends with a card saying, "We are grateful to Mr. Sherman Billingsley for his gracious cooperation in permitting scenes of this picture to be photographed at the Stork Club in New York City").

The Wrong Man began shooting in New York on March 26, 1956 (Miles arrived in New York on March 11), and ended its shoot in the city in mid-April. Some of the scenes were shot at the actual locations where the events depicted in the film happened. For example, the film was shot at the Queens County Jail, where the real-life prisoners recognized Fonda. One asked Fonda what he had been arrested for, and the actor reportedly quipped, "I'm accused of trying to steal scenes from Vera Miles, but they'll never make it stick. All the witnesses can testify she stole scenes from me."[14]

Although Miles and Scott were rumored to get married in New York while Miles was shooting *The Wrong Man*, immediately after the New York sequences were completed, Miles traveled to Yuma, Arizona, where, during the weekend of April 14–15, 1956, she and Scott wed. It was the same weekend that both Grace Kelly and President Truman's daughter, Margaret Truman, had their high-profile weddings ("We figured it was the perfect time to slip away without publicity," Miles later told the *Los Angeles Times*), though the couple intended to have a second ceremony in Los Angeles in June. The couple also intended to take a honeymoon but returned to Hollywood immediately after the wedding because Miles was needed to shoot interior sequences for *The Wrong Man* on set. Even in the wedding coverage, Miles couldn't avoid comparisons to Grace Kelly. She would remark to Bob Thomas about Kelly, "I married the king of the jungle and she married the Prince of Monaco." Gossip columnist Erskine Johnson quipped that Miles said she and her Tarzan husband were decorating their home in "early jungle" decor, and the November 1956 issue of *Screenland* reported that Miles joked she wore "an old leopard-skin loin cloth" from Scott as a good luck charm.[15]

On April 30, *The Wrong Man* resumed production in Los Angeles for interior shooting on sound stages and finished shooting by the first week of June. The dramatic range of Miles's role as Rose Balestrero was unlike any she had yet attempted on film, and, unsurprisingly, Hitchcock demanded much of her during rehearsals and filming. Though nothing was made of that in the press at the time, decades later it would become a source of controversy. In his 1983 book, *The Dark Side of Genius*, Hitchcock biographer Donald Spoto attributed Hitchcock's heavy attention to Miles during the production of *The Wrong Man* to an obsession with her, followed by resentment after she married Gordon Scott. Although Spoto never outright calls the relationship abusive, he asserts that Hitchcock demanded much time with her behind closed doors during the production of *The Wrong Man*. Spoto's book also contained Tippi Hedren's account of the mistreatment she faced while working with Hitchcock while she was under contract to him in the 1960s, and through that lens, it's apparent that Spoto was perhaps casting the Hitchcock–Miles relationship as a degree or two of intensity less than Hitchcock's later relationship with Hedren and maybe even a prototypical version of it.

While that makes for a biographical narrative arc, the thesis didn't sit well with the principals involved. Herbert Coleman, who spoke to Spoto for his book, believed that his discussions with Spoto ruined his friendship with Miles because he felt their conversation may have given Spoto the suggestion that Hitchcock was inappropriate with her. Coleman wrote in his memoir, "If I'd known he intended *The Dark Side of Genius* to be the title of his unauthorized biography, I would have been forewarned and would not have granted him the interview." Regarding Miles, Coleman wrote, "Donald Spoto's numerous misquotes, mistakes, and outright inventions damaged and destroyed many close friendships. The loss of my friendship with Vera Miles, a lady for whom I had and still have deep respect and affection, was, I believe, caused by Spoto's unfounded statement indicating a possible hidden affair between Hitch and Vera." Coleman also referred to Miles in his book as "a lady with high moral standards, which she would protect whatever the cost."[16]

Spoto's book doesn't outright accuse Hitchcock and Miles of having a physical relationship, but it certainly claims that Hitchcock forced Miles to spend a substantial amount of time with him behind closed doors. Unsurprisingly, Miles did not speak with Spoto for his book. She only conducted one interview on the topic of *The Dark Side of Genius*, a widely distributed June 1983 interview with Richard Freedman for Newhouse News Services (now Advanced Publications) to promote *Psycho II*. Miles stated that Patricia Hitchcock, Alfred's daughter, had "put me off" from speaking with Spoto and said his descriptions of the making of *The Wrong Man* and *Psycho* are "unfactual gossip" and "all wrong." As for the allegations of Hitchcock's abuse toward his lead actresses, Miles responded, "Anybody who knows me knows I would never put up with that sort of thing. There was always a great deal of respect between Hitchcock and me. Spoto says he (Hitchcock) rehearsed me for nine hours a day on *The Wrong Man*, which is nonsense." Specifically regarding any implication that Miles carried on an affair with Hitchcock, she said, "And as for playing casting couch to get the role, I'd have told him to go to hell. Neither of us had time for that kind of thing." Miles, having already allegedly ignored advances earlier in her career from Howard Hughes and Ward Bond, and likely others in the industry, too, was not inexperienced in the power dynamics that led to sexual harassment on set and behind closed doors. It's also worth noting that in his 2008 book about Hitchcock's actresses, *Spellbound by Beauty: Alfred Hitchcock and His Leading Ladies*, Spoto does not make the same kind of implications about Hitchcock's relationship with Miles as he did in *The Dark Side of Genius*, perhaps his way of backing off the assertion that he made in his earlier book.[17]

If Hitchcock indeed spent a significant amount of time working with Miles during the filming of *The Wrong Man*, the more likely explanation is that the role demanded more of Miles than any of her previous film roles, and Hitchcock wanted to ensure she was giving him the performance he envisioned for the challenging role. Furthermore, Hitchcock was using the film to debut the actress he intended to be his leading lady for the next several years; he wanted her public debut to be as successful as possible. As any student of filmmaking would know, it is not uncommon for a director to work very closely with an actor to ensure that they are striking the right performance for the film. Add that to the fact that Hitchcock was investing a substantial amount of both time and money into Miles's career, and it's not surprising that he worked very closely with her during the production of *The Wrong Man* to present Miles to audiences in what he envisioned was the proper way. As McCallum notes, Hitchcock was seeking a very particular performance from Miles. "Many women in Hitchcock films, like Tippi Hedren in *The Birds*, start very vibrant, in control, and dominant, and then become a different kind of woman," says McCallum. "I think there's an interesting correlation between her character and Rose that is interesting. When we get to Rose's breakdown—especially in the context of when the film was made in 1956—it's not an over-the-top, disrespectful, or prejudiced performance. It's nuanced and subtle."[18]

In addition, *The Wrong Man* was a learning experience for Hitchcock as well, since it was the first film he made in which he was heavily focused on reproducing actual events as accurately as possible. Lending from its docudrama style, *The Wrong Man* is slow-paced, even by the storytelling standards of the time. Fonda's Manny doesn't appear before a judge until fifty minutes into the film, and Miles's character doesn't start experiencing her mental breakdown until ten minutes after that, nearly forty minutes before the film ends. Much of the film is a symphony of confined spaces, from subways to prison cells, even after Manny is released from jail, because the Balestrero home is made up of small rooms (certainly not out of the ordinary for the urban sprawl of Jackson Heights, Queens). Though Manny's innocence is obvious to the audience from Hitchcock's opening monologue (if not from the title of the movie alone), Hitchcock does a masterful job of demonstrating the film's characters disbelieving Manny's innocence. This is particularly evident during the trial scenes as the jury, lawyers, reporters, and those in the gallery are shown losing interest in the proceedings, even appearing bored, as the evidence against Manny stacks up.

While the first hour of the film focuses almost exclusively on Manny, the last half hour of the film belongs to Miles in her startling portrayal of a woman having a nervous breakdown when she finds herself unable to reconcile her belief in her husband's innocence with the lack of evidence supporting it. At that point, Rose's breakdown becomes the film's most significant conflict because, by this point, the audience is aware that Manny did not commit the crimes he stands accused of committing. In the context of 1956 Hollywood releases, Miles's performance is one of the film's highlights. Dr. Bannay, who examines her mental state, dramatically describes her condition as follows: "She's living in another world from ours. A frightening landscape that could be on the dark side of the moon." This is why at the end of the film, when Manny comes face to face with the true culprit, his only words to the criminal are "Do you realize what you've done to my wife?" At this point, the conflict is no longer about proving his innocence—it's now about his wife's mental health. Regarding the ongoing comparisons between Miles and Grace Kelly, Miles's performance in *The Wrong Man* required her to do more than what Kelly had done in terms of an emotional performance in any of her three features with Hitchcock.

"While I don't find the terms 'Hitchcock woman' or 'Hitchcock blond' incredibly helpful, I think you can certainly look for trends, motifs, or repetitions in Hitchcock's casting of and representation of women," argues McCallum. "To me, Rose Balestrero is not the typical Hitchcock heroine but then I really don't think there is such a thing as a typical Hitchcock heroine—each woman is so dynamic and unique and of course finds herself in a very specific and individual circumstance. Miles communicates so much non-verbally and so terrifically in this film. She's very grounded and relatable as well. Here again, Miles is playing a housewife, but she communicates so much with her face—primarily her eyes, which I think are so emotive."[19]

On its release in New York City on December 22, 1956—though the film wouldn't be released in much of the United States, including Los Angeles, until after the new year—*The Wrong Man* received generally strong reviews, particularly for its cast. *Motion Picture Daily* called the movie "an exceptionally well-made film" and noted that Miles plays her role with "exceptional skill." *Harrison's Reports* largely praised the film as well (and said both Fonda and Miles are "highly effective in the principal roles") but called the film's subject matter "depressing." On the other hand, the *New York Times* review of the film criticized it for not being suspenseful enough, saying it "generates only a modicum of drama," though praised Miles for her ability to "convey a poignantly pitiful sense of fear of the appalling situation into which they have been cast." The review in *Variety* predicted that it would do strong business (and that Miles "registers strongly" in the film). The review in *Film Bulletin* also called the movie "grim" but commended Fonda's and Miles's performances as "high caliber." The *Motion Picture Exhibitor* also predicted that the film would have a strong box office return, calling the cast (including Miles by name) both "pretty near perfect" and "particularly outstanding."[20]

Yet despite those strong reviews and the compelling true-life back-story, as well as Hitchcock's significantly raised profile because of his television series, *The Wrong Man* was Hitchcock's lowest-grossing film released by Warner Bros. As it was the final film on his contract with the studio, it seems that Warner Bros. made less of an effort to promote it. Perhaps the film's darker tone—far different from Hitchcock's earlier (and more successful) 1956 release, *The Man Who Knew Too Much*—also turned audiences away. Whereas *The Man Who Knew Too Much* is full of color and shot in VistaVision, the starker, black-and-white cinematography of *The Wrong Man* is confined to small spaces, and the tone tells a much dourer story that was far from an audience-pleaser despite Manny being eventually declared innocent. The film's lack of commercial success did not seem to affect Hitchcock's attitude much, as, at the time of its release, he was distracted by health issues and deep into the preproduction of his next film, *Vertigo*. Years later, Hitchcock revealed he had no love lost for the film. In his interviews with François Truffaut, he called *The Wrong Man* "among the indifferent Hitchcocks" and said, "I don't feel that strongly about it."[21]

Curiously enough, for the actress Hitchcock was promoting as the "new Grace Kelly," Miles's role in *The Wrong Man* was nothing like the three characters played by Kelly in Hitchcock's previous films. Instead of playing a well-dressed socialite in glorious Technicolor (and, in the case of *Dial M for Murder*, also in 3D), Miles was presented as a working-class housewife in black-and-white cinematography. And while her role in *The Wrong Man* required her to emote far more than Kelly had to do in any of her films with Hitchcock, it didn't go unnoticed that this was perhaps not the right role to launch Hitchcock's next alluring star. *Picturegoer* critic Ernie Player savaged Miles's presentation in the film, calling the role a "morbid misfire" for Miles, explaining, "[Hitchcock] ought to have picked a role that fitted her like a velvet glove" and calling the character she plays in *The Wrong Man* "beyond her present strength" and "to blazes with the pun—miles wrong. For ANY actress the role would be painful and difficult." He also notes that this was nothing like the buildup that Hitchcock gave Kelly, the actress Miles was meant to replace.[22]

Player's hyperbole aside, he makes a strong point about the presentation of Miles in his remarks. Whether or not one agrees that Miles did a competent job of performing in the film—even if most critics would agree that she does—her presentation as a housewife suffering a breakdown in the film lacks the aura of the icy, ethereal Hitchcock blonde that had been established by her Hitchcock film actress predecessors. On the surface, there's simply no comparison between Kelly's upper-class Manhattan socialite Lisa Fremont in *Rear Window* and Miles's Queens housewife Rose Balestrero in *The Wrong Man*. Though both characters occupy the same city, they might as well have been from different continents.

It is equally untrue that Kelly was always presented by Hitchcock as a high-society character. "I can certainly see how she could have been his next iconic blond once Grace Kelly was out of the picture," says Gunz. "Remember, Hitch had displayed Kelly as a rather dowdy character in *Dial M for Murder*—all the better to surprise audiences with her glamorous side in *Rear Window*. It seems Hitch may have had similar plans with Miles, even going further to present her as an abject figure in *The Wrong Man* only to bewitch audiences next with her beauty and charm in *Vertigo*."[23]

While *The Wrong Man* shows off Miles's range as an actress—and Miles is quite excellent in the role—it did little to present her as the industry's next big star. Since the latter was Hitchcock's intention, it was one of his rare failures as a film promoter, though perhaps not as a filmmaker. "*The Wrong Man* often gets lost in the midst of the other films during Hitchcock at his peak, but for me, that makes it such a film of interest," explains McCallum. "That is why we should be turning to it. If Miles had starred in *Vertigo*, I wonder if that would change how *The Wrong Man* is perceived."[24]

6

Singing, Dancing, Scandal

For her part, Miles had been increasingly battling back against her "new Grace Kelly" label in the press now that she had completed filming what was meant to be her movie debut as Hitchcock's leading lady for the foreseeable future. A UPI story that began appearing in papers in late April 1956 described Miles as "sizzling upset" at being constantly compared to Grace Kelly and quoting her as saying, "Somebody once called me an 'earthy Grace Kelly.' Really! What is Grace Kelly without that wonderful sophistication? That's like saying somebody is a sophisticated Anna Magnani. I don't think I look anything like Grace." Of course, then the article went on to list the visual similarities between Miles and Kelly, including their hairstyles and standard wardrobe (such as wearing white gloves, though Miles would soon ditch the gloves because the style was so closely associated with Kelly). Whether or not Miles was actually upset about the frequent comparisons made of her to one of the world's most famous women, naturally this article was carefully coordinated publicity that sought to continue to draw a comparison between Miles and Hitchcock's previous star actress to pique the public's interest in Miles. At the same time, Miles disputing the similarities allowed her to have her own voice and sell herself as anything but Hitchcock's necessary replacement for Kelly.[1]

Still, the comparisons were typically careful not to slight Miles. Bob Thomas declared in his column that Miles was "destined for the top rung in Hollywood." He also made the inevitable comparison between Kelly and Miles, calling the former "cool and aloof" as compared to

Miles being "down-to-earth and friendly." The comparisons across the half-dozen syndicated Hollywood gossip columns were still obviously deliberate. Sheilah Graham described Miles in her February 16, 1956, column as having "the same dignity and quiet good looks as Grace Kelly." In his April 9, 1956, column, Harry MacArthur said of Miles that "a lot of people are thinking of as a logical successor to Grace Kelly (in Hollywood, that is, not Monaco)." Gossip queen Hedda Hopper would write, "I haven't seen Vera but am told she's as pretty as Grace Kelly, a good actress with a lot more warmth." Considering that Hopper had already written about Miles at least a half-dozen times in her column over the previous few years as well as Hopper's yearslong coverage of Hitchcock himself, that comment in particular sticks out as a planted remark meant to drum up interest in Miles.[2]

The calculated comparisons would continue for months, but the tone in the Miles–Kelly contrasts took a harsher turn in the press as time went on. Understandably, the repetitive nature of the Kelly questions appeared to eventually get on Miles's nerves. In her August 10, 1956, column, Sheilah Graham said that she stopped Miles while she was biking through the Paramount lot to tell her that in England she is referred to as "the new Grace Kelly." Miles responded, "They wanted to paint on this bicycle: 'This ain't Grace Kelly,' but I said I won't give her any more publicity." The September 1956 issue of *Screenland* said that Miles "gets fighting mad" whenever she is described as the "second Grace Kelly." In a bit of a turnaround, Sheilah Graham reported in her October 3 column that the Louis Shurr Agency was pushing their client Marion Ross as "another Vera Miles" (years later, Miles and Ross would later appear together in an episode each of *Ironside* and *Mannix*). However, the animosity appeared to cool after the December 1956 release of *The Wrong Man*, and the coverage became much more complimentary to Miles instead of presenting her as antagonistic to Kelly. In his January 10, 1957, column, the influential Walter Winchell wrote, "Vera Miles, in *The Wrong Man* movie, has the type of cool beauty that reminds you of Grace Kelly." The March 1957 issue of *Photoplay* declared that Miles was the "prime bet to take over the niche vacated by Princess Grace Kelly" and even complimented Miles by describing her as "more actress than the glamor type."[3]

With Miles starring in four films coming out in the last seven months of 1956 that costarred her with such luminaries as John Wayne, Henry Fonda, and Joan Crawford—in addition to being the only actress under personal contract to Hitchcock—the actress seemed finally poised for her long-awaited film breakthrough.

Unsurprisingly, with so much publicity casting Miles as the next big Hollywood star, Hitchcock began to receive numerous inquiries about her availability. Burt Lancaster and his agent, Harold Hecht, were interested in casting Miles in *Sweet Smell of Success* (presumably in the role ultimately played by Susan Harrison). Instead, Hitchcock first agreed to loan Miles to Paramount Pictures—the studio that he had signed a lucrative deal with in 1953—so she could costar with star comedian Bob Hope in the musical biopic *Beau James*, a film about a Prohibition-era mayor of New York City, Jimmy Walker, which would be Miles's most prominent role to date. While Hitchcock was in Italy after the African scouting trip for the abandoned *Flamingo Feather*, he received a telegram on June 29, 1956, from Paramount Studios head Frank Freeman inquiring about Miles's availability for the film. The deal came together very quickly; Miles's participation in *Beau James* was announced in early July 1956, with dance rehearsals for the film beginning July 10, approximately two weeks before filming began. While *Sweet Smell of Success* did not start filming until well after production on *Beau James* wrapped, the former film underwent well-documented issues in preproduction that Hitchcock may have wanted to steer his star clear from (the dates also would have clashed with Hitchcock's originally intended production dates for his next film that was supposed to star Miles).

Beau James was a passion project for Hope, who by 1956 was one of Hollywood's most successful funnymen, well known for his popular *Road to . . .* movies with costars Bing Crosby and Dorothy Lamour and his television specials that aired regularly since 1947. Hope had come up in vaudeville in New York during the years that Walker had served as mayor of the city, and Hope had been one of Paramount's biggest stars since the late 1930s. In 1955, he had a hit with the biopic *The Seven Little Foys*, about vaudeville performer Eddie Foy. The film's screenwriters, Melville Shavelson and Jack Rose, were nominated for the Academy Award for Best Story and Screenplay for the movie (Shavelson also directed the film in his directorial debut). Shavelson and Rose had met as writers on Hope's radio show and first wrote a screenplay together when they collaborated on the script for Hope's 1949 comedy film *Sorrowful Jones*. Based on the success of what was considered Hope's first "serious" role with *The Seven Little Foys*, Hope, Shavelson, and Rose decided to team up again for another dramatic biopic with *Beau James*.

Walker, who served as mayor of New York from 1926 to 1932, was a colorful and controversial figure who resigned from his office after a bribery scandal. Walker was also known for dating and later marrying *Ziegfeld Follies* showgirl Betty Compton. The relationship began as an affair while Walker was married to his first wife. When it came to *Beau James*, just securing participation agreements from the families of the principals involved cost the production $50,000 (including the mother of the late Compton, since Compton had died of breast cancer in 1944) and required three attorneys working nationwide. Compton's mother required in her participation agreement that the actress who played Compton physically resembled her daughter. However, Miles, who played Compton in the film, had very little resemblance to the former showgirl.

In what later became something of a publicity scandal, Hitchcock ordered some strict provisions in Miles's contract for her wardrobe in *Beau James* and any other film project she was loaned out to while under contract to him: Miles could only wear black, white, or gray clothing. Hitchcock's costuming provision was based on the insight of renowned Paramount Pictures costume designer Edith Head, who would later explain to Bob Thomas that when she tried to dress Miles for *The Wrong Man*, "I found her to be a beautiful girl. But when I tried to dress her in bright colors, something strange happened. They made her look washout, almost mousey-looking, though she certainly is not a mousey girl. So I decided that she would look the best in black, white, and gray." Hitchcock would then issue an edict that Miles could only appear in those shades in all films, including any film that he loaned her out for. To supplement this decree, Head designed Miles's entire wardrobe for her public appearances in those colors as well. Head would later design the costumes for other films starring Miles after *Beau James*: *A Touch of Larceny* (1960), *The Man Who Shot Liberty Valance* (1962)—for which she received one of her many Oscar nominations—and *Hellfighters* (1968). Another Hitchcock restriction was that Miles could only wear pearls as jewelry. Though seemingly limiting her wardrobe choices, Miles herself would publicly agree with Hitchcock's edicts regarding her clothing, telling James Bacon of the Associated Press in March 1957, "I don't look right in bright colors and I seem washed out in pastels, because my hair, skin, and eyes are almost the same color." Miles's Paramount dressing room was later redecorated in the same shades, and her lot bicycle was also black and gray.[4]

Hitchcock's instructions detailed that the limited palette was necessary because he believed that Miles had very delicate coloring. In fact, the wardrobe decree was just one of Hitchcock's several rules regarding the management of her career. He also did not allow her to be photographed with her husband or children to maintain an element of mystery about her, he told *Parade* in January 1957, because picturing her next to her adorable, smiling daughters and her husband, who had the body of a Greek god and was best known for playing a character on screen who spoke in pidgin English, would cast her in a very different light (one could presume that Hitchcock was also concerned that Miles being married to the then-current Tarzan actor could hurt the perception of her as a serious, sophisticated actress). However, this provision did not last long; Miles and Scott would be photographed together numerous times in event photos, and by the end of the year, they would appear in photos together in a feature in the September 1957 issue of *Photoplay*, among other publications. Miles also did a maternity shoot with her husband and daughters in the magazine's

November 1957 issue. But perhaps most daringly, Hitchcock ruled that Miles would no longer pose for "cheesecake" photos because he did not want the former beauty pageant contestant showing too much skin, believing it would prevent her from being taken seriously as an actress (some of the final cheesecake photos of Miles that were distributed by publicists as Hitchcock's rule came to light bore the caption "Perhaps the last leg shots ever of Vera Miles"). The August 1956 issue of *Photoplay* featured an image of Miles in shorts with her legs up in the "style fad" section. It would be one of the final "revealing" photos that she would take while under contract to Hitchcock. By September 1956, gossip columnists were reporting that Hitchcock refused any offers for Miles to pose for cheesecake photography.

Creating the "new" Vera Miles turned out to be a substantial investment for Hitchcock. In April 1957, the *Wall Street Journal* reported that Paramount Pictures and Alfred Hitchcock Productions had spent over $42,000 promoting Miles's new image. In the article, Herbert Coleman said, "We are trying to build an aura of mystery about this girl. Glamor, if you will. We avoid making her too commonplace. You don't go to the movies to see the girl next door. You can look at her over the backyard fence."[5]

"Hitchcock prepared her for *Vertigo*, grooming her to become a star, including dictating her dress not only on set but in her private life as well, and she seemed to go along with that standard Hollywood practice," says Joel Gunz, president of HitchCon International Alfred Hitchcock Conference and editor of *Hitchcockian Quarterly*. "It does seem that she wasn't as interested in being made into a star as he was in making her one. That might have been what attracted Hitchcock to her in the first place. Madeleine Carroll, Kim Novak, and Tippi Hedren also had a somewhat ambivalent relationship with stardom. A cool Hitchcock blond can't want her fame too much. Regardless, she was cooperative because that's what she signed up for when she signed the contract."[6]

Any filmmakers who borrowed Miles for their movies had to adhere to these provisions, and *Beau James*, being Miles's first non-Hitchcock film production while she was under contract to Hitchcock, was forced to serve as the trial subject for the rules. The same Associated Press story by James Bacon in which Miles confirmed her agreement with Hitchcock's costuming rules implied that a legal battle might ensue over the contract between Hitchcock and *Beau James* filmmakers Rose and Shavelson. The duo said they thought Hitchcock was "kidding" about these provisions, only to grow frustrated by them when they discovered they were unable to release cheesecake photos of Miles to promote their film. "Here we have this wonderfully talented and beautifully endowed creature playing a sexy, exciting true-life role as Betty Compton, the showgirl who won Mayor Jimmy Walker of New York away from his wife—and even made him resign as mayor," Shavelson said. "And yet the conditions of Mr. Hitchcock's contract on the loanout make it possible [*sic*] for us to give her the 'hot' buildup she should have." Hitchcock's response to their complaint? "The idea that the more shown of a girl the sexier she is, is pure nonsense. There must always be an element of mystery in building up a star." On November 25, 1956, the *Washington Evening Star* reported that Rose and Shavelson went to Edith Head to complain about the restrictions only to learn that Head was the one who had recommended the restrictions to Hitchcock in the first place. The row carried over into the new year months after filming had wrapped on *Beau James* and just weeks before its release, with Rose and Shavelson reportedly filing a suit against Hitchcock over the restrictions in March 1957.[7]

Ultimately, Rose, Shavelson, and Hitchcock were able to come to some compromises. The lone exception to the wardrobe rule that the filmmakers of *Beau James* were able to get into the film is when Miles performs in a pink period costume (a sequence they had already filmed). In addition, the production released publicity photos of Miles in her showgirl costume, and while they showed some skin—notably Miles's legs—they weren't the traditional cheesecake photos of other actresses, including Miles earlier in her career, that were standardly released by studios.

Another issue that arose during filming was entirely on Miles herself. Though she was playing a showgirl, Miles wasn't trained as a dancer, and Shavelson, Rose, and Hope were unaware of that until after she was signed for the film (of course, it was likely that her dancing prowess wasn't even a topic of conversation while Hitchcock was negotiating her role with Paramount). Miles blamed her lack of experience on the dance floor on her work schedule as a teenager, remarking, "I've just been too busy working all these years. When the kids in my high school class were out dancing, I had to work nights to keep in school." The filmmakers hired veteran choreographer Jack Baker, who had previously worked on *The Bob Hope Show*, to get Miles prepared for the sequence with just two weeks of rehearsals. Baker would tell Ron Burton of the United Press, "She's got beauty and a sense of humor and an analytical mind. But most of all she's got the courage and perseverance that all great stars have to have. Maybe that stuff that she did to put herself through school was terrific training. Wait till you see her dancing in the movie—she's a real pro." Miles clearly picked up the skill quickly; by mid-August, Rose and Shavelson decided to add an extra song, "When We're Alone (Penthouse Serenade)," to the film for Miles to dance to, and on September 15, Hedda Hopper reported in her column that none other than Fred Astaire, the silver screen's biggest dancing star, visited the *Beau James* set while considering casting Miles in his next film, a musical adaptation of silent movie actress Corinne Griffith's 1952 memoir *Papa's Delicate Condition*. Miles would even meet with iconic American songwriter Sammy Cahn, who was writing the lyrics for that project's music, about starring in the film. Though Miles took additional dancing lessons for the project (alongside Scott, who incorporated dancing into his Tarzan workouts), ultimately this version of the film was not made, and a version starring Jackie Gleason was released in 1963. Miles was still in consideration for the role for that version of the film, but actress Glynis Johns starred in the film instead.[8]

While Miles impressively mastered dancing for *Beau James*, singing was another question. All her vocals were dubbed by singer Imogene Lynn, who also dubbed the vocals for actress Mona Freeman in the 1948 Paramount musical film *Isn't It Romantic?*

Astaire wasn't the only individual considering Miles for a film project because of her increasing fame. Miles was also reportedly considered for the lead actress role in the 1957 film *The Joker Is Wild*, the biopic of Prohibition-era entertainer Joe E. Lewis, who was played in the film by Frank Sinatra (Mitzi Gaynor would star in the film instead). Miles was also considered for Bing Crosby's leading lady in the 1957 drama *Man on Fire* (the role would instead be taken by newcomer Inger Stevens). However, the shooting dates of both films would have conflicted with the originally planned shooting schedule of Hitchcock's next film that would star Miles, *From among the Dead*.

Miles may have missed out on starring opposite Astaire, Sinatra, and Crosby, but by the end of the year, Hitchcock was nonetheless commanding a $75,000–$100,000 fee per film for Miles, according to Hedda Hopper. Her star was certainly on the rise; Miles was number thirteen on the list of "Stars of Tomorrow" in the *Motion Picture Herald* as voted on by exhibitors in late 1956. Paramount executives were also impressed with Miles's performance in *Beau James*, with Sheilah Graham reporting in her September 27, 1956, column that the studio attempted to purchase some of Miles's contract from Hitchcock.

Under different circumstances and scheduling, Miles may have very well ended up in at least one of these roles. But Hitchcock held her out of these offerings in part because his planned next film that would star Miles was set to begin filming in early 1957, and he believed it would be her star-making performance. In fact, a Paramount advertisement that began running in the *Motion Picture Daily* on December 7, 1956, claimed that Hitchcock, Stewart, and Miles were already "rolling" on the film even though filming on that project, now titled *Vertigo*, wouldn't begin for another nine months, when Miles was no longer associated with it.

Early in the production of *Beau James*, Scott was in the hospital for minor surgery, Miles was bitten on the cheek by a cat named Rhubarb on set, and her daughter Debra came down with the mumps. Despite concerns, none of these domestic issues impacted the production of the film, which appeared to have gone smoothly. Hope heaped praise on working with Miles to Hedda Hopper, and an unnamed Paramount executive said that Miles had "the best legs we've seen around this studio since Dietrich," referring to the iconic actress and sex symbol Marlene Dietrich, who had been a Paramount star in the early 1930s. During filming, Miles celebrated her twenty-seventh birthday, and Hope threw a surprise party for her. Hitchcock was unable to attend but sent her four dozen roses. Three weeks after her birthday, Miles sent a belated thank-you note to Hitchcock to show appreciation for the roses she received from him on her birthday as well as for a set of flowers he sent to her when *Beau James* began production. Other commentators have suggested that Miles's delayed response was a sign of her rejecting an overbearing Hitchcock, yet the note in question is dated September 13, 1956—the day before production wrapped on *Beau James*, a project keeping Miles otherwise extremely busy up until just weeks before the originally scheduled production start of *Vertigo*.[9]

All things considered, Hope and Paramount were banking on *Beau James* being a big hit for the studio. In February 1957, Rose and Shavelson conducted a poll of exhibitors, columnists, and newspaper editors to determine the final title of the film—though *Beau James* had been used as the title throughout production, the producers offered *Love Me in December* as an alternate title. It had been taken from the name of the film's theme song, "Will You Love Me in December as You Do in May?," a popular tune that had actually been composed by Jimmy Walker in 1906. *Beau James* won by a significant margin, perhaps because the polled individuals were already familiar with the working title or perhaps because the title song was half-a-century old and had no buzz among audiences (another explanation is that the "December" reference in the title may have led audiences to think it was a holiday film).

Paramount executives promoted the film like they believed they had a hit on their hands. In May 1957, Paramount hosted a press screening of *Beau James* at the studio lot, which was preceded by a dinner at Lucey's Restaurant (located across the street from the studio) with Shavelson, Rose, and Miles in attendance. That month, Miles appeared on *The Bob Crosby Show*, a CBS variety television program hosted by the brother of Bing Crosby (Bob Crosby had appeared as himself in Miles's 1951 film *Two Tickets to Broadway*). She appeared on the cover of the May 1957 issue of *McCall's*, a then-popular women's interest magazine, and guested on the June 30 episode of NBC's *The Steve Allen Show*, which was entirely devoted to promoting *Beau James* by featuring both Hope and Miles on the program. Her appeal was even reaching children; in 1957, the Whitman Publishing Company released a Vera Miles paper doll set with a variety of costume options in many colors (Hitchcock's insistence on her strict black-gray-white wardrobe clearly did not pertain to the paper doll version of his starlet).

What appeared to be the film's biggest hurdle was its historical accuracy and the filmmakers' ability to depict Walker's controversial life by the standards of the Production Code. Walker's affair with Compton while still married to his first wife was public knowledge. He and his wife divorced in 1932, and Walker fled to Europe with Compton in the wake of a bribery scandal after resigning from office. Obviously, this history could not be depicted as it happened in a Hollywood production. The filmmakers and the Production Code Administration battled over the film's ending—while the PCA would not accept the affair to be depicted in the film as it happened, it also did not want the filmmakers to veer too far from historical fact. The film's final minutes depict Walker telling his wife he doesn't want a divorce and leaving on his own for Europe—until Compton greets him on the ship, and they speak about their future together as the boat sails away from Manhattan, with swelling music despite the bittersweet ending for Walker.

In what seemed to be an attempt to boost the film's box office chances in Walker's native city, on June 16, the *New York Times* published an essay by Rose and Shavelson defending their screenplay, noting that they heard many different perspectives on Walker from his various associates. "Maybe everything didn't happen the way we've depicted it," they wrote, "but we didn't write this screen play [*sic*] under oath." The duo's piece also defended Hope's portrayal of the city's former mayor and declared that "Miss Miles is going to be one of the biggest stars in Hollywood because she has understanding and depth and ability and lovely legs."[10]

For all its prerelease hype and production expenses, Hope's dream project turned out to be something of a nightmare on its June 26, 1957, release. Several of the initial reviews were generally positive but noted reservations. *Motion Picture Daily* said the film "rather vividly recreated" Walker's time in office and was "invested with a full measure of interest, entertainment, distinguished production values and some convincing if not memorable, performances by Bob Hope as Walker, [and] Vera Miles as Betty Compton." *Harrison's Reports* was confident that the film would face criticism for "whitewashing" Walker's controversial history but remarked, "As an entertainment, however, it is an enjoyable film." *Motion Picture Exhibitor* said that Hope "carries off the impersonation well enough" and hailed its nostalgia but questioned whether younger audiences would have any interest in a movie about a New York City mayor almost a quarter century after he left the office, suggesting that interest in the film would be largely regional. *Variety* declared that audiences would judge the film on its entertainment value and not historical merits and praised Hope's performance. But the *Los Angeles Times* noted that Hope's portrayal "never quite represents Walker" and also questioned the film's historical accuracy. *Film Bulletin* said Miles "gives a well tempered, touching performance," while the *New York Times* listed Miles among the actors who are "surprisingly convincing" in the movie.[11]

Variety reported that *Beau James* grossed an impressive $35,000 at the Astor Theatre in New York City in its first week, and it opened in Los Angeles at the Hollywood Paramount Theater on July 2, followed by an afterparty at the Cocoanut Grove. The Los Angeles premiere was a gala benefit to support Mount Sinai Hospital and Clinic and raised $10,000 or $15,000 (sources differ on the amount). Miles attended the gala, but Hope did not, as he was wrapping up shooting the film *Paris Holiday* overseas in the namesake city (Hope would make a personal appearance at the *Beau James* opening in London later that month). While the film overperformed in New York, in markets like Los

Angeles and Chicago, *Beau James* was considerably less popular, and the box office was strong, though not overwhelming. The following week, *Beau James* expanded to more cities with mixed results (*Variety* reported that the grosses were particularly weak in Boston). While there were some bright spots in scattered cities, *Beau James* lost much of its momentum after its first week of release and never rose higher than tenth place on the national weekly box office charts in *Variety*. On top of that, in November, Paramount had to pay a $1,500 out-of-court settlement to vaudeville actress Marion Sunshine for using one of her compositions in the film without credit or permission. While that settlement certainly didn't drop the film in the red, it didn't serve as a satisfying postscript to the film's underwhelming performance for Paramount.

According to the annual box office charts in *Variety*, *Beau James* ultimately grossed $1.75 million nationwide, the fifty-third highest-grossing film of 1957. It was less than half of the $4 million box office gross of the previous Shavelson-Rose-Hope film, 1955's Academy Award–nominated *The Seven Little Foys*, the film whose success the trio and Paramount hoped to build on for *Beau James*. Instead, *Beau James* was a box office disappointment and led to Hope splitting with Paramount after a twenty-year career with the studio. Of course, Hope would continue a successful career in comedy nearly through his hundredth birthday, but because he was so bitterly disappointed with the box office performance of *Beau James*, he never again attempted a dramatic role in a film.

Beau James is the type of film that should have made Vera Miles a star. In it, she dances and performs like in no other role she had ever had in her career—and none that she would ever have afterward—opposite one of Hollywood's most popular comedians. It was also unlike any role she would have ever done with Hitchcock. Considering the popularity of film musicals at the time, its lack of box office success might seem surprising on the surface. However, the fact that it was a part-biopic, part-musical based on a historical figure who meant very little to most audiences in the United States, let alone any audiences in international markets, meant it was a tougher sell than Paramount anticipated. As popular as Hope was as a comedian, neither he nor Miles was previously a bankable star of films like *Beau James*. Paramount was hedging its bet on Hope's popularity when they took a risk on this passion project—but unfortunately, it didn't pan out for anyone involved.

Though Rose and Shavelson would continue to collaborate—they released 1958's Academy Award–nominated *Houseboat*, 1959's *The Five Pennies* (which was originally slated to star Miles), 1960's *It Started in Naples*, and 1961's *On the Double*—*Beau James* was their last film with Hope in a starring role (though Hope appears in a cameo in *The Five Pennies*). After working with Miles in *Beau James*, Hope had plans for another film starring himself and Miles, which would be an adaptation of the comedic play *Anniversary Waltz*, written by Jerome Chodorov and Joseph Fields. The play ran on Broadway from April 1954 to September 1955, but Hope's plans to adapt it as a film were quickly abandoned. Though Miles and Hope would never make a film together again, Miles appeared alongside many of Hope's other film leading ladies from throughout his career in a 1966 episode of *The Bob Hope Show* titled "'15 of My Leading Ladies' or 'Richard Burton Eat Your Heart Out.'" The appearance was endearing but, in hindsight, highlights how the failure of Hope's passion project began a decline in his box office fortunes that even a 1962 reunion movie with Crosby, *Road to Hong Kong*, couldn't revive, though Hope would remain a popular entertainer for four more decades after the release of *Beau James*.

For Miles, the lack of success of the film didn't appear to be as heavy of a blow to her career. *Beau James* represented the first of what were expected to be many loan-outs of Miles's contract with Hitchcock for prestige films. While not every film was expected to be a box office hit, Hitchcock had confidence that his next project with Miles would make the box office disappointments of both *The Wrong Man* and *Beau James* a distant memory for audiences, who would surely have the same admiration of Miles on screen as he did.

7

The Woman in the Gray Suit

After production on *Beau James* wrapped in mid-September 1956, Miles turned her attention to what was supposed to be her next project with Hitchcock. On August 29, 1956, Hedda Hopper's column reported that it was "almost certain" that Hitchcock's *From among the Dead* would star James Stewart opposite Miles. *From among the Dead*—under its released title, *Vertigo*—marked Academy Award–winning actor James Stewart's fourth collaboration with Hitchcock after *Rope* (1948), *Rear Window* (1954), and *The Man Who Knew Too Much* (1956). Stewart, one of the biggest stars in Hollywood, was officially announced for the film by Paramount on August 31, with preproduction scheduled to begin on October 15. In the meantime, Miles filled her schedule with television work after she wrapped production on *Beau James*. On September 11, Miles appeared on *GE Summer Originals* in an episode titled "The Great Lady" on ABC, and on September 24, the *New York Times* reported that Miles would star in "Because of You" on NBC's *Lux Video Theatre* on October 25. The *Los Angeles Times* reported that Miles would receive more than six times the $750 she was paid for her last appearance on the program in June 1955 because of her vastly increased notoriety. In October 1956, Miles filmed a documentary short titled *The House without a Name* to raise money for the Motion Picture Relief Fund. It was later nominated for an Academy Award for Best Documentary Short. And just in time for the start of the college football season, *The Rose Bowl Story* was reissued once again to theaters by Allied Artists Productions.

Hitchcock believed that *Vertigo* would have been one of his most triumphant films. *Vertigo* focuses on San Francisco police detective Scottie Ferguson, who is forced into retirement when he develops vertigo after witnessing a fellow officer fall to his death during a rooftop chase. While working as a private investigator, he is hired by a friend from college, Gavin Elster, to track the whereabouts of his beautiful wife, Madeleine, because he is concerned about her mental well-being, suggesting that his wife's mental illness stems from her great-grandmother Carlotta, who committed suicide when her lover spurned her. With enough elements of the supernatural to throw Scottie off from the truth, he agrees to track Madeleine and soon becomes infatuated with her. While following Madeleine in her seemingly aimless wanderings, Scottie saves her life when he rescues her after she jumps into the San Francisco Bay. Though they begin to develop a relationship, Scottie witnesses Madeleine fall to her death from a church's bell tower—Mission San Juan Bautista, the childhood home of Carlotta—when his health conditions prevent him from chasing her and saving her as he did when she leaped into the bay.

Scottie takes Madeleine's death harshly until he has a chance encounter with another woman, Judy Barton, who remarkably resembles Madeleine. Scottie learns that Judy has been posing as Madeleine to cover up a scheme that Gavin created to murder his wife; in reality, Gavin threw his recently murdered wife, whom Judy resembled, off the bell tower because he knew Scottie would not follow "Madeleine" up the tower steps due to his vertigo. However, Judy has actually fallen in love with Scottie and feels guilty about her role in the plot. The story climaxes when Scottie confronts Judy in the bell tower where Madeleine had "jumped" and demands to learn the truth. Stewart was slated for the role of Scottie, while Miles was to star in the dual role of Madeleine and Judy.

While the script for *Vertigo* was not yet finished to Hitchcock's satisfaction by the mid-October start date for preproduction, he was eager to get to work on the project as soon as possible.

Three days before *Vertigo* was to begin scouting locations, Stewart's agent, future Universal Studios owner Lew Wasserman, called Hitchcock, who was already on location in San Francisco, and told him that at the insistence of Stewart's wife, Stewart needed time off, and Hitchcock had to delay filming *Vertigo* until January 1957. Stewart's wife, former model Gloria Hatrick McLean, thought her husband had been overworked on his current film, the Universal Pictures Western *Night Passage*, which would not finish shooting until late November. Hitchcock, likely seeing this as an opportunity to rework the not-yet satisfactory script, agreed to delay the film. Meanwhile, preproduction on the film carried on, and Miles began to receive her salary for the film on November 19 with no new start date yet set. On December 7, Miles posed for costume tests for *Vertigo* and was photographed wearing Madeleine's soon-to-be-famous gray suit that appears in the film. Unsurprisingly, she also continued with her television work, including starring in "The Letter" on *Schlitz Playhouse*, which aired on CBS on November 23.

In his column in the *Hollywood Reporter*, Mike Connolly suggested there was a bit more to Stewart's delay than exhaustion—on November 26, he reported that Stewart delayed the film because he "wouldn't okay Vera Miles as his leading lady." The following day, Connolly reported that Stewart was "livid" about the previous day's column, but Connolly stood by it, noting that if Stewart is denying that he said that, then he "should get over to Paramount, Jimmy, and meet the double who's using your name," suggesting that Stewart was backpedaling. It seems unlikely that Stewart asked to delay the film because he objected to working with Miles, based on the established claims of Stewart's wife's request to postpone production so he could take time off to rest. In addition, after three previous collaborations with Hitchcock and a long career as a top star in Hollywood, it seems unlikely that Stewart—represented by the powerful Wasserman—would pull "exhaustion" as an excuse to delay the film on the off chance that Miles would drop out or be replaced (even though that did come to pass) instead of negotiating for a different lead actress. Regardless, Stewart must have gotten over any concerns he may have had about Miles's abilities rather quickly, as he costarred with her in two other films within the next five years.[1]

The production of *Night Passage* was in fact very trying for Stewart not only because of the brutal weather conditions at the Colorado locations but because during preproduction, Stewart's longtime friendship with director Anthony Mann, who had previously directed Stewart in eight films, came to an end when Mann refused to direct the movie shortly before filming was scheduled to begin because he considered *Night Passage* to be a mediocre script. Stewart was also recovering from a critical shellacking that he took after the April 1957 release of *The Spirit of St. Louis*, a biopic of Charles Lindbergh that Stewart starred in as Lindbergh despite being nearly twice the age of the famed pilot during the events depicted in the film. Other sources indicate Stewart's main concern with *Vertigo* was with the as-yet unsatisfactory screenplay.

Stewart's delay ended up being fortuitous for the film and filmmaker—though, unfortunately, not Miles—for two reasons. *Vertigo* was now scheduled to begin shooting on March 4, 1957, with second unit production beginning on February 25. However, Hitchcock had several health issues early in the year that delayed the project. First, he was admitted to Cedars of Lebanon Hospital in Los Angeles on January 17, where he received surgery for a navel hernia. Additionally, he was diagnosed with colitis and was still recovering from it when he returned to Cedars of Lebanon on March 9 and had surgery to remove gallstones two days later. He would not return home from the hospital until April 9, after which he needed additional recovery time. Second, even though the film was supposed to be entering production, Hitchcock was still not satisfied by the screenplay by Alec Coppel, who had done an uncredited rewrite of Hitchcock's 1955 film *To Catch a Thief*. Hitchcock took his medical delay as an opportunity to bring in a third writer on the film, Samuel A. Taylor (the project's first screenplay, written by *The Wrong Man* cowriter Maxwell Anderson, was rejected by Hitchcock). Taylor began his writing career as a playwright and entered Hollywood when he cowrote the screenplay adaptation of his 1953 play *Sabrina Fair* as the 1954 Paramount Pictures movie *Sabrina*, for which he was nominated for the Academy Award for Best

Screenplay. Taylor began working with Hitchcock on the screenplay of *Vertigo* as the director recovered from his surgeries.

Unfortunately, Hitchcock's health issues in early 1957 snapped a very prolific streak in the Master of Suspense's career. Hitchcock released two films per year in 1954, 1955, and 1956 and directed six episodes of *Alfred Hitchcock Presents* across that period. He would not release any films in 1957 and only directed two episodes of *Alfred Hitchcock Presents* that year. His productivity would diminish considerably over the final two decades of his career, and while he would still produce some major projects after his 1957 health issues, he would no longer be the dominant creative force that he had been in Hollywood since he arrived in 1939. For someone under a long-term contract with him like Miles, this was significantly bad news for her career.

Nonetheless, all illness and production delays aside, Hitchcock's promotional push of Miles proceeded apace—indeed, her supporting role in *The Wrong Man* was meant to be the final step in his plan before Hitchcock launched her leading-lady career in *Vertigo*. As such, the release of *The Wrong Man* was shortly followed by another substantial publicity push. The January 13, 1957, issue of *Parade*, the Sunday magazine distributed in major newspapers nationwide, featured a photo of Miles and Hitchcock on its cover and the headline "ALFRED HITCHCOCK and His New Find, VERA MILES." The two-page feature expanded on the "quiet sex" concept and placed Miles among previous glamourous stars like Greer Garson, Ingrid Bergman, and, of course, Grace Kelly. The article detailed Hitchcock's plan to feature Miles in "half his motion-picture productions (at least two a year) and perhaps 25 television programs," adding that he would be loaning her out "at $100,000 to $200,000 per picture," while noting that it was a significant raise over the $1,200-a-week salary that she had pulled just two years before. Ultimately, Hitchcock himself was unable to keep up with that pace, and none of those marvelous terms came to fruition for either Miles or Hitchcock.[2]

Nonetheless, the article did hint at Hitchcock's not being completely satisfied with his new star. Hitchcock described Miles's performance in

The Wrong Man as "good" and "adequate," certainly not the words one would expect from a man touting his next big star. He then explains that Miles's role in his next film, *From among the Dead*, would require much harder work from her, with Hitchcock saying, "I've really got to Svengali this girl. It's an incredibly difficult dual role, opposite Jimmy Stewart. I'm going to have to work hard with Vera" (the article includes a small photo of Miles, Hitchcock, and Stewart discussing the project).[3]

While waiting for production to begin on *Vertigo*, Miles, for her part, kept up appearances in Hollywood befitting her growing stardom. On February 4, 1957, *Photoplay* named her as one of the year's most promising newcomers, certainly an odd honor considering that Miles had been appearing in film and on television for five years by that point but one that was likely bestowed on her by a bit of public relations pressure. Miles and Scott attended the awards banquet at the Beverly Hills Hotel on February 5, with Miles wearing a gown designed by Edith Head (with a veil) that included a black covering over her shoulders and arms. In its coverage of the event, *Photoplay* remarked that Miles deserved an award "for the most bouffant gown," noting, "The lovely blonde looked like something off a Swedish wedding cake in yards and yards of white nylon tulle." Regarding Head's design for the dress, Miles commented, "I don't think she counted on my tripping the light fantastic. This skirt is just too full for me to navigate [the dance floor]." The coverage noted that Miles's hair was trimmed and lightened for her upcoming film with Hitchcock.[4]

On Valentine's Day 1957, Miles and Gordon Scott attended Aladdin's Ball gala at the Shadow Mountain Club in Palm Desert alongside Sol Lesser and his wife, and then at the 14th Golden Globe Awards, held on February 28, 1957, at the Cocoanut Grove in the Ambassador Hotel in Los Angeles, Miles accepted the Most Promising Newcomer–Male Award on behalf of Anthony Perkins, the actor she would later work opposite of in *Psycho* and *Psycho II*. Perkins was shooting the drama *This Angry Age* on location in Thailand at the time of the ceremony. The Miles-Scott family also enjoyed some time together—Sheilah Graham reported that Miles and Scott started taking French lessons with the hope that Miles's daughters would pick up on the language—and columnist Erskine Johnson reported in his column on October 28, 1956, that Miles and Scott would be adopting a Korean War orphan. Though the couple did not end up adopting an orphan, Miles soon discovered several weeks later that she was pregnant with her third child.

On learning that Hitchcock had been admitted to the hospital in March 1957, Miles called Coleman to share with him the pregnancy news along with her realization that this latest delay because of Hitchcock's health would mean she would be too far along in her pregnancy to shoot *Vertigo* when Hitchcock would finally be ready to make the film. The September 1957 issue of *Photoplay* claimed Hitchcock wasn't told that Miles was pregnant for "six weeks for fear it would bring about a relapse" during his recovery. That was not that much of an exaggeration. Coleman was able to keep the news away from Hitchcock for about a month because, as part of his recuperation, Hitchcock did not have a telephone in his hospital suite, to prevent him from conducting any stressful business. Coleman revealed in his book that when Hitchcock finally did convince the hospital staff to put a telephone in his room, it was none other than gossip queen Hedda Hopper who called Hitchcock and told him that Miles was pregnant.[5]

Hitchcock briefly considered postponing *Vertigo* yet again in favor of directing *The Wreck of the Mary Deare* for MGM with Gary Cooper in the lead but decided against directing the film in favor of taking more time to recuperate. Cooper starred in a version directed by Michael Anderson that was released in November 1959, and Hitchcock later directed *North by Northwest* for MGM instead (the released version of *The Wreck of the Mary Deare* features no significant parts for women, and it was unlikely that Hitchcock's potential version would have offered a worthy role for Miles). Though Hitchcock was facing health issues, and *Vertigo* still did not have a final script, he determined that delaying the film even longer to wait for Miles to have her baby was not an option. In the meantime, Coleman, Wasserman, and Stewart had already begun looking for a replacement for Miles while

Hitchcock was still in the dark about Miles's pregnancy. The search was a challenge due to a lack of available candidates; Sheilah Graham reported in her March 30 column that Stewart told her, "There are just no available actresses to take Vera's place." Stewart was even franker in an interview a week later with Jay Carmody of the *Washington Evening Star*, saying, "Leading ladies are not to be found so readily that Hollywood can afford to have them behaving like normally happy wives who want babies." Ultimately, Coleman and Wasserman made a deal, subject to Hitchcock's approval, to borrow actress Kim Novak from Columbia in exchange for casting Stewart in a Columbia film (1958's *Bell, Book, and Candle*, starring both Stewart and Novak).[6]

Other sources argue that Novak was Wasserman's preference for the role all along. "There are a few conflicting stories regarding Miles dropping out of *Vertigo*," notes Joel Gunz, president of HitchCon International Alfred Hitchcock Conference and editor of *Hitchcockian Quarterly*. "MCA head Lew Wasserman wasn't keen on her because she wasn't represented by his agency, but Hitchcock had gotten his way and had signed her, and she was preparing for the role. Wasserman had advocated for his client, Novak, from the beginning but he'd accepted Hitch's decision and was willing to accept that as one time in business that he didn't get his way. Then, when Miles was forced to drop out, Wasserman finally prevailed."[7]

Three years younger than Miles, Novak had much less screen experience than the actress she would be replacing, though she had costarred in the Oscar-winning 1955 film *Picnic* and the Oscar-nominated 1955 film *The Man with the Golden Arm*. Her lack of experience and name value was concerning for Hitchcock, and in August 1957, he briefly reconsidered Novak and thought of going back to Miles for the role after she had her baby. With all the other delays on the film, Hitchcock could have delayed the film yet again for Miles but ultimately decided against it to get the project moving. By that point, Hitchcock felt comfortable with Novak in the role and had written off Miles's chance of becoming his future starlet of choice, though he would sour on Novak's performance in *Vertigo* later. The film went into production with Novak as scheduled on September 30. Miles gave birth to her son, Michael Scott, just before midnight on October 1, 1957, more than a week after her September 22 due date and just one day after *Vertigo* finally began filming.

Even though Novak became his lead actress in the film by necessity, Hitchcock would also maintain that he was ultimately dissatisfied with her performance in *Vertigo*, sharing in a 1962 interview with the *Saturday Evening Post*, "With a girl like Kim Novak you sometimes delude yourself into thinking you are getting a performance. Actually she is just an adequacy." Notably, Hitchcock never worked with Novak again. Miles was far more complimentary regarding her replacement in September 1958, after she finally had a chance to see *Vertigo*. "I saw it the other night and loved Kim in it," she told Mike Connolly. "But I got Michael instead and y'know what—it was worth it!"[8]

Though he would work with Miles several more times, Hitchcock was by all accounts deeply frustrated with the timing of Miles's pregnancy. Almost immediately, the massive media push that Hitchcock had behind Miles ceased and would completely dry up after the double shot of her pregnancy announcement and the disappointing box office performance of *Beau James*. In January 1958, Hitchcock shifted her contract payments from per-picture payments to $1,500 per week, likely because he had little interest in using her in another film at that point. Hitchcock planned her career rise as something akin to the buildup editing in his films, with a suspenseful climax that would reach its apex with *Vertigo*. Her having to withdraw from the film because of her pregnancy must have seemed to him like a commercial break interrupting the first few minutes of the thrilling Mount Rushmore sequence in *North by Northwest*.

As the years ticked away on her contract, Hitchcock showed decreasing interest in using Miles. In her April 21, 1961, column, Sheilah Graham revealed that Hitchcock intended his next film to be *Marnie*, based on the novel about a female con artist released that year by English writer Winston Graham. When asked if he would consider casting Miles to star in it, Hitchcock said he didn't think he would because he felt that Miles "broke her starring rhythm when she could not star in *Vertigo* because of pregnancy. She preferred to go up a tree with Tarzan." Of course, when Hitchcock said this, Miles was pregnant with her fourth child with her third husband, and *Marnie* would not end up being his next film anyway. Patrick McGilligan's 2003 biography *Alfred Hitchcock: A Life in Darkness and Light* claims that when Hitchcock finally started work on *Marnie* in 1962, he met with Miles about the lead role in the film after Grace Kelly, who was going to make her return to acting with the film, dropped out likely because a tenuous political situation between Monaco and France made it a difficult situation for her to return to Hollywood, especially in a role as a kleptomaniac. Miles reuniting with Hitchcock for the role would have been an intriguing choice for the film. "Maybe everyone would have been better off if he'd gone with that instinct," notes Gunz.[9]

However, Tony Lee Moral, author of the 2005 book *Hitchcock and the Making of "Marnie,"* found nothing in the Hitchcock archives to indicate Miles was ever considered for the role. Hitchcock ultimately cast Tippi Hedren, whom he had under contract, in the 1964 film. Considering Hitchcock's loss of interest in Miles and the fact that Hitchcock had Hedren under contract as his next big star at the time, it is extremely unlikely that he considered Miles for the lead in *Marnie* at any point. Once Hedren was cast, much like how Grace Kelly was name-dropped in articles promoting Miles as Hitchcock's latest discovery, in early 1964, both Miles and Kelly were name-dropped in articles promoting Hedren as Hitchcock's latest discovery while promoting *Marnie*.[10]

In a 1963 interview with Italian journalist Oriana Fallaci, Hitchcock lamented the timing of Miles's third pregnancy. "I was offering [Miles] a big part, the chance to become a beautiful sophisticated blonde, a real actress. We'd have spent a heap of dollars on it, and she has the bad taste to get pregnant," Hitchcock said, then infamously adding, "I hate pregnant women, because then they have children." It likely didn't help Hitchcock's temperament that his significant media push behind Miles as his next big star had taken place barely two months before she revealed her pregnancy to him as if she were intentionally pulling a fast one on him. The August 1957 issue of *Modern Screen* noted that behind the scenes, Hitchcock and Miles were having "disputes" but discounted that the duo was having a "feud."[11]

Years later, Miles told her side of the story to Don Alpert of the *Los Angeles Times* in a March 29, 1964, article, unapologetically explaining, "I set out in life to make some roots. I never questioned whether it was wise to have four children or not. When I was under contract to Alfred Hitchcock I had my third and he was overwhelmed. He said, 'Don't you know it's bad taste to have more than two children?' I don't think glamor is a matter of age or how many children you have. It's a state of mind. I resent the connotation that children limit a woman's life. They don't. They make a girl a woman. I don't care what the number is. Each successive experience is more broadening." The statement again highlighted Miles's commitment to being a mother over her career, no matter what the professional cost. Years later, she added a quip to her exchange with Hitchcock in another retelling, remarking, "He told me it was in bad taste to have more than two children. I took his advice into consideration and had four."[12]

It did not help Hitchcock's attitude toward Miles's pregnancy that on its release, *Vertigo* was Hitchcock's second theatrical release in a row that was a box office disappointment. According to *Variety*, *Vertigo* grossed $3.2 million at the US box office after costing nearly $2.5 million to produce. *Vertigo* received extremely positive reviews in the *Hollywood Reporter* and *New York Times*, but other outlets were less taken with the film, including *Variety* and the *Los Angeles Times*. For a film that Hitchcock spent nearly two years of his life trying to produce while facing numerous health problems, it's not hard to see why he took the less-than-stellar reception personally.

In his memoir, Coleman defended Miles, noting that Hitchcock ignored the original reason production was delayed in the first place to blame her for the film's lack of box office success. "For the rest of his life," Coleman wrote, "[Hitchcock] refused to blame Jimmy Stewart's request to move the original starting date back almost three months so he could have a vacation as the root cause of our problems." It's also worth noting Coleman's point that even if Stewart had jumped right into production on *Vertigo* instead of demanding vacation time, neither Hitchcock nor Stewart was satisfied with the screenplay until Taylor rewrote the script in the first half of 1957. Regardless of whether Stewart was ready in time and Miles was available, Hitchcock was not yet ready to shoot the film. Wish-casting aside, the timing to get Stewart and Miles in *Vertigo* simply would not have worked out for either party.[13]

To a degree, Hitchcock did pin some of the blame for the failure of *Vertigo* on Stewart but not because of his requested vacation. In hindsight, he expressed that the graying, nearly fifty-year-old Stewart looked too old in the film, particularly because of the pairing with the youthful Novak. Perhaps because of this concern, *Vertigo* would be the final film that Hitchcock and Stewart would make together, though Hitchcock did consider him for other projects that never came to fruition.

After the poor reception of *Vertigo*, it nearly seemed like Hitchcock was trying to bury the memory of the film. For over two decades after its initial release, *Vertigo* was one of the most difficult, if not the most difficult, American Hitchcock films to screen. After Hitchcock gained full ownership of four of the films that he directed for Paramount Pictures in 1961, including *Vertigo*, as per the terms of his unique contract with the studio, he withdrew them from circulation (the rights to a fifth film that was also withdrawn, 1948's *Rope*, were already owned by Hitchcock outright). During his lifetime, Hitchcock did not allow any of these five films to be reissued. Infamously, when the UK's National Film Theatre (NFT) intended to screen *Vertigo* as part of a Hitchcock retrospective in 1969, the director would only agree to allow the screening if the source of the *Vertigo* print was disclosed. The NFT declined to identify the source (Paris's Cinémathèque Française film archive) for fear that Hitchcock would order that the print be destroyed after the screening to further secure his control over exhibiting the film.

After Hitchcock died in 1980, his agent, Herman Citron, still demanded such high fees for the screening or television rights for these five films that they remained virtually unseen by the public. Even Stewart was denied permission to screen *Vertigo* by Citron when he requested to showcase it as part of a retrospective of his films when he was honored with the first-ever Honorary Golden Bear at the 1982 Berlin International Film Festival.

In 1983, Universal Pictures, Hitchcock's home studio for the final years of his career, brokered a deal with Citron and the Hitchcock estate for ownership of the rights to the five films (not coincidentally, Lew Wasserman, the agent who had secured the unique ownership deal with Paramount for Hitchcock in 1953 and demanded Stewart's three-month vacation before *Vertigo*, was now head of Universal). Universal didn't hesitate to rerelease all five films to theaters, and an October 1983 limited theatrical rerelease of *Vertigo* was very success-ful, grossing $5.3 million—over $2 million more than the box office in its original 1958 release. The theatrical rerelease was followed by a 1984 home media release on VHS and laser disc, and *Vertigo* (as well as the other four so-called "lost Hitchcock" films) has remained in cir-culation, including television airings, ever since.

Though Hitchcock was disappointed with the initial box office per-formance of *Vertigo*, that was unlikely the primary reason he withheld the film from circulation, as another one of the five withheld films, 1954's *Rear Window*, is also one of Hitchcock's most highly regarded films and another, 1955's *The Trouble with Harry*, is believed to be one of Hitchcock's personal favorites. The most likely explanation for Hitchcock's withholding the films is that he was not confident that their theatrical rereleases would be profitable and that he already had enough content on television to promote through his other films and television series. However, in contrast, his 1960 film *Psycho* remained a reliable moneymaker for Universal through frequent screenings and television airings after the studio acquired the rights to it in 1968, though it already had proven success by being Hitchcock's most finan-cially profitable film ever since its original release.

While *Vertigo* was not a critical or financial success in its initial 1958 release, the return of *Vertigo* to the public eye in the 1980s aided its critical reevaluation. The film is now recognized as one of Hitchcock's masterpieces, with some critics and Hitchcock scholars declaring it his greatest film. Indeed, in 2012, it dethroned *Citizen Kane* as the greatest film ever made in the British Film Institute's *Sight and Sound* critics' poll after fifty years with *Kane* topping the list (it ranked seventh in the directors' poll). In 2022, it was bumped to second place in the critics' poll but tied for sixth place in the directors' poll. By that measure, it's hard to fathom if the film would have been any greater with Miles in the Madeleine role instead of Novak, though it certainly would have boosted Miles's profile as an actress and solidified her status as Hitchcock's preferred leading lady.

The almost-casting of Miles in *Vertigo* has long been a point of fascination for Hitchcock enthusiasts. "Between her acting skills that support an almost weightless presence and her remote, ethereal beauty, I can see Miles naturally epitomizing Madeleine and needing very little direction from Hitch," argues Gunz. "By contrast, and by her own admission, Kim Novak required more process to bring her performance to perfection."[14]

Miles's pregnancy was reported publicly on March 21, 1957, citing a mid-October due date. Almost immediately, she capitalized on the news—naturally, Miles was not going to let anything stop her working for long. While she couldn't star in *Vertigo*, she still had plenty of acting opportunities. The following month, she received $5,000 for just three hours of work for a Pampers diaper commercial. She also appeared on the April 18 episode of *Lux Video Theater* on NBC titled "The Taggart Light" opposite Roger Moore on NBC. Miles also starred as an expectant mother who inherits half a million dollars in an episode of *Climax!* titled "The Hand of Evil," which aired on May 23, 1957. On June 19, CBS aired another episode of *Climax!* starring Miles, "House of Doubt," and on July 27, NBC reaired "The Golden Flower" as part of its summer repeat series Encore Theatre, ensuring that Miles still maintained a regular presence on television while pregnant.

To highlight her status as the next big star of Hollywood, Miles was to be honored in a spotlight event in Dallas, Texas, hosted by the Texas-based exhibitor Interstate Circuit on June 10, 1957, to promote the importance of new film stars to the industry and her role in *Beau James*, which was released that month. The coming-out party would have invited VIPs from around the region for a screening of *Beau James*, followed by a banquet featuring Miles as the guest of honor. However, because of her pregnancy, the event was rescheduled to April 23, 1957, as a less formal luncheon held to honor Miles at Paramount. Business-man Robert J. O'Donnell, the vice president and general manager of Interstate Circuit, spoke at the luncheon and said, "It isn't often that one is privileged to look $200,000,000 right in the eye, even in Texas," noting that this was an estimate of what O'Donnell believed was the ten-year minimum box office potential of a new star like Miles.[15]

This was far from the only recognition Miles would receive during her third pregnancy despite Hitchcock's already falling interest in pro-moting her. The July 24, 1957, edition of *Variety* included Miles on its list of "Youngsters with 'Star' Potential," written by Alfred F. Corwin, a representative of the Motion Picture Export Association of Motion Picture Producers, and *Motion Picture Exhibitor* crowned Vera Miles with the Laurel Award for Top New Female Personalities for 1956–57 (her future *Psycho* costar Anthony Perkins was named Top New Male Personality). In October 1957, the *Motion Picture Herald* declared Vera Miles one of the runners-up in its "Star of Tomorrow" poll of exhibitors. Interestingly enough, Perkins was voted number one.

Miles's popularity was expanding beyond the gossip columns too. *Los Angeles Times* beauty columnist Lydia Lane wrote about Miles's secrets to losing "10 Pounds Quickly by Avoiding Overprocessed Foods" in her April 28, 1957, column. The material was based on a conversation that Lane had with Miles after Lane saw her "when she walked into the commissary at Paramount the other day." However, by late April, Miles was nearly three months pregnant and not a regular on the Paramount lot. Since the article was in part a promotional piece for the upcoming *Beau James*, it's likely that if the conversation took place at all—and with a beauty column during that era, its substance is in question—it did so during the production of *Beau James* at Paramount. In the article, Miles also says that she is twenty-six years old (Miles was four months shy of her twenty-eighth birthday at the time of the article's publication). Of course, Hollywood stars shaving several years off their birth year was a common practice, but it also indicates that this column was based on older material (this is not the only Lydia Lane column that featured Miles that had questionable facts and timing). Regardless, Miles's pregnancy is not mentioned at all in the column, and the actress credits her weight loss to avoiding overprocessed foods "like white bread, pastry, potato chips." Postpregnancy, Miles's beauty tips would again feature in Lane's column on November 28, 1957, Thanksgiving Day, appropriately titled "This Thanksgiving Day, Go Easy on Starches" to promote that evening's airing of Miles's *Playhouse 90* episode "Panic Button" and on December 15, 1963, when Miles extolled the health benefits she felt after quitting smoking.[16]

In July 1957, several months before Michael's birth, Gordon Scott and Vera Miles legally changed their last name to Scott, though Miles continued to use Vera Miles professionally ("Wouldn't you feel sorry for your children starting to school and trying to spell the name of Werschkul?" Miles reportedly asked the judge). While pregnant, Miles dedicated herself to domestic chores in her Sherman Oaks home once she couldn't work as an actress, telling *Photoplay* in a November 1957 feature on her pregnancy, "I work as long as I can in pictures. Then, when I'm no longer in shape, I do all the things I ordinarily don't have time for. Last summer, while I was carrying the baby, I papered and painted three rooms, and made curtains, draperies, and the girls' fall school clothes. I also got a lot of reading done." Weeks after the baby was born, Miles and her family still stayed busy. At the end of January 1958, Miles, Scott, and their children vacationed at Wonder Palms Hotel in Palm Springs. Soon afterward, the couple began construction on an $80,000 beach house in Malibu.[17]

That same *Photoplay* feature on Miles's pregnancy claimed that, ever eager to get back to work, she asked her agent to "find her a picture that started two weeks after September 22" (the due date for her third baby). However, whether Hitchcock was too preoccupied with shooting *Vertigo* or still annoyed at her pregnancy, he did not approve her for another film project that fall. In hyping Miles's appearance on *Climax!* on January 23, 1958, Hedda Hopper remarked in her column, "I'll wager Jimmy Stewart and Alfred Hitchcock are mighty sorry they didn't get her for *Vertigo.*" Of course, the remark oversimplifies the situation, since Hitchcock had cast Miles in *Vertigo* in the first place and felt it was her "fault" in getting pregnant that prevented her from appearing in the film.[18]

Miles wouldn't begin shooting another American film until nearly a year later when she started production on *The FBI Story* in August 1958, which would not come until after her agent, Milt Rosner, renegotiated her film contract with Hitchcock to owe him just one film a year instead of three. In between, Miles returned to television—an episode of *Playhouse 90* ("Panic Button") that aired on November 28, an episode of *Studio 57* ("Emergency Care") that aired on January 23, two episodes of *Climax!* that aired on January 23 ("Sound of the Moon") and June 19 ("House of Doubt"), an episode of *Schlitz Playhouse* ("Penny Wise," a comedic turn in which she portrays four different roles and stars alongside legendary *King Kong* actress Fay Wray) that aired on May 2, and the September 9 episode of *Colgate Theatre* ("Mr. Tutt," also known as "Strange Counsel"). *Colgate Theatre* was a short-lived NBC anthology series for unsold television pilots—"Mr. Tutt" had been shot more than four years earlier and never aired—that was used to fill the time slot abruptly abandoned by the hugely popular quiz show *Dotto* in the wake of being one of the first of several quiz shows that would be caught up in an infamous fixing scandal. Columnist Mike Connolly claimed that the *Climax!* episode "House of Doubt" was Miles's one hundredth television role. While that was an exaggeration, the note demonstrated how frequently Miles had appeared on television over the previous several years. Miles continued to keep up appearances in 1958 after Michael's birth, appearing on the variety show *The Ford Show* (starring country singer "Tennessee" Ernie Ford) on January 9 and presenting honorees at the Muscular Dystrophy Awards luncheon at the Statler-Hilton Hotel in Los Angeles on March 24.

Increasingly, Miles's television programs, like most programs at the time, were taped and no longer broadcast live. In a July 1958 column syndicated by the Newspaper Enterprise Association, Miles was interviewed—likely because of her extremely prolific career on television—regarding why the number of live television broadcasts had been shrinking. The actress certainly wasn't reserved in her response, blaming the change on both producers and stars.

"The producers of live television began digging their own graves when they came to Hollywood," she began. "Not because of Hollywood, but because of the original reasons all the shows moved to Hollywood. They came here to get big star names for their productions. This was the big mistake. They concentrated on creating vehicles for big stars, rather than concentrating on strong stories." It was a theme that Miles would often return to in her interviews—that Hollywood sacrificed well-written stories for glamour, which especially impacted the quality of roles for actresses. She later added, "Live television died in Hollywood because the producers came here to live off the production of motion pictures—the big star names—rather than to bring anything creative of their own."[19]

Still, even though Miles often took on as many projects as her schedule would allow, she did try to work with acclaimed writers when she could. Less than two weeks before its broadcast date, Miles's first project after giving birth—the *Playhouse 90* episode "Panic Button"—faced prerelease controversy from the airline industry, which protested the inclusion of a commercial airline crash in the teleplay for fear that it would negatively impact the industry even if an actual flight company was not named in the program. Writer Rod Serling, who would later create *The Twilight Zone*, subsequently revised the story to make the aircraft company of the lost plane named Charter Line to imply that the plane was a charter aircraft and not a commercial plane. Serling's brother, Bob, who was then an aviation writer for the United Press's Washington, DC, radio bureau, served as technical adviser for the episode. In comparison to Serling's previous highly acclaimed episodes of *Playhouse 90*—including the boxing drama "Requiem for a Heavyweight," which won Serling his second of six Emmy Awards for television writing and was later adapted into a 1962 feature film— "Panic Button" received lukewarm to negative reviews. The *New York Times* said it was overlong ("Mr. Serling might have done an even more effective job on the same script if he had not needed to fill so much time"), while *Variety* said, "String some tin cans to the tail of a dog, let it go, and hear the interesting noises. This somewhat approximates the effort of Rod Serling in his 'The Panic Button' script" and called Miles's performance "strictly stock."[20]

While Miles was keeping busy with her television roles, it was nearly two years after production wrapped on *Beau James* before she began shooting another film. After the cool reception and box office returns for *Vertigo*, it became obvious that Hitchcock had nearly completely lost interest in the actress he had touted as his next big star just a year earlier. During preproduction for his next film, *North by Northwest*, he did not consider Miles for the female lead. Then, in June 1958, Hitchcock and Miles's agent, Milt Rosner, renegotiated their contract to allow Miles to accept roles without consulting Hitchcock first. The agreement extended Miles's contract with Hitchcock for six more years but committed her to only one film a year for Hitchcock. "The [previous] deal was causing consternation on all sides," Miles told *Picturegoer* several months later, pointing to the contract as the reason for her lack of film appearances. "I was not dissatisfied with Hitch's treatment, but he is such a perfectionist that he would not loan me out for anything that he didn't consider to be a masterpiece. There are very few masterpieces and an actress must keep working in this business." Later in the interview, she added, "I want to show the versatility I've revealed on American TV. Let's hope we can look forward to the new Vera Miles." However, Hitchcock's fading interest in Miles as a leading lady did not stop him from working with her on several more projects over those six years, some of which wouldn't be considered "masterpieces" by either party.

Curiously, over a year later, Hitchcock signed another actress, Joanna Moore, to an exclusive contract in December 1959 after she had appeared in three episodes of *Alfred Hitchcock Presents*. Moore, who was another former beauty contestant, had even less success working with Hitchcock than Miles did. Hitchcock never directed her in a film or television program, though she made three more appearances on his television show, and by the time he met Tippi Hedren in 1961, he already had no future plans for Miles or Moore. While Hitchcock and Miles would make their best-known film together just months later, the bountiful relationship they both had hoped for had long since fizzled out.[21]

8

Bald in Italy

After the renegotiation of her contract with Hitchcock, Miles was immediately considered for roles in two United Artists films—1958's *Lonelyhearts* and 1959's *The Man in the Net*—though she ultimately appeared in neither film. Instead, Miles chose to star alongside her would-be *Vertigo* costar James Stewart in the Warner Bros. film *The FBI Story*. "I appreciate my not being exclusive to anyone," Miles told Hedda Hopper in her March 1, 1959, column. "I can do outside pictures and on those my salary is my own affair. People love to exaggerate. I'm getting $75,000 a picture. You really can't keep much of it, you know." On finally working with her would-be *Vertigo* costar, she told Hopper, "Jimmy was wonderful to work with—no nonsense or temperamental bits."[1]

The FBI Story was based on the nonfiction book *The FBI Story: A Report to the People*, by the Pulitzer Prize–winning journalist Don Whitehead. The book chronicles the history of the FBI and was a national bestseller. The concept behind the film was to present the career of a fictional agent (John Michael "Chip" Hardesty, played by Stewart) who is involved in some of the agency's most famous cases, including investigating the Ku Klux Klan in the early 1920s and battling Prohibition-era gangsters like John Dillinger and Baby Face Nelson. Miles portrays Chip's wife, Lisa, whom he meets while working in the FBI (Lisa works in the organization's library). Lisa feels torn by Chip's dedication to the FBI—she wants him to become a lawyer instead—versus the obligations of their domestic life, including raising their children. The film was produced with the full support and technical assistance of the FBI—J. Edgar Hoover, the first director of the FBI, appears as himself in the film—and, while well-made and entertaining, is largely a piece to promote the agency.

In his August 20, 1958, column, Mike Connolly said that Miles's daughter "Linda" auditioned to play Miles's character's daughter in *The FBI Story* but was unable to take the role because it would interfere with her schooling (of course, Miles didn't have a daughter named Linda, so Connolly likely got her name wrong). The film was behind schedule and did not start shooting until August 11. The delays forced Miles to bow out of a film with Paramount, *The Five Pennies*, a biopic of famed jazz performer Red Nichols opposite Danny Kaye, which was supposed to be her first film after her pregnancy. The project was directed, written, and produced by the *Beau James* team of Melville Shavelson and Jack Rose and featured a cameo by Bob Hope as himself. Miles ultimately was unable to take the role despite an attempt to shuffle the filming schedules of both movies, and the role was instead played by Barbara Bel Geddes (incidentally, Bel Geddes appeared in *Vertigo* as Midge, and she would later star with Miles in *Five Branded Women*).

To star in *The FBI Story*, Miles and the rest of the principal cast and crew underwent what FBI agent Edward Kempler referred to as a "routine name check" to ensure that the agency wouldn't be embarrassed by any scandals that might have come to light involving those making a film about the FBI. Not only did Miles and Stewart pass the background check, but their personal characters were also determined to be stellar enough that in November 1958, both received Americanism Awards from the American Legion for their "outstanding contributions in making motion pictures depicting the American way of life." It was the second time Miles had been honored by the veterans' organization; in May 1953, she was made an honorary colonel of Hollywood's American Legion Post 43 along with nine other actresses designated as "stars of tomorrow" (even just five years later, Miles had by far the most notable career of the ten "colonels").

Filming for *The FBI Story* began in Hollywood in August, later moving to Washington, DC, for seventeen days in November, including shooting in the actual headquarters of the FBI. After Stewart and Miles completed their roles, the crew traveled to New York City to shoot a subway pursuit sequence. The crew also shot at Yankee Stadium, Central Park, and Midtown. Singer Anita Gordon, a close friend of Miles, worked as Miles's stand-in on the movie (Gordon would occasionally also babysit Michael while Miles was filming abroad). Miles met J. Edgar Hoover during production on November 5, 1958, and was photographed with him in his office in Washington, DC. After Hoover saw the film, he wrote Miles a letter saying, "To be perfectly honest this is the first fan letter I've ever written. Your truly great acting has added richly to this fine entertainment."[2]

The FBI Story had its premiere at Radio City Music Hall on September 24, 1959, and entered theaters with very strong advanced reviews. The *Variety* review said that Miles "plays particularly well with Stewart" and that "her success contributes importantly to the film." *Harrison's Reports* declared that Miles "does a superlative job as his wife and shows off to particular advantage in the early scenes when she bravely faces the disadvantages of being married to an FBI agent." *Film Bulletin* called Miles "appealing" in its otherwise average review of *The FBI Story*. The *New York Times* review noted that "Vera Miles has that air of bearing the Seal of Approval, the same as June Allyson" (Allyson was a frequent costar of Van Johnson, whom Miles worked with in *23 Paces to Baker Street* and *Web of Evidence*). In her column, Hedda Hopper said that she advised "every man, woman, and child over the age of 12 to see *The FBI Story*," calling it "the best picture Mervyn LeRoy ever made; same goes for Jimmy Stewart, Vera Miles, and everybody connected with it." While many did heed Hopper's advice—*Variety* reported on October 14, 1959, it was the top-grossing film in the United States in its weekly national box office survey—it was not a substantial hit. Stewart's *Anatomy of a Murder* and Hitchcock's *North by Northwest*, both released in early July, were significantly bigger hits.[3]

Nevertheless, Miles's return to film was occurring at the same time as her husband's career appeared to take interesting turns of its own. After spending time and money in litigation to resolve the television rights for Tarzan, Sol Lesser Productions abandoned its plans for a Tarzan television series by June 1958, when NBC, which showed interest in the series, was unable to secure a high-dollar sponsor for what would have been an expensive program—it cost nearly $250,000 to shoot three pilot episodes. The footage shot for the first three episodes was later edited into a feature film, *Tarzan and the Trappers*, which aired on television in 1966, six years after Scott had ceased playing Tarzan. Nonetheless, the Tarzan film series, which celebrated its fortieth anniversary in 1958, remained highly profitable for another decade.

The July 1958 entry of the series, *Tarzan's Fight for Life*—Scott's third Tarzan film—was the final Tarzan movie to be produced by Sol Lesser and was filmed before shooting started on the jettisoned television series. Earlier that year, Lesser sold his production company to television producer Sy Weintraub. After twenty-five years of producing Tarzan films and shortly after having a heart attack, Lesser felt it was time to step down from the series and retire from the film industry.

Weintraub's stewardship of the character would result in immediate changes to the series formula. Under Weintraub's watch, Tarzan was revamped to be a more eloquent adventurer, and Jane was banished from the series. In addition, Weintraub cut down on comic relief (chimpanzee sidekick Cheeta's screen time was significantly reduced) and aimed to shoot in exotic locations whenever possible instead of shooting on a back lot. Whether he fully realized it at the time, Weintraub was reinventing the character for the 1960s, a decade that would see a significant change in action and adventure films later influenced by the launch of the James Bond series (incidentally, future Bond star Sean Connery plays a villain in Weintraub's first Tarzan movie, 1959's *Tarzan's Greatest Adventure*).

Even with a new producer coming on board, Scott was losing interest in playing the character, particularly when it became clear that the television series would not come to pass at that time. Unlike Lesser,

Weintraub was against the idea of a television series, because he felt it would hurt the box office of theatrical releases.

After only three films as the Lord of the Jungle, Scott was looking forward to life after Tarzan. Previous Tarzan franchise actors Johnny Weissmuller and Lex Barker still made respectable livings as actors after they each retired from wearing the loincloth. Weissmuller starred in just one non-Tarzan film from 1932 to 1948, 1946's *Swamp Fire* (opposite fellow Tarzan actor Buster Crabbe), and then moved on to the Jungle Jim movie series about a big-game hunter and adventurer. He later starred in a *Jungle Jim* television series from 1955 to 1956, after which he retired from Hollywood. Lex Barker had a more varied career after portraying Tarzan in five films from 1949 to 1953, though he mostly appeared in Westerns until moving to Europe to make films in Italy, a career move that Scott would also make several years later.

Scott initially announced to the press that he would no longer play Tarzan shortly after the release of *Tarzan's Fight for Life* and punctuated his leaving the series by growing a large, very non-Tarzan beard, telling columnist Bob Thomas, "When I quit the Tarzan series, I wanted to get as far away from it as possible. The only way I could get producers to look at me differently was to change my appearance. And it has worked. I've had some pretty good offers for Westerns."[4]

However, none of those projects would pan out for Scott—if they were indeed actual projects and not just a negotiating tactic by Scott for a new Tarzan deal. In fact, a rumor floated that MGM, which still held the rights to remake its 1932 Tarzan movie, *Tarzan, the Ape Man*, considered teaming with Scott for a remake of that film that would be a stand-alone film separate from the main Tarzan series, which would now be released by Paramount (the remake, released in 1959, starred former UCLA basketball player Denny Miller in his only appearance as Tarzan).

Scott's time away from Tarzan was brief. On December 2, 1958, it was announced that he signed a multiyear contract with Weintraub to play Tarzan again. In February 1959, Scott told Sheilah Graham that he agreed to return to the role even though he considered other projects, adding, "But I decided the other pictures were not important," though it was also reported that the new deal allowed Scott to play a non-Tarzan role with Weintraub's approval (with the general caveat that he could not play a villain). *Variety* reported that to sign the deal, Scott fired his agent Milt Rosner (who also represented Miles) and returned to working with Walter Meyers, who had discovered him in Las Vegas, as his agent when Rosner objected to Scott resigning to play Tarzan. The new deal gave Scott royalties for Tarzan merchandise, and he was allowed to keep all revenue from personal appearances. Scott would return to the Tarzan series as the new version of the Lord of the Jungle in 1959's *Tarzan's Greatest Adventure* and 1960's *Tarzan the Magnificent* before retiring from the series (the next movie series Tarzan actor, Jock Mahoney, appeared in the latter film as the movie's villain). Plans for a Tarzan television series, now to be shot in London and Africa, came up again in early 1959, but the idea was again abandoned. Scott's final two Tarzan films are highly regarded by fans of the series for their more serious take on the character.[5]

Almost immediately after filming concluded on *The FBI Story*, Miles went to London to reteam with her *23 Paces to Baker Street* costar Van Johnson to shoot the thriller *Beyond This Place* (also known as *P.O. Box 303* during production and released in the United States as *Web of Evidence*), which began shooting on November 3. The film was based on the titular 1950 mystery novel written by A. J. Cronin, in which an American man (played by Johnson) travels to Liverpool to find out the truth about his father, whom he believed died during World War II as a war hero but is, in reality, in prison for murder. Miles portrays a librarian who helps Johnson investigate the circumstances behind his father's imprisonment. Early in the production, Allied Artists acquired the Western Hemisphere distribution rights. By the beginning of December, Scott joined Miles in London before traveling to Nairobi, Africa, to film *Tarzan's Greatest Adventure*. Miles returned home shortly before the holidays without Scott. When he did come back to the States, Scott brought Miles back a pair of leopard shoes and a crocodile bag from the African shoot as Christmas gifts. Miles must have been making an impression on English audiences; Sheilah Graham wrote in her December 12, 1958, column, "They named Vera Miles 'Miss Quiet Sex of 1958' in England," though she did not clarify exactly who or what "they" were. However, on its release, the reviews of *Beyond This Place* were not positive. The *Variety* review of *Beyond This Place* calls Miles "adequate in a colorless role as a timid librarian." *Harrison's Reports* had a similar take on the film and called Miles "attractive in the underdeveloped role" of the love interest.[6]

Early in the new year, Miles shot an episode of the popular hit Western television series *Wagon Train* titled "The Sister Rita Story," with Miles playing the titular Sister Rita, a leader of a group of nuns who are caring for a group of orphaned Navajo children. The episode reunited Miles with her *The Searchers* costar Ward Bond, who was the star of the series until he died in 1960. Miles would appear in two other episodes of the series (though as different characters) after Ward's death. The episode aired on March 25, 1959. She then shot "Nora," based on Henrik Ibsen's play *A Doll's House*, for *General Electric Theater*, replacing Oscar-nominated actress Gene Tierney in what was to be a comeback role for the actress after a series of serious health issues. The episode aired on May 3, 1959, on CBS.

After shooting these episodes, Miles returned to England early in the year to film *A Touch of Larceny*, a romantic comedy to be distributed in the United States by Paramount in which Miles starred opposite James Mason, a few months after the English actor wrapped production on Hitchcock's *North by Northwest*. *A Touch of Larceny* was directed by future James Bond series director Guy Hamilton. In the film, Mason plays an English former World War II naval war hero who, now in a cushy position, trades on his reputation to spend most of his time as a playboy. However, after he meets a rich man (played by Oscar-winning actor George Sanders), Mason's character is immediately taken by his partner, played by Miles. To make himself rich to impress her, he plots to plant evidence that he has defected to the Soviet Union so he can sue the press for libel once the newspapers report the false story.

The film's producer and cowriter, Ivan Foxwell, cast Miles in the film because it was an attempt by the veteran producer to shoot a feature in England that would have a strong appeal to American audiences. While *A Touch of Larceny* was largely shot at MGM British Studios, a few scenes were shot in Scotland, including scenes set on the remote Scottish island of An Dubh-sgeir.

While Miles was shooting the film in London, Scott also returned to London to shoot the interior scenes of *Tarzan's Greatest Adventure* at Shepperton Studios and brought along Miles's two daughters. While working on *A Touch of Larceny*, Miles stayed in an apartment rather than a hotel, explaining, "I like to be able to fix coffee for myself if I want to instead of ringing for room service. But I lost weight the first two weeks before my family arrived. I don't like to eat alone, and I won't cook just for me. But after my husband brought the two girls over it was different. They're nine and six and a half. We left Michael, the baby, at home. He's 15 months." Miles returned home to Los Angeles in early May, although she would return right back to Europe in July to shoot her next film. Though Miles would spend most of her career in Hollywood, she praised the British performers' mindset in their approach to acting in an interview with Hedda Hopper published in her March 1, 1959, column, saying, "They'll take a bit part, if it's good, and never lose face by doing so. If you did that [in Hollywood] you'd be washed up since prestige is based on dollars. In England they're actors who want to work at acting. Billing, a major issue here, is relatively unimportant there: they take the same pride a painter has for what he puts on canvas." She later added, "The English like me. They say I look well-bred, and no matter how much I try to convince them I'm nothing but a farm girl from Kansas, they still insist I'm an aristocrat."[7]

Because of that mindset, and perhaps also because of marital issues with Scott that would soon become public, in the spring of 1959, Miles agreed to star in *Jovanka*, a war film based on the novel *Jovanka e le altre* by Italian novelist Ugo Pirro about five Yugoslavian women during World War II who are deemed traitors when they are accused of fraternizing with a Nazi sergeant and are punished ("branded") by having their heads shaven. Though the women are unfamiliar with one another, their shared status as social outcasts leads them to bond as they go on the run to survive. However, Miles, who plays one of the branded women, reveals after a suicide attempt that she never slept with the sergeant in question. After a period of fighting for survival, the women join a group of Yugoslavian partisans to battle the Nazis. The film was certainly a risk for Miles—not only was she not known for war dramas, but she also was required to shave her hair during the production of the film. One of the other American stars who played another of the other branded women, Barbara Bel Geddes, refused to have her head shaved and wore a wig instead.

Jovanka was initially announced to star American actor Van Heflin, best known for his work in Westerns and a variety of other genre films, and Italian actress Gina Lollobrigida, who was one of Howard Hughes's discoveries, and was set to be shot in Italy, Austria, and Yugoslavia. However, much of the production would change, including its title. After cycling through several other title choices, it would finally be titled *Five Branded Women*. The title change came so late in the process that even after the film premiered in Rome, it was still being referred to as *Jovanka* in the press before its May 1960 release in the United States. In addition, plans to shoot in Yugoslavia fell through after the film was rejected by the country's government. Furthermore, Lollobrigida would leave the film before shooting began and was replaced as Jovanka by Silvana Mangano, then wife of the film's producer, Dino De Laurentiis. Though De Laurentiis would become one of the most well-known Italian film producers by his death in 2010, by the time *Five Branded Women* went into production, he was largely known for producing both low-budget Italian comedy films and acclaimed productions including films directed by venerated Italian filmmakers Roberto Rossellini and Federico Fellini. However, De Laurentiis began making an effort to expand his audience beyond Italy and arthouse cinemas with international productions like the 1956 version of *War and Peace* directed by renowned American director King Vidor and

Five Branded Women, which was directed by American filmmaker Martin Ritt, who had directed the hit 1958 film *The Long, Hot Summer*. The film's screenplay was initially solely credited to Italian screenwriter Ivo Perilli, who was also one of the many writers who contributed to the screenplay of De Laurentiis's *War and Peace*, but it was cowritten by two American writers, Paul Jarrico and Michael Wilson, who both moved to Europe after being blacklisted by Hollywood when they were named as unfriendly witnesses by the House Un-American Activities Committee. Infamously, Wilson cowrote the Oscar-winning screenplay for the 1957 film *The Bridge on the River Kwai* but did not receive credit for writing the script, because he was blacklisted. He was awarded his Oscar posthumously in 1984. Though Wilson and Jarrico cowrote the screenplay for *Five Branded Women*, they were not given credit for their work by the Writers Guild of America until 1998.

Five Branded Women began shooting with its international cast on July 13 in Rome, but before leaving Hollywood, Miles shot episodes of two series that had yet to premiere: an episode of *Riverboat* (which aired on September 27, 1959) and an episode of *Rawhide* titled "The Incident at the Buffalo Smoke House" (which aired on October 30, 1959). In her June 30, 1959, column, Hedda Hopper quipped that Miles squeezed in these projects—she shot the episode of *Rawhide* the same day that she left for Europe—before leaving, because Miles "never turns down hard cash." Miles was also under consideration for the female lead in a film adaptation of the novel *Ice Palace* by *Giant* author Edna Ferber, but the role was ultimately taken by Carolyn Jones (Miles was still shooting *Five Branded Women* when *Ice Palace* began production). Filming of *Five Branded Women* moved to Austria in mid-August—with the cast and crew traveling by chartered train from Italy to Austria—and lasted until the beginning of October.[8]

In August 1959, photos of Miles with her crew cut appeared in newspapers worldwide after she was photographed with Hollywood legend Clark Gable in Rome. Gable was shooting the film *It Started in Naples*, the last movie he made that was released during his lifetime. "I didn't really mind it," Miles would later tell the press about getting her head shaved. "With hair on my head, I had a very ordinary face. Now my features have become important" (of course, few would support the notion that a former Miss America finalist's features were "ordinary"). Miles would later tell James Bacon of the Associated Press in a piece that was syndicated throughout the country over the next several weeks, often with photos of Miles sporting the crew cut, "I like it. I never realized how much time a woman spends on her hair" and that she "thought nothing of" shaving her hair, explaining, "The role called for it and I did it. I've always been a good-natured slob about such things." Miles also noted to Bacon that she enjoyed her time in Rome, adding, "There's something about Rome. There are so many unusual sights that a bald-headed American actress created no stir."[9]

Though the production of *Five Branded Women* was troubled, De Laurentiis was sufficiently impressed by Miles's performance in the film and sought to match her again with Van Heflin for *Love in the North Atlantic*, a romantic adventure screenplay about a couple who steal abandoned cargo on the German coast. In February 1960, Mike Connelly reported in his column that De Laurentiis was casting Ernest Borgnine as the male lead in the film. While Borgnine went on to make three films produced by De Laurentiis that were all released in 1961—*Barabbas*, *Il giudizio universale*, and *Il re di Poggioreale*—*Love in the North Atlantic* was ultimately never made.

Paramount executive George Weltner, who would later serve as president of the studio from 1964 to 1967, was gifted a unique keepsake for his New York City office from the film's production—a framed photograph of the five female leads with locks of their shorn hair (even from the actresses who did not completely shave their heads), with each lock wrapped in a different color ribbon to note that the film was shot in Technicolor.

Like during the filming of *A Touch of Larceny*, Miles's daughters joined her in Europe for part of the shoot. In a June 1962 interview with Hedda Hopper, Miles reflected on the experience of having her daughters with her, noting, "But I had fun in Rome. Barbara Bel Geddes and I had good times together, and I had the children with me. It's a fantastic place for kids; you take them to the best eating places and they're welcome. The Italians love kids. We shot from noon straight to 8 p.m. The youngsters slept late and had naps in the afternoon, and we'd all dine around 9. We had a great time."[10]

Miles had about a week off after returning from Europe before starting her next film, but of course, she filled that week with two projects ("I haven't had a real vacation in years. I guess I'm lucky to be the way I am," she told James Bacon of the Associated Press). She shot an episode of the CBS Western anthology series *Dick Powell's Zane Grey Theatre* titled "Miss Jenny," which was directed and cowritten by soon-to-be-renowned filmmaker Sam Peckinpah. The episode aired on January 7, 1960. She was also considered for the female lead in the 1960 Western *Cimarron* opposite Glenn Ford, but the project failed to meet her salary requirements.[11]

Miles also shot an episode for the first season of Rod Serling's iconic science fiction television series *The Twilight Zone*, the instant classic "Mirror Image," in November 1959. At the time the episode was shot, *Twilight Zone*, which had launched in September 1959, had not been an instant ratings success. Perhaps because of that uncertain future, "Mirror Image" is one of the series' more compact episodes as nearly the entire episode takes place in a nondescript bus depot in upstate New York. Miles stars as Millicent Barnes, a young woman dressed for travel and waiting for a late-night bus to Cortland to take her to Buffalo, where a new job is waiting for her. While anxiously waiting for the late bus in the nearly empty station, Barnes approaches the ticket counter to ask if there is an updated time for its arrival. The ticket agent remarks that she doesn't need to keep asking him what time it will arrive, only for Barnes to respond that she wasn't sure what he meant, because it was her first time approaching the counter. She soon begins to believe she has a doppelgänger in the bus depot, a fear that appears to be confirmed as more than just delirium right before she exits the ladies' room and sees another version of herself with the same suitcase sitting in the seat she just vacated reflected in the bathroom mirror (in an excellent camera trick by the director of photography, George T.

Clemens, who would shoot over a hundred episodes of the series and win an Emmy Award for his work on it). Nervous, she befriends a man also waiting for the Cortland bus, Paul Grinstead (Martin Milner, star of the popular television series *Route 66*, which Miles would appear on in 1964), who offers to help her. However, when the Cortland bus finally arrives, Barnes faints when she sees another version of herself, with a sinister look on her face, sitting on board. After awakening, she explains to Grinstead, in a key piece of exposition, that she has read about parallel dimensions and that her "other self" may be trying to supplant her. Grinstead, fearing for her sanity, calls for the police, and they take her away—only to see a double of himself, with a face full of mischievousness, running out of the bus station. Grinstead gives chase, but his double escapes.

"A remarkable piece of science fiction," notes Andrew Ramage, editor of the book *Forgotten Gems from the Twilight Zone, Vol. 1* and webmaster of the long-running *The Twilight Zone Museum* website, about the episode. "Rod Sterling wasn't a sci-fi writer, nor did he pen many sci-fi-type entries of *The Twilight Zone*, but 'Mirror Image' is a polished gem. One of the finest 24 minutes in TV history, it is superlative in every regard. Interesting aside, Rod never was good at writing female roles. He was a very masculine writer. While almost all *The Twilight Zone* episodes have a resolution, a few don't, and this is one of them, and it makes for a chilling, unresolved situation."[12]

"Mirror Image" aired on February 26, 1960, as *The Twilight Zone*'s twenty-first episode. The episode was one of many written by Serling himself, a television writing pioneer who also served as the narrator for the series, and was directed by John Brahm, a prolific television director who would later direct Miles again in the 1962 *The Alfred Hitchcock Hour* episode "Don't Look behind You."

Ramage continues,

1960 was a good year for Vera Miles. She did *Psycho* and this episode of *The Twilight Zone*, which were the highlights of her career. Her performance as the disbelieving Millicent Barnes can be described in a word—spooked. But yet, she remains resilient right up until she is snatched by the police after her near-mental breakdown. One of the most chilling moments in all of *The Twilight Zone* comes near the end of the episode when the lemon-gnawing bus station attendant, played to perfection by Joe Hamilton, says to Paul Grinstead, somewhat eagerly, "Get her off, alright?" right after Millicent is hauled away. It's as if he knew it was going to happen. Then all is suddenly quiet. Grinstead removes his jacket and loosens his tie, preparing to get a few hours of sleep. He goes to the water fountain and swallows deep and long. As he raises his head, he sees his briefcase gone and [hears] the last couple footsteps of a darting thief. Pretty disturbing and directed and filmed amazingly well. Bravo, John Brahm, and bravo, George Clemens. It's a quiet but disturbing series of incidents that has no resolution. *The Twilight Zone* at its very best.[13]

"Mirror Image" marks one of many television programs in which Miles plays a woman unraveling from her sanity, which would turn out to be one of her archetypal roles in her career. Because of the enduring popularity of *The Twilight Zone* in subsequent decades, "Mirror Image" may be the most widely viewed episode of television starring Miles. Coincidentally, the episode of the popular series features the concept of the double, though in a very different way than depicted in *Vertigo*.

Though Scott told Sheilah Graham in early 1959 that he and Miles planned on having more children (and the family added a fifteen-hundred-square-foot extension to their house for precisely that purpose), in June—just weeks before she left for Europe to shoot *Five Branded Women*—Miles announced that she and Scott had separated the previous month. For some, the separation was not a surprise; as early as August 1958, Mike Connolly was questioning the stability of the relationship in his column ("Are Miss Miles and Gordon Scott REALLY Happy?" he asked without any additional explanation). The couple had seen little of each other in the preceding months of 1959, with Scott in Nairobi shooting *Tarzan's Greatest Adventure* and Miles in England shooting *A Touch of Larceny*. However, columnist Dorothy Manners (covering for a traveling Louella Parsons) noted in mid-July the "separation had to be sudden," pointing out, "Just four days before the rift announcement, their press agent asked Louella Parsons to do a Sunday interview on them at their newly remodeled home 'so you can see how happy they are.'"[14]

For the rest of the year, Scott's movements were covered thoroughly by the gossip columns. Erskine Johnson reported in his column in late July 1959 that "friends" of Miles and Scott "are hearing reconciliation talk," even though Miles was just starting the long shoot in Europe for *Five Branded Women* at the time of publication and was nowhere near Scott. She even told columnist Sidney Skolsky, "I got tired, very tired, of having men say to me—'Me Tarzan—you Jane.' Since I'm getting a divorce they don't say it to me on the set." Earlier that month, Scott was reportedly dating a young actress by the name of Marilyn Walker in a short-lived relationship. In August, Mike Connolly, perhaps taking Miles's "side" in the split, reported that Scott "sat through five hours of strip sessions" at the Sunset Strip gentlemen's club Largo. Later that month, Connolly reported that Scott "took dancer Gwen Dolan out to his Malibu hut to teach him some non-Tarzan type terping." In September, New York–based gossip columnist Lee Mortimer linked Scott to actress Linda Williams (it is unclear if it was the same Linda Williams who was later known as Linda Hutchings), while in October, Skolsky reported that Scott was preparing to marry a German actress named Cathy Bonn once he was divorced from Miles. Whether or not it was a coordinated public relations blast, the gossip columns were making it no secret that Scott was keeping himself very occupied with several women while his estranged wife was working in Europe regardless of what he said in the press about reconciling with Miles, and after their divorce, Scott was regularly linked to many actresses in Harrison Carroll's column through the early 1960s.[15]

Any realistic chance of reconciliation had long passed by the time the *Van Nuys News* reported on October 8 that Scott no longer had a car after his station wagon was discovered and subsequently impounded by a police officer the previous day in Sherman Oaks when it was found "blocking a driveway and pointing in the wrong direction on a one-way street" less than a third of a mile from Scott and Miles's home. The article incorrectly describes Scott as "Hollywood's former Tarzan" (Scott would shoot his final Tarzan film, *Tarzan the Magnificent*, in early 1960), ribbing him by saying that he may need to swing from vines instead for transportation because he was now without a car. On her return from Europe, Miles filed for divorce, with Sheilah Graham noting in her October 30 column that Scott was "disappointed" because "he had hoped to reconcile" with her despite his now well-publicized dalliances.[16]

Shortly after *Psycho* wrapped production, Miles flew to Juarez, Mexico, on March 2, 1960, to obtain a divorce from Scott, telling the *Los Angeles Times* that she went south of the border "to get the thing over as quickly as possible" (it was over so quickly that gossip columnist Harrison Carroll reported that Miles left Los Angeles at 7:30 a.m. and returned home by 3 p.m.). Miles received custody of their son but didn't file a suit asking for child support from Scott until May 1961. At the time of the divorce, Scott was filming *Tarzan the Magnificent* in London. Later that month, Miles was spotlighted in Louella Parsons's column (under the humorous title "Tarzan Is Left in the Tree by Jane but Vera Miles Not Sour on Marriage"), with Miles remarking, "Now I'll be content with my three wonderful children and my career," though Parsons noted that she added "as quick as lightning," "I shouldn't have said that. I really have nothing against marriage. If I can find a man who would make me happy and whom I could make happy I would like to marry again but not for a long time." However, unmentioned in the article was that by that time, Miles was already steadily dating her former costar Keith Larsen, whom she began seeing shortly before the December 1959 reshoots of *Five Branded Women*. As for her explanation of why her marriage with Scott failed, Miles simply stated, "We just weren't meant for each other." After Miles married Larsen in 1960, Scott told columnist Harrison Carroll,

"Vera is entitled to a little happiness. I couldn't give her the intellectual stimulus she needs."[17]

Scott's final film as Tarzan, *Tarzan the Magnificent*, was released in July 1960. After wrapping the production of the film, Weintraub loaned Scott to Italian film producer Paolo Moffa just weeks later to star in the 1961 film *Maciste contro il vampiro*, or *Goliath and the Vampires* as it was titled when it was released in the United States in 1964. *Maciste contro il vampiro* was Scott's introduction to the Italian *peplum* (sword-and-sandal) film, the genre that would dominate the rest of his career. Scott's muscular body was seemingly built for him to star in such films as legendary strongmen, and the Italian film industry was in a *peplum* film craze that began with 1959's *Hercules*, starring bodybuilder-turned-actor Steve Reeves. Many of the *peplum* films centered on the character Maciste, a long-standing Hercules-like strongman of Italian cinema. Because the character was unknown in the United States, he was typically renamed after a biblical or mythological muscleman whom Americans would be more familiar with, like Samson (or, as in the case of *Maciste contro il vampiro*, Goliath), when the films were dubbed and released in the United States. Of course, the simplistic plots of the typical *peplum* film made the character's name relatively unimportant when translated and localized. *Maciste contro il vampiro* was codirected by Sergio Corbucci, who is best known today for directing *Django*, the 1966 spaghetti Western (the genre that succeeded *peplum* in Italian cinema). By the time Scott finished his first *peplum* film, he decided he was through wearing Tarzan's loincloth and reportedly turned down a contract extension to play the Lord of the Jungle for several more years to make more films in Europe. Other sources indicated that it was Weintraub who decided to release Scott despite having two more films on his contract because he wanted to cast the leaner Jock Mahoney as the next Tarzan.

Though *Maciste contro il vampiro* was shot and released in Italy first, Scott's first Italian film to be released in the United States was his second feature, *Maciste alla corte del Gran Khan* (released under the title *Samson and the Seven Miracles of the World* after several other titles evoking Goliath were considered), in which he again played Maciste. In his third *peplum* film, *Romolo e Remo*, Scott starred alongside old colleague Steve Reeves as Romulus and Remus, the legendary founders of Rome (Reeves, by then a huge Italian film star, had reportedly recommended Scott for the role). By the time it was released in the United States in June 1963, Scott had moved to Rome to take full advantage of his new status as an Italian film star. He appeared in twenty European films from 1961 to 1967. The films were very low-budget, but several were highly profitable; *Variety* reported that the American release of *Romolo e Remo*, titled *Duel of the Titans*, grossed over $1.25 million in the United States, and Paramount had acquired the American distribution rights for only $70,000.

As the trends changed in Italian cinema, Scott's career changed with them; he starred in two spaghetti Westerns (1964's *Buffalo Bill, l'eroe del far west* and 1965's *Gli uomini dal passo pesante*) and two Eurospy films (1967's *Il Raggio infernale* and 1967's *Segretissimo*, Scott's final film), the genre that exploded after the success of the first James Bond films. Scott also starred in a failed television pilot for a Hercules series that aired in the United States as the 1965 television film *Hercules and the Princess of Troy*. In a 1993 interview with *Starlog* magazine, Scott claimed he made forty-two films in Italy. The Internet Movie Database and other sources only list twenty, but it's not unlikely that additional films Scott starred in were lost to time, especially if they were never released outside of Italy. Whatever the actual number, Scott made a substantial number of films in Europe between 1961 and 1967. However, it's not clear how much contact, if any, there was with Miles or their son during this prolific period for the former Tarzan. Author Richard Lamparski, who profiled Scott in the tenth volume of his long-running Hollywood profile series *Whatever Became Of?*, bluntly stated, "Although legally bound to support their son, he has contributed very little financially. [Miles] repeatedly juggled schedules so the boy could spend time with his father, but he was canceled at the last minute or just stood up." Harrison Carroll (who appeared to have a friendly relationship with Scott based on how often he was mentioned in his column, even years after Scott was no longer appearing in Hollywood productions) would occasionally mention Scott's visits to his son in his column, often also noting the name of an actress Scott was seen out with at the time.[18]

After 1967's *Segretissimo*, Scott never made another film, and he returned to the United States in 1970 (in a March 1973 column, Sheilah Graham reported a rumor that at one point, Scott owned two Ferraris while he lived in Italy but was unable to afford a ticket home by the time he returned to America). Little is known publicly about his whereabouts over most of the next two decades except for Lamparski noting in his profile that Scott was living in a friend's houseboat in Marina del Rey, California, while working a series of odd jobs as well as trading in on the affinity people still had for his version of Tarzan. A press agent told the *Toronto Star* in 1987 that Scott developed the same reputation in Rome that he did in Hollywood for "standing people up and for not paying his bills" and that he had little contact with his family. By the 1980s, Scott stepped back into the public eye as he became a regular on the fan convention circuit, including making occasional public appearances with other actors who played Tarzan, like Jock Mahoney and Denny Miller. Scott spent the final six years of his life living in Baltimore in a spare room of a devoted fan who became a close friend. He passed away in April 2007 at the age of eighty, just eighteen days after the death of Miles's first husband, Bob Miles.[19]

VERA J. RALSTON
Wichita, Kansas

Training in voice and music is the ambition of 18-year-old Vera Ralston. Her favorite hobby is photography and her favorite sport swimming. A graduate of Horth High in Wichita, Vera has had basic photographic and modeling training, and believes right living, plenty of hard work and a definite goal in mind are a girl's best forte. Her birthday falls on August first.

Vera J. Ralston's entry from the 1948 Miss America Yearbook Program. Note the inaccurate high school and birthday information. Atlantic City Heritage Collections, Atlantic City Free Public Library.

Publicity photo for *The Charge at Feather River* (1953). Warner Bros. / Photofest.

Vera Miles with Ralph Meeker in *Alfred Hitchcock Presents* 1955 episode "Revenge." CBS / Photofest.

Gordon Scott presents Vera Miles with a birthday cake on the set of *Tarzan's Hidden Jungle* (1955). Photofest.

Publicity photo for *The Searchers* (1956). Warner Bros. / Photofest.

Vera Miles with Jeffrey Hunter in *The Searchers* (1956). Warner Bros. / Photofest.

Alfred Hitchcock directing Vera Miles, Henry Fonda, and Anthony Quayle in *The Wrong Man* (1956). Warner Bros. / Photofest.

Vera Miles and Henry Fonda in *The Wrong Man* (1956). Warner Bros. / Photofest.

(*left*) Vera Miles poses for her *Vertigo* costume test on December 7, 1956. Paramount Pictures / Photofest.

(*bottom*) Vera Miles meets with J. Edgar Hoover, director of the FBI, on November 5, 1958, in his Washington, DC, office during the production of *The FBI Story*. National Archives photo no. 65-HN-4856-A.

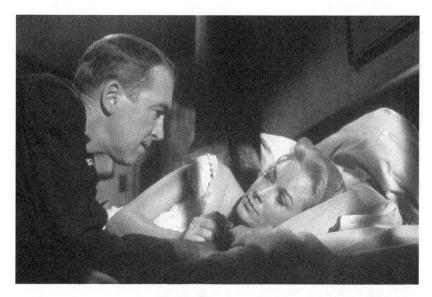

Vera Miles with James Stewart in *The FBI Story* (1959). Warner Bros. / Photofest.

Publicity photo for *Psycho* (1960). Paramount Pictures / Photofest.

Publicity photo for *Psycho* (1960). Paramount Pictures / Photofest.

Vera Miles and Keith Larsen celebrate their recent marriage in 1960. Photofest.

Vera Miles on the set of *The Man Who Shot Liberty Valance* (1962) with James Stewart, John Wayne, and director John Ford. Paramount Pictures / Photofest.

Vera Miles with Meg Tilly in *Psycho II* (1983). Universal Pictures / Photofest.

9

Scream Queen

After spending the last half of the 1950s facing both disappointing box office returns (*The Wrong Man, Vertigo*) and massive successes (*The Man Who Knew Too Much, North by Northwest,* and his television series), Alfred Hitchcock was looking for a new project to fulfill his final movie obligation to Paramount Pictures. After he determined that big-budget, large-in-scope projects like *The Flamingo Feather* would be too difficult to film, his eye turned to the idea of creating an effective film on a more modest budget. In 1959, Hitchcock's personal assistant, Peggy Robertson, shared with him a positive review in the *New York Times* of a suspenseful novel titled *Psycho* by author Robert Bloch. The book depicts a series of murders committed by the owner of an isolated motel, Norman Bates, while under the influence of his domineering mother, though she is ultimately revealed to be deceased at the time of the murders, and Bates has been impersonating her. After Hitchcock read the novel on a transatlantic flight, he was convinced it would be the ideal source material for his next project, despite (or perhaps because of) the content being far more sensational than Hitchcock's usual films and most Hollywood films of the period in general, for that matter.

In part because of the box office disappointment of *Vertigo*—but even more so because Paramount felt the source material was lurid and unsuitable for film and completely different in style from Hitchcock's MGM film *North by Northwest,* one of the biggest hits of 1959—Paramount wanted as little to do with *Psycho* as possible. A studio reader had previously rejected the novel, deeming it unsuitable source material for a movie. "Paramount opposed the film and told Hitch they didn't have any space for it," author Robert Bloch told comic book legend Jim Steranko in a 1982 interview. "Hitch's contract gave him control of the subject matter, and he *wanted* to make *Psycho*, but Paramount did everything possible to block the project. They hated the title, the whole concept; they knew it was going to be a catastrophe. They cut the budget. Hitch had to use his television cameraman, John Russell, and shoot in black-and-white, without his usual Cary Grants or Jimmy Stewarts."[1]

Bloch's recollection is accurate—with a reduced budget, Hitchcock largely invested his own money to make the difference. He also relied on using behind-the-camera talent from his television series to shoot the film. However, Hitchcock's use of black-and-white photography in the film, his first black-and-white feature since *The Wrong Man*, was not just for budgetary reasons; it was also an attempt to avoid censorship since he believed the gore in the film would make the ratings organization, the Motion Picture Association of America, deem it unreleasable if it were depicted in color.

To adapt *Psycho* as a screenplay, Hitchcock hired newcomer Joseph Stefano after approving a sample scene he had written. Before *Psycho*, Stefano had received credit on just two film screenplays, but Hitchcock felt strongly about his submitted material and take on the novel. The first half of the film focuses almost entirely on one character, Marion Crane, as she runs off with a large sum of her employer's money. She stops for the evening at the Bates Motel and is shockingly murdered in the shower by Norman Bates (though the audience is led to believe that Bates's mother committed the murder). Since most of Hitchcock's American films had been toplined by male stars like James Stewart, Cary Grant, and Harry Fonda, Hitchcock felt he needed a bigger name for Marion who could carry such a prominent role than the actresses whom he typically cast as his male lead's love interests—like a Kim Novak, Eva Marie Saint, or, of course, Miles, whom he still felt had lost her "momentum" to becoming a star and had little interest in attempting to build her back up again. Hitchcock would ultimately cast actress Janet Leigh in the role.

Leigh was a familiar face to audiences in 1959 not only because of her career as an actress but also because of her high-profile marriage to fellow Hollywood star Tony Curtis (with whom she starred in several films). She was the female lead in the 1958 United Artists adventure film *The Vikings* opposite Kirk Douglas and Curtis, which was a box office hit. That year, she also appeared in Orson Welles's film noir *Touch of Evil*, which, while not a runaway commercial hit, would later be recognized as one of Welles's best and most important films. What Leigh was not generally known for were sultry, "bad girl" parts befitting someone who would run off with her boss's money as Marion does in *Psycho*, making Hitchcock's casting of her in the role even more curious. Most importantly, Hitchcock cast Leigh because he believed the audience would not expect that her character would be murdered halfway through the film, based on her prior roles.

The *Psycho* screenplay called for another actress to play Lila Crane, Marion's sister, who investigates her sister's disappearance in the second half of the film alongside Marion's boyfriend, Sam Loomis. For this role, which was far less sexy than Leigh's Marion, Hitchcock selected a capable actress who was already on his payroll in part to keep costs on the low-budget project down—Vera Miles. Hitchcock considered other actresses for the Lila role before casting Miles, most notably Carolyn Kearney, whom he had seen in an episode of *Playhouse 90* (Kearney would later appear in a 1961 episode of *Alfred Hitchcock Presents*, "You Can't Be a Little Girl All Your Life"). Despite feeling burned by Miles's withdrawal from starring in *Vertigo*, Hitchcock didn't appear to have an issue with casting her in *Psycho*. However, in his 1990 book *Alfred Hitchcock and the Making of "Psycho,"* author Stephen Rebello argues that Hitchcock cast Miles in the less-glamorous role as an act akin to retribution for his previous slight against her and quoted Rita Riggs, who worked on the costumes for the Hitchcock films *Psycho*, *The Birds*, and *Marnie*, who remembered Miles as being unhappy during the making of the film because of the role. Rebello also quotes *Psycho* makeup artist Jack Barron as saying, "Vera was a pretty headstrong lady. She'd do things *her* way and stand up to anybody. Even him."[2]

Many Hitchcock enthusiasts dispute the notion that Lila's part in the film is weak. "People look at this film as some kind of retribution on Hitchcock's part for Miles after the episode of *Vertigo* with this being a dull, underwhelming part, but I don't see Lila's part as dull because Miles brings the part to life with her capabilities and working with arguably what little she has," explains Rebecca McCallum, writer, speaker, editor, and creator/host of the *Talking Hitchcock* podcast. "I guess if I look at Lila's dialogue on a page maybe it doesn't spring off, but what Miles does with it is incredible. Yes, some of that is Hitchcock, but it's so much Miles and what she brings. I really get a sense that the purposefulness, directness, and refusal to be intimidated by men that we see in Lila feels like a lot of that is in Miles as well and that is why she can handle that material so well. In Lila, Miles brings a very modern woman to the screen."[3]

In that vein, Hitchcock's close collaborator Herbert Coleman wrote in his memoir, "There was never any disagreement for Lila Crane. Vera Miles was a sure bet for the part. No one could have been better." Leigh's own memoir about the making of the film, 1995's *Psycho: Behind the Scenes of the Classic Thriller* (cowritten by Christopher Nickens), does not mention any on-set animosity between Hitchcock and Miles during the making of the film, though it's worth noting that Leigh and Miles did not work together during the production of *Psycho* except for shooting publicity stills together, because of the film's split narrative.[4]

Of course, Miles was not interviewed for either of these books, and Miles herself did not publicly speak about any ill will between herself and Hitchcock during the production of the film. Miles would later recall that she had faith in Hitchcock that he wouldn't make a tasteless movie despite the lurid content it was based on, saying, "I read the book but was not concerned because I knew Hitchcock's style was not overt. I never felt Hitchcock would be guilty of extreme gore and eyeballs popping out of the screen." Miles was paid just $10,000 for her role in the film, a fraction of the $75,000 per film she told Hedda Hopper she was getting paid in a March 1959 interview. Of course, starring in *Psycho* would fulfill her yearly obligation to make a film for Hitchcock in her contract, so the incentive was still there for Miles to appear in the film. The low-budget nature led to everyone working on it taking cuts—for example, Leigh was paid $25,000, about a quarter of her usual fee. Despite being the female leads, Leigh and Miles each only appear in about half of the film and likely wouldn't have received their standard payments anyway because of that. Leigh worked about three weeks on the film, with almost the entirety of one week's shooting devoted to filming the famous shower sequence.[5]

Miles had undergone a physical transformation that the production would need to address—her hair was still short from the shaving she endured for *Five Branded Women*. During the production of *Psycho*, Hitchcock even ribbed Miles by referring to the short-haired star as "the prettiest boy in town." As a result, Miles wore a wig throughout production.[6]

To play Norman Bates, Hitchcock cast Paramount contracted actor Anthony Perkins, a thin, handsome actor who was, before *Psycho*, best known for dramatic roles like 1956's *Friendly Persuasion* (for which he was nominated for the Academy Award for Best Actor) and 1957's *Fear Strikes Out* as well as romantic films like 1958's *The Matchmaker* and 1959's *Green Mansions*. Perkins had been hailed since his screen debut in 1953's *The Actress* as a future star for his boyish good looks and expressive body language. The casting of Perkins was virtually opposite of the way Bates is depicted in the novel as an overweight, middle-aged, balding alcoholic who becomes "Norma" after drinking too much and blacking out. Not only was Perkins cast against type, but his casting also made Norman a far more sympathetic character than how he is depicted in the novel. In addition, Hitchcock suspected that audiences would not expect a leading man of Perkins's stature in the industry to be revealed as a psychotic murderer.

In her October 10, 1959, column, Hopper announced that Hitchcock had cast Miles in his upcoming film, which would start shooting just weeks after her return from Europe filming *Five Branded Women*. In his remarks to Hopper, Hitchcock wouldn't "confirm or deny" that the film would be based on the novel *Psycho* but said that he would not be shooting it on a studio lot. Of course, Hitchcock would ultimately shoot almost all of *Psycho* on the Universal Studios lot—a fact that Universal still promotes to this day on its studio back-lot tour—utilizing the production space of Revue Productions typically used for his television show. That secrecy and misdirection prevailed throughout the production of the film. In an interview with gossip columnist Louella Parsons before the release of *Psycho*, Miles shared, "I would like to tell you the plot, but when we started to work we all had to raise our right hands and promise not to divulge one word of the story."[7]

To help control costs, Hitchcock utilized crew members from the *Alfred Hitchcock Presents* television series, including cinematographer John L. Russell, who shot nearly one hundred episodes of Hitchcock's show. One of the few collaborators Hitchcock carried over from his film work was editor George Tomasini, who had edited Hitchcock's films starting with 1956's *Rear Window* (and would continue through 1964's *Marnie* before his death the following year). The film's editing, particularly the dozens of shots that make up the shower sequence, has been acclaimed since its release.

As Lila, Miles features in the second most memorable sequence in the film (ranked after the iconic shower sequence). Searching for clues regarding her sister's fate and suspecting Norman is hiding something, she descends the stairs in the Bates mansion into the fruit cellar. She sees Mrs. Bates sitting down there and, after turning her chair around, makes a startling discovery: "Mother" is a mummified corpse, and the true hand behind the murders is Norman, who had been driven insane by his overbearing mother's abuse and takes on her persona after her death to commit violence. Perkins standing at the top of the basement stairs dressed as Mother with a crazed look on his face is one of cinema's unforgettable images, and Miles's scream instantly launches her to the top of any list of the best "scream queens" in horror movie history. "With Janet Leigh and Anthony Perkins, Miles seems to get sidelined," notes McCallum. "But she is a character that looks, knows, and refuses to be told lies. She wants to go to the motel and inside the Bates house. She refuses to settle. I love the quality that Miles brings to that performance."[8]

Hitchcock shot Stefano's script virtually as it was written except for a single scene between Lila and Sam Loomis—Marion's boyfriend, played by John Gavin—after Bates is arrested when they both realize that Marion had been murdered (according to Stefano, the scene was cut before it was shot).

Hitchcock did as little as possible to publicize the plot of his new project—it was even rumored that Hitchcock had bought up as many copies of the *Psycho* novel as possible to avoid the story being revealed to too many people—in an endeavor that is standard in filmmaking today but very unconventional at the time. The *New York Times* remarked that Hitchcock treated the production "with greater secrecy than surrounded the old Universal Studios of the silent era," comparing it to the earliest days of the studio, when Universal hired armed guards on horseback to chase off spies from other production companies. Even with the press digging into every rumor about the film, Hitchcock also attempted to present Mother as the killer instead of Norman, including floating names in the press of whom he might cast as Mother, and he told the *New York Times* that the film is about "a young man whose mother is a homicidal maniac." Miles was one of several cast and crew members (including Hitchcock) who were hit with the flu in mid-January, one of the few details about the production that was shared with the press.[9]

Knowing the seriousness of the material, Hitchcock decided to add his customary cameo—by now expected by moviegoers—very early in the film. The filmmaker inserted himself in an understated appearance outside Marion's office to avoid distracting the audience from Marion's fateful journey and the subsequent search for her after her murder.

In the opening credits and on the film's poster, Miles is second-billed after Anthony Perkins (third-billed total if counting Hitchcock's possessory credit with the title, which comes even before Perkins's credit), while Leigh receives the last billing as her credit comes at the end of the acting credits ("and JANET LEIGH as Marion Crane"). Miles is not featured on the film's primary poster, which is dominated instead by an image of Leigh in a white bra (other posters did include a publicity still of Miles—much smaller than Leigh—covering her face in horror).

To promote *Psycho*, Hitchcock shot an ingenious six-and-a-half-minute trailer that features him giving a tour of the film's Bates Motel and house sets while vaguely describing the "most dire, horrible" plot of the film (the filmmaker stops himself whenever he's about to give away too much about a particular sequence). The trailer was shot about a week after filming had wrapped, before the movie's sets had been dismantled. While, a decade earlier, Hitchcock had been known mostly for his brief, humorous cameos in his films, by 1960, he was a television personality well known by audiences. The trailer serves as almost an opening sequence to the film, much like the role Hitchcock played in the opening of his television series (the filmmaker opens the trailer by saying "good afternoon" in a similar tone to his customary "good evening" that greeted viewers of *Alfred Hitchcock Presents*).

Cleverly, the trailer features no actual footage from the film. The sequence ends when Hitchcock enters the motel room's bathroom (with his famed silhouette cast on the wall behind him) where Marion is murdered, and after he describes the horrific state of the bathroom after the murder ("You should've seen the blood"), he pulls back the shower curtain to reveal a screaming woman, whose face is covered by the film's title. Pausing the trailer before the title appears reveals that the screaming woman is not Janet Leigh but is, in fact, Miles wearing a wig (but a different wig, stylized to be like Leigh's hair in *Psycho*, than the wig Miles wears in the film). The trailer was filmed after production wrapped on *Psycho*, when Leigh had already moved on to her next project and was no longer available to appear in the trailer, so Hitchcock used Miles instead.

The extended trailer was just one of the ways that Hitchcock used his masterful ability for showmanship that he had developed from forty years of show business experience and, perhaps more importantly, the public recognition he had gained from *Alfred Hitchcock Presents* to promote the film. In fact, Hitchcock's visage was so dominant in the marketing of the film—from the trailer to life-size Hitchcock stand-ups in theater lobbies and a worldwide promotional tour—that one could easily mistake him for the most unlikely leading man of all time. Some of the posters feature Hitchcock pointing to his wristwatch with a dour schoolmaster's look alongside text that insists that absolutely no one would be admitted to the theater after the movie begins. Of course, those threats were tongue-in-cheek, such as suggesting that the theater manager was to stop latecomers from entering "at the risk of his life" and that the policy meant that "no one—and we mean no one—not even the manager's brother, the President of the United States, or the Queen of England (God bless her)" would be allowed in late, but Paramount did expect exhibitors, particularly those in larger markets that featured the film first, to adhere to the rule.

With Hitchcock focusing most of the marketing on himself and his no-late-admittance-allowed policy, the stars, including Miles, were not asked to make the typical promotional appearances for the film, though Miles appeared in a Hobe Jewels store counter advertising campaign to promote *Psycho* displayed in over five thousand retail and department stores. Now that her hair had grown back, Miles also appeared in print ads for Lustre-Creme shampoo that promoted her as the costar of *Psycho*, which, of course, ironically featured Miles in a wig. She shot a commercial for Lustre-Creme as soon as her hair was long enough, and she would also appear in Lustre-Creme ads promoting her 1961 film *Back Street*.

Miles also received the highest honor in her career, a star on the Hollywood Walk of Fame, as one of the more than 1,500 initial honorees cited during the groundbreaking on February 8. Her star is located at 1652 Vine Street, around the corner from the famed Pantages Theatre. Miles's star was awarded for her television work. Like all the other sidewalk stars marking the debut of the landmark, it would be several weeks before construction on Miles's star was completed.

Before the film's release, Miles described *Psycho* as "the weirdy of all times" and "of all Hitchcock thrillers this will be the one to get people right out of their chairs." Hitchcock did not even allow critic screenings, forcing the press to line up with the public in the massive lines forming around theaters to view his latest thriller.[10]

Psycho premiered in two New York City theaters on June 16, 1960. Hitchcock's stark departure from glamorous suspense in films like *Vertigo* and *North by Northwest* divided critical opinion, though most fell on the side of declaring that Hitchcock had created something unique that was destined to be a big hit. The *Hollywood Reporter* called *Psycho* "a first-rate mystery thriller, full of visual shocks and surprises which are heightened by the melodramatic realism of the production" and remarked, "Vera Miles is splendid as the devoted sister." *Variety's* Gene Arneel said that *Psycho* is "an unusual, good entertainment, indelibly Hitchcock, and on the right kind of boxoffice beam." Of course, not every major critic saw the film as among Hitchcock's best. *Film Bulletin* called the film's ending "not very surprising" and expressed that Hitchcock had "gone in for the gruesome," favoring "shocker effects and weird camera angles for effect, rather than his more subtle suspense techniques." Noted *Esquire* writer and cultural critic Dwight Macdonald labeled *Psycho* as "third-rate Hitchcock" and "a nasty little film," being "a reflection of a most unpleasant mind, a mean, sly, sadistic, little mind." Rebello's *Alfred Hitchcock and the Making of "Psycho"* attributes a line from a review calling *Psycho* "a blot on an honorable career" to Bosley Crowther of the *New York Times*, though that line does not appear in Crowther's June 17, 1960, review of the film. Indeed, Crowther's review is tepidly positive, though he does say that the film's "denouement falls quite flat for us." Crowther even listed *Psycho* on his top ten of 1960 list at the end of the year, now calling it an "old-fashioned horror melodrama [that] was given a new and frightening look in this bold psychological mystery picture." The misattributed "blot" quote and Crowther's top-ten list have been cited by Rebello and others to represent the remarkably quick turnaround of some critics' opinions of the controversial film; however, Hitchcock himself attributed the "blot" line to a London critic instead of Crowther in a 1969 interview with *Chicago Sun-Times* critic Roger Ebert. The true origin of the quote is not clear unless the misquote originated from Hitchcock himself in that interview.[11]

One of the critics of *Psycho* includes Miles herself. In a thirtieth-anniversary retrospective of the film, she said, "I don't think *Psycho* was Hitchcock's best work. He did so much better work but, unfortunately, *Psycho* has become his trademark and I think that's sad."[12]

Another successful move by Hitchcock to bolster the box office of *Psycho* was the film's slow rollout—though it opened on June 16 at the DeMille Theatre and the Baronet Theatre in Manhattan, the film did not enter general release until September 8, after playing various big-city markets throughout the summer. Just two weeks after *Psycho* entered general release, *Variety* highlighted the financial success of this booking strategy, as well as Hitchcock's clever financial move to take a bigger cut of the box office instead of salary. "Alfred Hitchcock could author a book on how he struck gold with a motion picture," the trade reported. "It was disclosed in New York this week that the producer-director will walk away with a profit of at least $5,000,000 from his *Psycho* entry. This is gross income, i.e., before the Internal Revenue 1040 statement, but nonetheless a tidy amount of coin for an enterprise that took about nine months of his time and effort." *Psycho* was the most financially successful film of both Hitchcock's and Miles's careers, and because of the film's low cost, it was far more profitable than nearly any other studio release of the year. In addition, because of Hitchcock's ownership stake in the film, he made more money from *Psycho* than from any other film he produced in his career. He would end up trading the rights to the film and his television series to Universal for a substantial ownership piece of the studio, and Universal would remain his home studio for the rest of his career after *Psycho*.[13]

After a three-day break following the end of filming of *Psycho* in February, Hitchcock directed Miles in the one-hour telefilm "Incident at a Corner" for the *Ford Startime* program, a short-lived anthology program spearheaded by Universal head (and Hitchcock's agent) Lew

Wasserman, whose participation in the program enabled it to utilize film talent on the series. While Miles was by that time a longtime television veteran (and now had the Hollywood Walk of Fame star to prove it), outside of *Alfred Hitchcock Presents* and *The Alfred Hitchcock Hour*, *Ford Startime* would be Hitchcock's only foray into dramatic television. "Incident at a Corner" would be the final time Hitchcock would direct Miles and the only time he would do so in color. Like *Psycho*, "Incident at a Corner" was filmed at Hitchcock's Revue Studios stage at Universal Studios and included other key production principals from *Psycho* such as cinematographer John L. Russell, second unit director Hilton A. Green, set decorator George Milo, and several others. Unlike in *Psycho*, Miles was able to appear on screen with her own hair (though sporting a short cut).

"Incident at a Corner" is based on the 1957 short novel by Edgar Award–winning mystery writer Charlotte Armstrong and was adapted by Armstrong herself. It depicts an elderly crossing guard for an elementary school, James Medwick (portrayed by Paul Hartman), who is fired from the job he loves after an anonymous note accuses him of being "too fond" of the "little girls" at the school. However, the accusation follows an incident in which Medwick reprimands an influential parent of a student, Mrs. Tawley (Leora Dana), for ignoring a stop sign. This situation, the titular "incident" at the corner, is shown in the opening of the program from three different angles, with the final angle showing a woman, Georgia (Eve McVeagh), watching the exchange between Medwick and Tawley. She complains to her partner that she wants Medwick to "go away" because she recognizes him from decades earlier and is running from an embarrassing past. As such, the audience is aware from the opening minutes that Georgia and her partner are the likely culprits behind the accusation, though the principal characters, including Medwick's granddaughter, Jean (Miles), and her fiancé, Pat (portrayed by future *Breakfast at Tiffany's* star George Peppard), initially suspect Mrs. Tawley because of the earlier argument. The investigation into the accusation, primarily conducted by Jean and Pat, is mostly carried through by conversation, and the program is more of a domestic melodrama that is less action-oriented than Hitchcock's typical film work, yet it succeeds as a portrayal of how a careless and baseless accusation and ensuing gossip—similar to *The Wrong Man*—can ruin an innocent man's reputation. Like *The Wrong Man*, "Incident at a Corner" also lacks many of Hitchcock's more humorous touches, though that may have been the influence of *Psycho* creeping into the project. Interestingly enough, after Georgia answers the door when the investigation turns to her, she identifies herself as "Mrs. Crane," the same surname as Janet Leigh and Miles's characters in *Psycho*.

Though it was shot after *Psycho*, "Incident at a Corner" was announced by NBC in a press release on March 15 with an air date of April 5, about nine weeks before the release of *Psycho*. The *Los Angeles Times* review was ecstatic in its praise for "Incident at a Corner," calling the cast "uniformly excellent" and stating that "Miss Miles and Peppard were eloquent and moving." The unsigned review in the syndicated "TV in Review" column called the program "a welcome change" to Hitchcock's more explicit television show, noting, "Hitchcock's flamed flashes of directorial genius were less in evidence than usual. But I guess that's because he was operating under a severe handicap. No corpses."[14]

While Miles is top-billed in "Incident at a Corner," Peppard's Pat is the true driving force of the plot. Yet the program fulfilled one of the films that Miles owed Hitchcock on her contract, though it would ultimately mark the last time she and Hitchcock would work directly together. Nonetheless, Miles still expressed warm affection for Hitchcock and a desire to continue working with him in a March 20, 1960, interview with Louella Parsons, remarking, "I would like anything Mr. Hitchcock directs. If he told me to jump over the moon, I have such confidence in his judgment I probably would try it. To me he is the greatest."[15]

In an interview with Cecil Smith, Miles spoke about how different the shoot for *Psycho* was from the shoot for "Incident at a Corner" (which she called "a wonderful story") despite the projects being filmed back to back and reflected on her grueling schedule over the past year: "It's strange—even with the same director—going from a movie to a TV play. We shot *Psycho* at the rate of three pages a day and 'Incident' at the rate of 17. Perhaps I'm just weary. In the last year and a half, I've made five films and seven TV shows. My children are beginning to wonder. I've spent three Sundays with them in the last three months. Still, I don't think they REALLY care how hard I slave."[16]

The constant state of work that Miles was in did not go unnoticed in the industry. In his February 11, 1960, column, Earl Wilson noted that Paramount "has an $8,000,000 bet on Vera Miles" since she would be starring in three films released by the studio in the first half of 1960—*Five Branded Women*, *A Touch of Larceny*, and *Psycho*. Though *Psycho* was a huge hit, her other two Paramount films made little impression in the United States even if Miles received positive notices for her performances.[17]

In its review of *A Touch of Larceny* after its release in January 1960, *Film Bulletin* said, "Miss Miles conveys the right amount of sophistication to make her an appropriate reformer for a reformless rogue." The *Los Angeles Times* review called Miles "winsome and appealing," while the *New York Times* review describes Miles as "properly pretty and receptive in a glacial sort of way." The film was not without its fans; in a 1974 column, film critic James Meade called the slow dance between Mason and Miles to the classic standard "The Nearness of You" "the all-time sexiest fully-clothed movie scene." The sequence in question runs just over two minutes with the pair dancing closely, filmed in a tight silhouette, and features no dialogue beyond the implications of affectionate stares. As Meade remarked, it is a masterful display of suggestiveness that communicates the sensuality between the two characters without a word or loss of clothing and is the type of romantic sequence that Miles would not often have the opportunity to perform throughout most of her career.[18]

On the other hand, *Five Branded Women*, released just two months later, faced much harsher criticism. The *Hollywood Reporter* said Miles was "wasted" in *Five Branded Women* in a negative review of the film.

For her part, Miles didn't think highly of the film either, once remarking to Hedda Hopper, "Marty Ritt directed and the film didn't turn out too well. As Marty said, 'All De Laurentiis wants in his picture is excessive sweat and blood.'"[19]

For once, Miles took some time off after filming "Incident at a Corner." Around the time of her divorce from Scott, she purchased a second home on six acres in Thousand Oaks and decided to take time to enjoy it, but she was still searching for her next film role. In her July 14, 1960, column, Sheilah Graham said that Miles "is hunting for a 'sexy, glamorous role.' She is tired of being good, drab, or mixed-up, career-wise. Are you listening, Alfred Hitchcock? (He owns her contract)." While she made a few public appearances at the time— including participating in the fashion show at the Women's Adoption International Fund Ball on June 4, 1960, at the Beverly Hilton, which included European royalty in attendance: Crown Princess Margrethe of Denmark, Princess Astrid of Norway, and Princess Margaretha of Sweden—her main focus at that moment was her relationship with her *The Rose Bowl Story* and *Wichita* costar, Keith Larsen, who was her date at the WAIF Ball. On July 31, Miles appeared at the Researchers' "Magic Moments Dance" at the Embassy Room of the Ambassador Hotel to receive the organization's first-ever Humanitarian Award for her "contributions to juvenile decency." Proceeds from the event went to the Eleanor Roosevelt Institute for Cancer Research.[20]

However, the biggest development of Miles's career in 1960 was in her contract status. After nearly five years of Miles being under the employ of Hitchcock, on November 22, 1960, Miles's agent Milt Rosner and attorney Richard Kleinrock notified Hitchcock that she "no longer considers herself under contract" to Alfred J. Hitchcock Productions. Miles's agent and lawyer argued that because Hitchcock loaned her out for *A Touch of Larceny* and she starred in *Psycho*, she had fulfilled her obligations to the filmmaker. Naturally, Hitchcock's team argued otherwise at first and asserted that there were still three years left on their deal, but because of the filmmaker's waning interest in her, the parties eventually negotiated to release her from her contract in August

1961. Hedda Hopper devoted her entire June 24, 1962, column to a profile on Miles, which marks one of the few instances in which Miles, now out of her contract with Hitchcock, spoke disparagingly about the director. "I found him difficult to work with because he had a preconceived image of me which made it hard for us to communicate," Miles told Hopper. She later expanded, "Over the span of years he's had one type of woman in his films—Ingrid Bergman, Grace Kelly, etc. Before that it was Madeleine Carroll. I'm not their type and never have been. I tried to please him but I couldn't. They are all sexy women but mine is an entirely different approach." Three years later, Miles echoed similar sentiments in another interview, remarking, "Hitch has a favorite type of woman he wants for his pictures and I guess I look similar to that woman but I never had that kind of temperament. I accused Hitch of making me into something I wasn't, a Grace Kelly type. Altogether I wouldn't call it an ideal producer-actress relationship."[21]

Unfortunately for the story of Miles and Hitchcock's relationship, those words have been quoted in dozens of articles and books detailing Hitchcock's relationships with his actors, including works judged as definite sources, like Stephen Rebello's 1990 book *Alfred Hitchcock and the Making of "Psycho,"* as evidence that Miles disliked working with Hitchcock. But those statements are truly outliers when it comes to Miles's postcontract comments about working with Hitchcock. In the case of Rebello's book, he also fairly quotes Miles as saying that while she had disagreements working with Hitchcock, it "wasn't a nasty situation" and that she "look[s] back on him very fondly."[22]

Speculation that Miles had more to say to Hopper at the time on the topic of any issues with Hitchcock can be dismissed; the original transcripts of Hopper's interview with Miles, located in the Academy of Motion Picture Arts and Sciences, archives show that Hopper quoted Miles's words nearly verbatim without any missing context. It's clear that Miles didn't hold deep animosity toward Hitchcock; she still appeared in two episodes of *Alfred Hitchcock Presents* after this interview, though neither episode was directed by Hitchcock. By the end of that year, Miles was again praising the way Hitchcock worked, this time to the *Washington Evening Standard* on December 30: "Hitch will explain the entire technical process in a scene, hoping to instill the mood he desires. He seldom raises his voice, but he has little patience with an actor who asks too many questions" and "Hitch usually has the entire movie or TV show shot by the time he comes on set. He has it all sketched out in his mind."[23]

In a 1973 in-depth feature on Miles's career in *Films in Review*, Miles elaborated on her complicated relationship with Hitchcock, particularly his restrictions on cheesecake photos and wardrobe, but implied that the breakdown in their working relationship was because she was too headstrong to accept his plans for her. "I chafed at the bit," Miles admitted. "I was unable to be anybody's Pygmalion. I was unwilling to allow anyone to guide my career and groom me properly. I admire Hitch as a director and am very grateful for the help he gave my career, though." Miles largely echoed those sentiments in comments in *The Book of Movie Lists*, a 1981 book authored by her son-in-law, Gabe Essoe. "Hitch was not always a pleasant man, and he liked to control people too much," she remarked. "I admired him as a director but we often butted heads over what was or was not right for me."[24]

Twenty years after her frequently quoted interview with Hopper, Miles struck a balance on her thoughts on Hitchcock by speaking of his strict expectations of professionalism when she told the *New Orleans Times-Picayune* in 1981, "Hitchcock always had a reputation for being contemptuous of actors, and I'm not sure whether he *really* wasn't. But, basically, I think the reputation was a lot of baloney. My God, he *adored* Cary Grant! . . . He expected an actor to show up absolutely prepared, ready to take direction, which was mostly technical. He expected you to have worked on your part, your approach before you got on the set." Nonetheless, in all her interviews afterward when she was asked about Hitchcock, and she commonly was, Miles hardly had a cross word to say about him. As noted elsewhere, Miles strongly rejected the assertion by Donald Spoto in his Hitchcock biography *The Dark Side of Genius* that Hitchcock was inappropriate with her behind the scenes, and she, alongside nearly every major star who worked with him, saluted him in person and briefly spoke when Hitchcock received the American Film Institute's Lifetime Achievement Award in March 1979.[25]

After their partnership ended, Hitchcock directed a half dozen more features, and Miles continued to have a successful career in film, television, and the stage, including making another film with Ford and establishing a long-term partnership with Walt Disney and the Walt Disney Studio. Regardless, the end of the Hitchcock–Miles partnership after just two features and two television programs in the wake of the filmmaker's substantial buildup of her career has remained one of the most curious subjects among fans of both Hitchcock and Miles.

In 2012, Fox Searchlight Pictures released *Hitchcock*, a fictionalized adaptation of Stephen Rebello's 1990 book *Alfred Hitchcock and the Making of "Psycho."* The film stars Academy Award–winning actors Anthony Hopkins as Hitchcock and Helen Mirren as his wife, Alma Reville. Actress Jessica Biel, then best known for starring in the television drama series *7th Heaven* and films like the 2003 remake of *The Texas Chainsaw Massacre* and 2004's *Blade: Trinity*, appears in the film as Vera Miles. Not surprisingly, Miles refused to meet with or speak with Biel about the younger actress's portrayal of her. "She's not interested in having a public life and just wasn't interested in speaking to me at all," Biel said in a press conference. "I don't think that was an insult in any way." Instead, Biel spoke with one of Miles's grandchildren, actor and artist Jordan Essoe, about his grandmother and her work.[26]

Though the film takes many liberties with the true-life events it depicts—most notably, it includes many scenes with Miles and Leigh interacting, even though the two spent very little time together during the making of *Psycho*—it does include an intriguing sequence in which Hopkins's Hitchcock and Biel's Miles discuss why his plans for her did not work out as intended. "Why didn't you stay with me?" he asks her. "I would have made you as big a star as Grace Kelly." Biel's Miles responds, "Well, unlike Grace Kelly, I can pick up my own dry-cleaning. I've got a family, Hitch, a home. That blond woman of mystery you're always after? She's a fantasy. She doesn't exist."

While a conversation between the real-life Miles and Hitchcock would not have happened anywhere like that on the set of *Psycho*, the response of the fictional Miles is in line with what she has said about working with Hitchcock. Being a mother and in charge of her career was far more important to her than fulfilling Hitchcock's vision of making her the second coming of Grace Kelly. She wanted to work as an actress, not be shaped into a star she never intended to become.

10

Print the Legend

On July 19, 1960, Miles announced to the press that she and Larsen had wed on July 16 at the Last Frontier Chapel in Las Vegas. The Associated Press report inaccurately called Larsen her "second" husband, also noting that she only officially "shed her first husband" just four months prior (the report also said that Miles and Scott shared a "daughter" named Michael with no mention of Miles's two older children).[1]

Larsen, born Keith Larsen Burt, hailed from a Mormon family in Salt Lake City and, after a nomadic childhood during the Depression, was a standout tennis player at the University of Utah, where he was majoring in law. His studies were interrupted by his service in the navy in World War II, which in turn was interrupted when his ship was bombed. Larsen was hospitalized with an eye injury in California and resumed his studies, now at the University of Southern California. However, while in Los Angeles, Larsen got bitten by the show business bug and explored acting. He was cast as the lead in a production of the Clifford Odets play *Golden Boy* in Santa Monica and appeared in bit parts of the 1951 John Wayne films *Operation Pacific* and *Flying Leathernecks*, both of which were primarily shot in the fall of 1950.

Unfortunately, Larsen initially had little luck in his acting career in Hollywood, even though Polish filmmaker Rudolph Maté, best known at the time for directing film noir movies like 1949's *D.O.A.* and 1950's *Union Station* and had served as the cinematographer on Hitchcock's second Hollywood film, 1940's *Foreign Correspondent*, visited him backstage after a performance of *Golden Boy* and praised his acting.

Looking elsewhere for opportunities, Larsen moved to New York City. He eventually landed in Paris, and after a chance meeting with Maté, who was in Paris for preproduction for the French American coproduction *The Green Glove*, the director hired him to help with casting the film. After assisting Maté with the production (and having a bit part in the film too), Larsen went back to California to assist Maté with his 1952 film noir movie, *Paula*, which also features Larsen in a small part. Following this work, Larsen signed a contract with Monogram Pictures, which led to his appearance in several films, including *The Rose Bowl Story*, his first of two films with Miles. In one of Larsen's earliest films, *Hiawatha*, he played an Indigenous American character, which led to Larsen, who was primarily of Norwegian descent, frequently portraying Indigenous Americans in films throughout his career, including in the films *War Paint* (1953), *Chief Crazy Horse* (1955), and *Apache Warrior* (1957).

Since Miles and Larsen had first worked together, Larsen had become a television regular in several television programs, most notably the 1955–56 series *Brave Eagle*. Larsen portrayed the title character, a Cheyenne chief, in one of the few Western television series of the era to have an Indigenous American character in the lead role. Unfortunately for Larsen, the CBS series was programmed opposite ABC's *Disneyland* and did not have much of a fighting chance against the popular Walt Disney anthology series. He had another opportunity to star in a series with *Northwest Passage*, a 1958–59 adventure series about pioneers during the French and Indian War. At the time of their wedding, Larsen was in the beginning stages of filming his newest television series, the underwater adventure series *The Aquanauts*, which would debut in September 1960.

Though the marriage was something of a surprise to the public, the notices mentioned that the actors had long been acquainted. Miles and Larsen had been linked together in the press as early as March 1960, though she was also noted by gossip columnists to be seen in the company of actor Tom Tryon. But Miles told Hedda Hopper, "It was a surprize [*sic*] to us, too, even though we have known each other for nine years." The November 1960 issue of *Modern Screen* noted that the nuptials "caught most of Hollywood off guard," including Finish American actress Taina Elg, who was reportedly dating—or was at least under the impression that she was dating—Larsen for two years before he married Miles. Elg had appeared with Larsen in a 1959 episode of his adventure series *Northwest Passage*—it was one of three episodes combined to make the theatrical feature *Mission of Danger*, which was distributed internationally in 1960 and 1961—and the two were reported as engaged as recently as Mike Connolly's January 7, 1960, column in the *Hollywood Reporter* while Elg was finalizing a divorce from her then-current husband. Elg was starring in a musical in Dallas titled *Redhead*, for which Larsen reportedly flew out for the opening night, at the time she received the surprising news that Miles and Larsen had wed.[2]

Regarding his courtship with Miles, Larsen told *TV Radio Mirror*, "We both dated others and, up to the day we got married we never 'went steady' although we had vowed our love to each other." As for her side of the story, Miles told Hedda Hopper in June 1962, "When we first met I was married and expecting a baby. The second time, I'd just gotten a divorce: I had two children. My thinking was that I now was a mature woman and must conduct myself accordingly. So when Keith asked for a date I condescendingly told him that he could come some day and take me and the children for a drive. He turned and fled. Then he called up, out of the blue, when I got back from Rome with my bald head—it had been shaved for that De Laurentiis picture, and we began going out together." Though Larsen owned a house in the exclusive Malibu Colony that formerly belonged to Frank Capra, the family primarily lived in Sherman Oaks at Miles's house until shortly after the birth of their baby in May 1961. Almost immediately after the marriage, the pair held a small gathering in Hollywood to celebrate before Larsen returned to production on *The Aquanauts*. Louella Parsons reported in her July 28, 1960, column that Gordon Scott, who around that time had been spotted in New York with bombshell Sabrina (English model Norma Ann Sykes), had sent Miles a telegram congratulating her on the marriage. However, whatever good feelings this gesture may have had were long gone by the end of May 1961, when Miles sought a court order to force Scott to pay $300 a month for child support for Michael (Miles had not sought support from Scott in her quickie Mexican divorce).[3]

The Aquanauts also would only last one season, and Larsen departed the series partway through the season because of a needed sinus operation. *The Aquanauts* was an attempt to replicate the success of the similarly themed television series *Sea Hunt*, starring Miles and Larsen's *Wichita* costar Lloyd Bridges, that began airing in 1958 in first-run syndication after all three networks passed on it. After *Sea Hunt* became a big hit following its debut, *The Aquanauts* was a less successful attempt by CBS to recreate the success of the series it and the other networks had passed on. Incidentally, both the half-hour *Sea Hunt* and hour-long *The Aquanauts* were produced by producer Ivan Tors and Ziv–United Artists productions. Meanwhile, another similar syndicated series, *Assignment: Underwater*, also premiered in September 1960 as another attempt to cash in on the success of *Sea Hunt*. At the very least, Larsen and Miles got a honeymoon out of the series— Miles tagged along with Larsen when he shot some of the series in Bermuda in August 1960.

As was standard in Hollywood at the time, over the next several months, the gossip columns were filled with saccharine stories about the newlywed Miles and Larsen. Sheilah Graham's September 7, 1960, column called the couple "very TV happy" and mentioned that Larsen had recently gifted Miles a $500 knitting machine. In her September 26 column, Graham reported that Miles and Larsen "bought a half-interest in a gown shop with Parisian designer Andre d'Aulan" and that Miles turned down an offer to shoot another film in London because it would have separated her from Larsen for three months. Larsen told Ruth Waterbury in her October 2, 1960, *Los Angeles Times* column, "[Miles is] the greatest. Gets up at 3:30 a.m. to get me my breakfast before I go to work. We have to shoot that early to have the water clear enough for photography. Often I don't get home till 10 at night. What kind of new bridegroom is that? But Vera never complains. A doll, that's what." Waterbury then reported in her October 23, 1960, column that while Larsen was promoting *The Aquanauts* in New York City, he racked up an $853 long-distance phone bill because of his calls to Miles.[4]

In what seemed like a virtual rewrite of the puff pieces about Miles's marriage to Gordon Scott, the February 1961 issue of *TV Radio Mirror* featured a similar piece about Miles's marriage to Larsen, titled "Built-in Happiness." The article portrays the couple at the height of domestic bliss, Larsen as a devoted stepfather and Miles as a working mother who still had time to run a house. The article went as far as calling Miles "one of Hollywood's most accomplished and ardent chefs." However, the article, as well as most of the press surrounding their marriage, made no mention of Larsen's first wife, German American actress Susan Cummings, or their child together. Nonetheless, the article detailed Larsen's impromptu proposal, in which he mentioned to Miles while they were poolside at her Sherman Oaks home that they could fly to Vegas, get married, and be home before 10:30 p.m., with Larsen saying, "I myself wasn't sure whether or not I was kidding. But then I knew I wasn't, that I meant every word, that we just had to get married, that the love we knew we had for each other had to be fulfilled."[5]

Despite all the happiness that was reportedly going around in the Miles-Larsen household, it was right around the time of the marriage that Larsen's once-promising career as an actor began to go south. According to Hedda Hopper's October 3, 1960, column, Larsen was supposed to shoot a film in Italy, titled *My Italian Affair*, with producer Herbert Coleman, who worked regularly with Hitchcock, after wrapping the first season of *The Aquanauts* (in his memoir, Coleman wrote about the project, "Gossip columnist Hedda Hopper helped create studio interest with an item in her column"). However, the project didn't materialize. In his September 28, 1960, column in the *Hollywood Reporter*, Mike Connolly reported that Miles would guest star on *The Aquanauts* alongside Larsen in an episode filmed at Niagara Falls after she finished shooting *Back Street* in late 1960. However, that project also didn't materialize, most likely because Larsen himself wasn't long for the series.[6]

At the end of October, Larsen was hospitalized with pneumonia in Boulder City, Nevada, while filming a scene for *The Aquanauts* in the Colorado River outside Las Vegas (Miles left the set of *Back Street* to be at his side). The health of the series wasn't faring much better. In mid-November, *Variety* reported that two major sponsors, Kellogg's and General Foods, bailed on the series effective January, and by December 1960, just three months after *The Aquanauts* debuted, mediocre ratings already put the show on the chopping block. Larsen would soon depart the series midseason in January 1961 because he needed a sinus operation that would make the series' trademark diving scenes impossible for him to film (*Weekly Television Digest* described Larsen's condition as "A World-War II-incurred head injury 'aggravated by constant exposure to water pressure'").[7]

Curiously, shortly after Larsen was replaced because he could no longer film the underwater sequences, the series jettisoned most of the underwater photography anyway in an attempt to alter the format to a cheaper one under a new producer, Perry Lafferty. The name of the retooled series changed to *Malibu Run* in March 1961 to reflect its focus on more land-based adventures. Despite the format change, the series was doomed to be short-lived because it aired opposite NBC's far more popular *Wagon Train*. The final episode of *Malibu Run* aired on June 7, 1961. *The Aquanauts* marked Larsen's final regular television role. He would make just one more appearance on episodic television, in a December 1961 episode of the ABC drama series *The Roaring 20's*, before shifting his focus to an uneven career in directing and producing films while also frequently playing in celebrity tennis tournaments in Palm Springs and Palos Verdes, sometimes with Miles as a doubles partner.

Miles's next film was a romantic drama, *Back Street*, based on a novel by popular American writer Fannie Hurst. It was the third film adaptation of the novel after 1932 and 1941 versions, all of which were released by Universal Pictures. The film reunited Miles with her *Psycho* costar John Gavin, who plays Miles's husband. Miles stars against type as Gavin's character's troubled alcoholic wife, and the film focuses on his character's desire to be with another woman, played by Susan Hayward, instead of the unstable Miles. Miles later described the character simply as "very rich, very bad, very bitchy." Hayward had recently won the Academy Award for Best Actress for her remarkable performance in the 1958 drama *I Want to Live!* During production, Hayward would tell John L. Scott of the *Los Angeles Times*, "Vera has the type of role that allows her to steal the movie," to which Miles replied, "Susan has paid me my finest compliment. Now I know how she felt when she won her Oscar."[8]

Miles initially turned down the lead in *Back Street* because it was scheduled to be shot in London, and she did not want to shoot a film overseas again after shooting three films in Europe in the previous two years. When the production eventually was moved to Stage 20 on the Universal lot, Miles agreed to take the role, and the film started shooting on September 21, 1960 (part of the film was also shot in Monterey). During production, Miles suffered from bruising after a scene that involved Susan Hayward pushing her down a flight of stairs required thirty takes, and she was also injured after going through breakaway glass with too much force during a scene in which her character is inebriated.

Back Street was produced by Ross Hunter, known for his romantic melodrama films, and was released by Universal. Hunter told Hedda Hopper that Miles would have "14 lovely Jean Louis gowns, plenty of mink, sable, and real jewels" to wear in the film. Jean Louis was a famous French American costume designer whose career achievements included designing costumes for Marlene Dietrich, Joan Crawford, Kim Novak, and many others as well as the gown that Marilyn Monroe wore when she famously sang "Happy Birthday, Mr. President" to John F. Kennedy in 1962. Miles reportedly was able to keep the $78,000 wardrobe, the first time she had the opportunity to do that after starring in a film.[9]

Because of the heavy focus on the film's wardrobe, Universal promoted the film with a seven-minute fashion-reel trailer highlighting all of Miles's and Hayward's costumes worn throughout the film. Miles would later tell the Associated Press, "Amazingly, I've gotten more reaction from that picture than any I've ever done. All Ross has to do is ask me. He knows how to please women—both on the screen and in the audience. I think from now on I'm going to select movies on the basis of wardrobe." Miles was supposed to go on tour to promote the film while wearing the glamorous clothing at each stop, but the release would come a few months after the birth of her fourth child, and she decided not to tour. Instead, Miles and Gavin both recorded interviews that were distributed to radio stations that were timed with question gaps to simulate a live interview with the local disc jockey.[10]

Despite not going on a full promotional tour, Miles participated with the cast in a parade down State Street in Chicago on October 11 in advance of the premiere screening (the Los Angeles premiere was held on October 26 at the brand-new New Warners Hollywood theater on Hollywood Boulevard, which Miles also attended). The review in *Variety* said, "Miss Miles is a skillful, accomplished actress. She does all that is humanly possible with her role." *Harrison's Reports* said that Miles "endows her work with charm, cynicism, bitterness, emotional turbulence." John L. Scott's review in the *Los Angeles Times* said, "I for one would have welcomed more emphasis on Miss Miles." While *Back Street* proved to be a box office hit (*Variety* estimated its final gross would amount to $3.5 million), it was the only time Miles worked with Hunter on a film, even though he produced another dozen movies and several television productions before he retired from film production in 1979. However, Hunter directed her in a play twenty years after the release of *Back Street*.[11]

After finishing filming *Back Street*, Miles wrapped up the year with a few television projects and public appearances. On October 23, she appeared in the *General Electric Theater* episode "The Camel's Foot" on CBS. The following month, Miles was honored at the *Los Angeles Mirror*'s "Best Dressed for Her Life" fashion show, which was hosted by Ronald Reagan and held at the home of *Los Angeles Times* publisher Norman Chandler. Miles was demure about winning the award, later telling the *Washington Evening Star*, "You know how it is with children, you don't always put on your nicest things because of those sticky fingers." Just days later, Miles was scheduled to be one of five judges of the Fast Draw Contest between Western television actors, staged at the Sahara in Las Vegas.[12]

By the end of 1960, Miles decided to take on a new acting challenge: the stage. She began her foray into the theater on the production side in November 1960 when she directed a production of *Our Town* staged by members of the Flyers Club of Sherman Oaks Methodist Church with her friend Anita Gordon as assistant director. Proceeds from the production went to the church. On December 31, 1960, the *Los Angeles Times* announced that the pregnant Miles would make her stage debut opposite actor Jeff Morrow in *The Country Girl* on February 15 (with previews starting February 12) as the first-ever production at the new Teddy and Dorothy Hart Theatre 90 at 870 N. Vine Street in Hollywood (the ninety-seat house was advertised as "the little theater with big stars"). The play was written by Clifford Odets, who directed the original production on Broadway in 1950.

The Country Girl is a behind-the-scenes look at the production of a new musical starring a once-popular actor, Frank Elgin, who has fallen on hard times. Frank initially convinces the musical's director, Bernie Dodd, that his wife, Georgie, is the reason for his troubles. In reality, Frank's fading star, fueled by alcoholism and suicidal thoughts stemming from the death of their son, is propped up by Georgie. While Bernie takes Frank at his word about Georgie, he realizes that Frank is truly the troubled one and begins to develop an attraction to Georgie. The play had been previously adapted as a film in 1954 starring Bing Crosby and Grace Kelly, which was a hit and earned Kelly her Academy Award for Best Actress.

Leon Charles, who was the dialogue coach on Miles's *Back Street*, directed the new production. Also initially announced among the cast members was Larsen, though he departed the production before it was staged for a personal appearance tour and was replaced by Robert Christopher. However, Larsen was far from the only cast member to be replaced. Another actor, James Drake, was replaced by Robert Osborne—later host of Turner Classic Movies—just two weeks before opening. A third actor, Tom Barnes, withdrew because of a death in his family and was replaced by Bill O'Connell. Another actor, Bob Danielson, became the show's stage manager and was replaced by an actor named William Ramage. On top of that, opening night was then pushed back to February 16 as the theater underwent some finishing touches.

After years of comparisons between Miles and Kelly, it was ironic that Miles was making her stage debut in a role so closely identified with Kelly, especially since Miles initially intended to take time away from acting because she was pregnant with her fourth child. She remarked to the *New Orleans Times-Picayune* in 1981, "I was about to go into one of my periodic retirements for a while—to have another baby, by the way—and the offer to do the play came along. I enjoyed it, the involvement of it all. . . . In the movies you work 16 hours a day, hard work, but suddenly, for the first time, I found acting to be terribly involving, absorbing fun in a way the movies weren't." Unfortunately, one week after opening, the *Los Angeles Times* published a review of the play under the title "*The Country Girl* Revival Disappoints." Reviewer Geoffrey M. Warren almost entirely laid the blame for a production that "fails to come up to par" at the feet of director Leon Charles, noting Miles as both "lovely" and "very well cast." Miles also received good marks in much more positive reviews in the *Hollywood Reporter* and the *Hollywood Citizen News*, the latter noting, "With little exception she dominates each scene in a portrayal that is at once sensitive, kind, rebellious, patient, and impatient. There is little doubt the role has lent her greater emotional structure as an actress." The praise for Miles made no difference—the now very pregnant Miles lasted just one more week in the role before being replaced by Anna Karen, who was also Morrow's wife (Karen appeared in *The Wrong Man* as Miss Duffield, one of the insurance office secretaries who wrongly identifies Henry Fonda's Manny as a robber). [13]

Despite the troubles behind the production, the March 29 issue of *Variety* reported that the play was being shopped for an East Coast summer stock theater with Miles, Larsen, and Morrow, though this ultimately failed to materialize. Miles gave birth on May 1 to a son, Erik, at St. Joseph's Hospital in Burbank, her fourth and last child and her only child with Larsen.

In the summer of 1961, both Miles and Larsen shared their acting knowledge when they were featured as guest speakers at an eight-week acting seminar hosted by actress/writer Jenna McMahon at the Cameo Playhouse on Santa Monica Boulevard in Hollywood. Then, just a few months after their first time working together on stage ended early because of Miles's pregnancy, Miles and Morrow would again take another chance at working together with director Leon Charles. On August 27, 1961, the *Van Nuys Valley News* reported that Miles, Larsen, and Morrow would star in a production of an original mystery play titled *The Deadly* directed by Charles starting October 6 at the Valley Theater in Woodland Hills, Los Angeles (the play would run only on Friday, Saturday, and Sunday nights) and, in some standard preshow hype, noted that the "production is possibly headed for Broadway." *The Deadly* was written by *The Parent Trap* screenwriter David Swift and produced by William Robert Obrecht. However, before the play debuted, Jeff Morrow was replaced by Harry Townes, an experienced stage and television actor who had appeared in the second episode of Larsen's *The Aquanauts* and would later appear with Miles in the pilot episode of *The Fugitive*. Miles would go on to work with Morrow again; in 1963, she appeared with him in an episode of *The Virginian* ("The Man Who Couldn't Die"), and several years after that, she appeared with him again in an episode of the legal drama *Judd for the Defense* ("Everyone Loved Harlan but His Wife"). Also among the cast was Yvonne Craig, the future Batgirl actress on the Adam West *Batman* television series. In the play, Miles portrayed a promiscuous woman named Johanna Chapel, who spends much of the time wearing bandages covering her face after her character is allegedly shot by her jealous husband, only for the husband (played by Townes) to then turn the gun on himself. Miles rehearsed for *The Deadly* in the evenings while filming *The Man Who Shot Liberty Valance*.[14]

Previews for *The Deadly* began on October 14, 1961, with the play opening on November 3. Unfortunately, reviews for *The Deadly* were even worse than those for *The Country Girl* earlier in the year. Two days after opening night, the *Hollywood Reporter* reviewer James Powers said the play must have come "from the bottom of the old trunk" and that "Leon Charles' direction does not help as much as it might and lacks cohesiveness." Powers also noted that Miles was not successful at acting with her face covered in bandages. Later that week, the *Los Angeles Times* published a review by Philip K. Scheuer that was also largely negative, noting that "Swift's dozen characters are barely two-dimensional." The review in *Variety* was also negative, outright declaring that Swift's play "comes off badly" and calling it a "cliche thriller with redundant and repetitive dialog, and irrelevant comedy attempts." The review didn't spare the Larsens from any criticism, calling Miles's and Larsen's roles "trite" and adding, "Miles plays adequately but without punch and Larsen looks like a lumbering robot." On the other hand, at least the *Van Nuys Valley News* praised the play in a more puff-than-professional review, declaring, "If this play isn't a commercial success then we miss our guess."[15]

The *Van Nuys Valley News* wasn't wrong in that aspect—despite the poor reviews, the play was a commercial success and ran through the new year, with the January 21, 1962, performance held as a fundraiser for the Valley University Women. The production finished its run at the end of January. In January 1964, the *New York Times* reported that Swift rewrote the play and mounted an attempt to get it on Broadway with Broadway and film producer Frederick Brisson, who had produced such notable Broadway productions as *The Pajama Game* (1954), *Damn Yankees* (1955), and *Under the Yum-Yum Tree* (1960, which Swift adapted for a 1963 film starring Jack Lemmon that Brisson produced), with plans to adapt the play as a film after its Broadway run. However, the production never materialized, and whether Miles's and Larsen's names were still in the mix at that point isn't clear.

Miles didn't let the bad reviews dissuade her from pursuing acting on the stage. Though it never became the primary focus of her career, Miles would regularly perform short runs in various plays in Los Angeles and, later in her career, other significant theater cities throughout the United States.

Miles's new interest in the theater did not stop her from continuing her regular work on television, of course. Most notably, in January 1961, she filmed the pilot episode of *The Asphalt Jungle*, a short-lived crime series that was inspired by the 1950 film noir classic *The Asphalt Jungle*. However, in postproduction, the episode, titled "The Lady and the Lawyer," became the series' second episode and aired in April. Though some early reports said that Miles would be playing the character played by Marilyn Monroe in the original film, the only resemblance is that both characters are named Angela; the characters' storylines are entirely different (Miles portrays a legal secretary who is having an affair with her boss, played by Robert Douglas, and aids him in his scheme to stage a robbery to steal a substantial amount of money from the mafia). After the series was canceled in June, MGM repurposed the episode by reediting it into the feature film titled *The Lawbreakers*, which was released later in 1961 in international markets. In June, Miles filmed an episode of the detective show *Checkmate*, "The Crimson Pool," which aired on November 22. She also played a blind equestrienne in an episode of *Frontier Circus*, a CBS series about a traveling circus in the American West, which aired on October 19.

On August 24, 1961, Hedda Hopper reported that Miles, who "has more jobs than she can fill," was wanted by John Ford for his next film, *The Man Who Shot Liberty Valance*, a Paramount film based on a Western short story by Dorothy M. Johnson that Ford had purchased the film rights to earlier in the year. Johnson's novella *The Hanging Tree* had recently been adapted as a 1959 Warner Bros. movie starring Gary Cooper. The very next day, Miles was announced as part of the cast for a September 5 start.[16]

The Man Who Shot Liberty Valance tells the story of a US senator, Ranse Stoddard, who attends the funeral of a rancher named

Tom Doniphon. At the funeral, Stoddard recalls to a reporter that he and Doniphon had been associates years earlier and worked together to put an end to the notorious outlaw Liberty Valance in the frontier town of Shinbone. Stoddard's political career was built on being known as the titular "man who shot Liberty Valance," although, in actuality, Doniphon was the true gunman who shot Valance but let Stoddard take the credit. In April 1961, Ford cast his frequent collaborators James Stewart as Stoddard and John Wayne as Doniphan, and he later cast notorious tough-guy actor Lee Marvin as the outlaw Valance. It was the first of only two films (the second being 1976's *The Shootist*, Wayne's final film) to feature Wayne and Stewart together in the same movie (although both Wayne and Stewart appeared in 1962's anthology film *How the West Was Won*, which was released several months after *The Man Who Shot Liberty Valance*, they are featured in different segments). Regarding the rare dual-headlining film (though Stewart is billed first on the posters), Patrick Wayne says that his father didn't question the arrangement. "If John Ford ever asked my father to do anything, he did it," he explains. "That was the case with *Liberty Valance*. Jimmy Stewart is the star of the film. Although my dad's presence takes over a great deal of it, it was definitely somebody else's film. My father felt that he owed this to Jack Ford because of the great start that he gave my dad in *Stagecoach*. He was a loyal man, and that was his core value."[17]

In *The Man Who Shot Liberty Valance*, Miles portrays Hallie, a waitress in Shinbone whom both Stoddard and Doniphan romantically pursue. Ford hadn't worked with Miles since they had shot "Rookie of the Year" for *Screen Directors Playhouse* shortly after production wrapped on *The Searchers*. However, that was more out of scheduling issues than a lack of interest. Ford had wanted Miles to star in his 1958 ensemble political film *The Last Hurrah*, but Hitchcock passed on the opportunity. Ford and Stewart wanted Vera Miles to play the female lead in their 1961 film *Two Rode Together*, but the part was ultimately played by Shirley Jones because Miles was committed to *Back Street*. Before Miles, Ford considered casting Carolyn Jones in *The Man Who*

Shot Liberty Valance, but this time the schedules aligned to allow Miles to take the role, and her casting was announced in early August 1961, around the same time that Hitchcock released Miles from their contract and just weeks before filming was scheduled to begin.

As usual, *The Man Who Shot Liberty Valance* would feature many of Ford's frequent collaborators who had also worked with Ford, Wayne, and Miles on *The Searchers*, including uncredited appearances by actors Gertrude Astor, Danny Borzage, Jack Pennick, and Chuck Roberson as well as stuntmen Chuck Hayward, Bryan "Slim" Hightower, and John Hudkins. Ford's frequent assistant director Wingate Smith also served that role on both films. Most notably, the film also stars John Qualen, who plays the father of Miles's character as he did in *The Searchers*.

However, what set the production of *The Man Who Shot Liberty Valance* apart from the production of *The Searchers* was the budget. Whereas *The Searchers* was bankrolled by business magnate C. V. Whitney to launch his new production company and spared little expense on shooting the film on location in Monument Valley in VistaVision, *The Man Who Shot Liberty Valance* was largely shot on the Paramount lot on black-and-white film, which, even just two years removed from the monochrome success of *Psycho*, was increasingly rare for a studio feature with major stars. It was Ford's first Western filmed in black and white since 1950's *Rio Grande*. A common explanation for Ford's choice to film *The Man Who Shot Liberty Valance* in black and white that has persisted in the decades since the film's release has been that it was an attempt to help both Wayne and Stewart, who were both over fifty, appear younger on screen, though Ford himself said he felt the material was better suited for black and white, particularly in the use of shadow in the film. It has also been speculated that the film's high costs, much of which were taken up by the salaries of the two leads, left little room in the budget provided by Paramount for the project to be an on-location color shoot. Ford even reused some of the score from his 1939 20th Century Fox film, *Young Mr. Lincoln*, for scenes featuring Miles in *The Man Who Shot Liberty Valance* (Ford later remarked to filmmaker and author Peter Bogdanovich in an interview for his 1967 book *John Ford* that he reused the score because it was one of his favorite pieces of music). However, at a budget of over $3 million, *The Man Who Shot Liberty Valance* was still one of Ford's most expensive productions.

In the film, Miles's Hallie starts as the girlfriend of Wayne's character, Doniphan. However, when she begins to care for Stewart's Stoddard after the young lawyer is beaten and robbed by the notorious Liberty Valance, she starts to fall for him instead. While Stoddard wants to bring the outlaw to justice through the legal system, Doniphan is convinced the only way to stop Valance is with a bullet. Stoddard and Doniphan form a bond over their shared goal of eliminating Valance from Shinbone, though Doniphan notices that Stoddard is now a rival for Hallie's affection and tries to warn him away. However, Hallie's interest in Stoddard grows as he teaches her how to read. Stoddard is later selected to be a delegate for Shinbone for the statehood convention for the territory, a move that Valance opposes on behalf of the cattle barons who want the area to remain a territory. When Stoddard and Valance have a showdown in town over the issue, a gunfight ensues, and Stoddard believes that he has shot and killed Valance—only for Doniphan to reveal that he was the one who actually fired the fatal shot. Believing that Stoddard's reputation will lead him to great things—he enters politics and eventually becomes a US senator—Doniphan also acknowledges to him, "Hallie's your girl now." The narrative is framed by an older Stoddard and Hallie attending Doniphan's funeral. Stoddard tells a reporter there the truth about who really shot Valance, even though his political career was launched on the idea that he shot the outlaw, but the newspaper's editor refuses to print it and offers Stoddard one of the great lines in the history of Hollywood movies: "This is the West, sir. When the legend becomes fact, print the legend," a reflection of the mythmaking of the American West that Ford, Wayne, and Stewart all played substantial roles in creating in Hollywood.

In many ways, Miles's Hallie is similar to her spirited character Laurie, whom she played in Ford's *The Searchers* nearly a decade earlier. She represents the possibility of domestic life for both the rough Doniphan and idealistic Stoddard at a time when Shinbone itself faces a more civilized future with the opportunity of statehood. Though Doniphan is in love with her, in a memorable sequence after he has shot Valance, he attempts suicide by burning down his house (where he has been building a new addition for Hallie for when they get married) while inside it once realizes that Hallie has fallen for Stoddard. Though Doniphan is rescued by his friend Pompey (portrayed by NFL player–turned-actor Woody Strode), he still lets Hallie go and encourages Stoddard to pursue her.

The Man Who Shot Liberty Valance started filming in September 1961 at the Paramount lot. In a June 1962 interview with Hedda Hopper, Miles spoke about shooting the film, noting, "My stand-in and I had a wonderful time working with all those tall, handsome males. They are John Ford's ideal types. He wouldn't let me wear anything but Mary Janes because he wanted me to look 4 feet tall. He's terrifying to work with, so bright, fast, and keeps you busy. I've never been on a set where there wasn't time to read, knit, or sit around gassing; but Ford keeps everyone hopping trying to second guess him." While Miles recalled making the film as a positive experience, Ford allegedly lost interest in the project early on and instead found more enjoyment in pitting Stewart and Wayne against each other behind the scenes. Luckily, Miles avoided being a target of this quarreling.[18]

For a film that is today viewed as one of Ford's greatest Westerns, *The Man Who Shot Liberty Valance* did not receive stellar reviews on its release. The *Variety* review said, "Yet, while it is both an enjoyable film and a promising contender, it falls distinctly shy of its innate story potential, and this will both the more discerning filmgoer" but noted that "Vera Miles is consistently effective." *Film Bulletin* called it a "lukewarm Ford western" that "lacks sustaining action" and said that it would "disappoint fans intended for." The review in *Box Office* outright stated that the film should be considered a comedy and that during the press screening the audience "laughed, groaned, and commented so audibly and derisively that a well-disposed reviewer could only be embarrassed for its makers." The *Harrison's Reports* review was far more positive, at least in the case of Miles's role, noting that she "grows in dramatic stature with each succeeding picture." Nonetheless, *The Man Who Shot Liberty Valance* became a box office hit, likely on the strength of the popularity of its two stars. It also managed to get some awards recognition: Edith Head received an Oscar nomination for Best Costume Design, Black-and-White, and Miles was one of many members of the production who was cited on the Bronze Wrangler trophy awarded to the film in April 1963 by the National Cowboy Hall of Fame and Western Heritage Center, located in Oklahoma City, in Miles's birth state of Oklahoma, for her work in the film along with Ford, producer Willis Goldbeck, screenwriter James Warner Bellah, and the rest of the primary cast. The award was accepted by Paramount executive Peter Adams.[19]

Like *The Searchers*, *The Man Who Shot Liberty Valance* has maintained a stellar reputation since its release. In 2007, it was selected for preservation in the US National Film Registry by the Library of Congress, joining *The Searchers* (one of the first twenty-five films selected in 1989) and *Psycho* (selected in 1960) with that honored status.

Though *The Man Who Shot Liberty Valance* was a hit and Miles received strong reviews for her performance, Ford and Miles never had the opportunity to work together again. If Edith Head had her way, Ford, Miles, Wayne, and Marvin would have reunited the following year for *Donovan's Reef*, which was the final film in which Ford directed Wayne after decades of working together. Head felt the actress cast as Wayne's love interest in the film, Elizabeth Allen, was unsuitable for the role and unsuccessfully lobbied Ford to cast Miles instead. Wayne also felt uncomfortable with the age difference between him and Allen; though Allen was nearly two years older than Miles, Wayne felt she looked too young on screen compared to him. However, Ford kept Allen in the part, and Wayne would have to wait several more years before working with Miles again.

Ford largely retired after his last feature film, 1966's *7 Women*, and passed away in 1973. From her perspective, Miles felt that the two films she made with Ford were the finest of her career. In a 1989 interview with *USA Today*, Miles said, "If I were to go back and look at the films, I think the most joyous and creative times were the John Ford films" and later added, "They were highpoints for me."[20]

11

The Disney Mom

After completing work on *The Man Who Shot Liberty Valance*, it would be nearly two years before Miles was cast in another film. In April 1961, the *Hollywood Reporter* noted that Miles would be starring in *In the Wrong Rain*, presumably an adaptation of *Los Angeles Times* literary critic Robert R. Kirsch's 1959 novel, but the project never materialized. While she was considered for several films, including George Cukor's *The Chapman Report* (1962) and Otto Preminger's *Advise and Consent* (1962), Miles was not cast in any new film projects.

Meanwhile, Miles continued her prolific television work and her live theater pursuits. On January 11, 1962, she was announced as the lead in the two-part "Three Blind Mice" episode of the crime drama series *The Detectives,* which aired on March 30 and April 6. On January 25, Miles was announced to appear on the popular NBC medical drama series *Dr. Kildare* as a neurotic patient with then president of the Academy of Motion Picture Arts and Sciences Wendell Corey—who had appeared in Hitchcock's *Rear Window*—as her doctor. However, on April 9, NBC announced that the episode would be pulled from the series and instead be reworked as the pilot episode of a new medical drama series titled *The Eleventh Hour* that would star Corey (about half of the original episode was reshot to remove Richard Chamberlain, who played the titular Dr. Kildare, from the narrative). The episode, "Ann Costigan: A Duel on a Field of White," features Miles as a woman accused of murdering her husband, while Corey, as Dr. Theodore Bassett, is assigned to review her mental state to evaluate her plea of insanity. The pilot aired on October 3, 1962. It marked a successful launch for the series; the *Los Angeles Times* review called the premiere "an engrossing piece of work with a beautiful script" and cited Miles's performance as "fascinating." Miles was personally surprised with how popular the episode became with viewers, later remarking, "Of all the things I've done in the past few years, more people remember and comment on my performance in the first show of *The Eleventh Hour*. I thought it was good, but not that good, although I'm pleased to hear it."[1]

Just over two years later, Miles and Corey were supposed to work together again in the Actors Theater production of Budd Schulberg's *The Disenchanted* (based on his 1950 novel that was partially inspired by the life of F. Scott Fitzgerald), which opened on May 7, 1965, in Los Angeles. However, Miles pulled out of the play because of illness just a few days before opening and was replaced by Sally Kellerman. The *Los Angeles Times* noted in its review that "the entire production seemed rough and unsteady, possibly because of the tension caused by the change in leading ladies."[2]

During the time that *The Eleventh Hour* was being retooled, Miles appeared on several other notable television broadcasts. She reunited with her *The Searchers* love interest, Jeffrey Hunter, for an episode of *The Alfred Hitchcock Hour* titled "Don't Look behind You," a thriller about women being assaulted in a small college town, which aired on September 27, 1962. The episode also reunited Miles with director John Brahm, who had directed her acclaimed episode of *The Twilight Zone* two years earlier.

Over the final months of the year, Miles also appeared in episodes of *Sam Benedict* (October 27), *Route 66* (December 14), and an adaptation of F. Scott Fitzgerald's short story "Crazy Sunday" for *The Dick Powell Theatre* (December 18). She also appeared in another notable pilot episode that was shot that year opposite fellow guest actor Brian Keith for the television series *The Fugitive*, "Fear in a Desert City," which was shot in November and December 1962 in Tucson, Arizona, and Hollywood (the episode aired on September 17, 1963). Miles later admitted she felt the pilot and the series premise—about a man on the run after being wrongfully convicted of his wife's murder—was not going to be picked up. She later explained that she initially thought, "This thing will never sell. A show with the same man on the run every week? No way." Miles later admitted she couldn't have been more wrong about the series' potential as *The Fugitive* became a hit and ran for four seasons.[3]

In the new year, Miles and Larsen made a brief return to the live stage together at the Pasadena Playhouse in *Rain*. The play was written by John Colton and Clemence Randolph in 1922 and based on the short story written by W. Somerset Maugham and first published in 1921 about a missionary, Davidson, who attempts to reform a prostitute, Sadie Thompson. The play had already been adapted three times into film, including a 1932 version starring Joan Crawford. In this production, Miles starred as Sadie, while Larsen was cast in the Davidson role. Opening night was scheduled for March 7, with the play running nightly (except Mondays) through April 7. The *Los Angeles Times* review of the production called Miles's and Larsen's casting "questionable," noting, "Miss Miles is an admirable actress in the right role and a marvelously pretty one in any setting but her Sadie is hardly more than a caricature," but still recommended the production. Similarly, the unsigned *Hollywood Citizen-News* review made sure to praise Miles as "lovely" before saying that the fault of her performance "lies in the casting" and explaining that Miles is "inevitably, a naturally 'nice' girl type with a voice much too high-pitched and girlish for Sadie." On the other hand, the *Arcadia Tribune* called Miles's performance "powerful" and named the production the "finest vehicle in years" at the Pasadena Playhouse. While Miles and Larsen both wanted to hone their craft on the stage, even if it was simply a way to keep busy between Miles's frequent television projects and infrequent film projects, critics were largely not buying into their performances.[4]

When Miles finally reemerged in film, it marked the start of the next long partnership in her career with another iconic entertainment personality of the twentieth century.

Even after the box office disappointment of *Vertigo*, Alfred Hitchcock and James Stewart considered working with one another again on another film that would be titled *The Blind Man*, about a blind pianist who becomes able to see after receiving the donated eyes of a man who was murdered in an unsolved crime. While visiting the Western-themed Frontierland in Disneyland with his family and witnessing a simulated gunfight, the pianist has a flashback to the murdered man's death in a shooting through his eyes and then embarks on a search for the murderer of his donor.

Hitchcock worked on the screenplay for *The Blind Man* with his *North by Northwest* collaborator, Ernest Lehman, though Lehman later claimed that Walt Disney had no interest in working with Hitchcock in any capacity, reportedly because Disney was disgusted by *Psycho*. While Hitchcock could have likely set the scene at another theme park, the project was ultimately abandoned. Curiously, Miles was considered for the female lead opposite Tony Curtis in the 1962 film *40 Pounds of Trouble*, a comedy that was the first-ever production to film scenes at Disneyland (despite being a Universal Pictures release), though the role was eventually played by Suzanne Pleshette (who also appeared in Hitchcock's next film, *The Birds*).

Disney's reported disgust with *Psycho* may have been exaggerated over time, as Hitchcock employed Disney's optical effects team, including Mickey Mouse cocreator Ub Iwerks, to work on *The Birds*, and in 1962, Disney even wrote Hitchcock a letter suggesting that he cast actress Susan Hampshire to play the title role in *Marnie*. In January 1964, Hitchcock also filmed the horse-riding scene in *Marnie* at Disney's Golden Oak Ranch, a movie ranch owned by the studio, located outside Los Angeles. As such, Disney's personal dislike of *Psycho*—if that story is indeed true—clearly did not stop him from collaborating with Hitchcock in the years following. Indeed, the two titans of Hollywood also had far more in common than most acknowledge, including both serving as host of their eponymous television programs that helped create immense brand value for their respective public images.

Regardless of Disney's true feelings on *Psycho*, any edict he had about not allowing Hitchcock to film in Disneyland did not extend to working with the Master of Suspense's frequent collaborators. On April 9, 1963, Hedda Hopper announced the cast of Disney's latest live-action film, *A Tiger Walks*, including Miles, in her column (Walt Disney had given Miles's daughters free tickets to Disneyland earlier that year, perhaps as a whimsical negotiating tactic with their mother). Though Disney had built his studio's fortunes on his famous cartoon shorts and features, his studio began releasing live-action family films, starting with 1950's *Treasure Island* and, by 1964, released about five live-action films per year, often with their releases timed to coincide with school breaks to maximize their box office earnings with family trips to movie theaters. After the completion of their theatrical runs, the movies would typically air on Disney's anthology television series, *Walt Disney's Wonderful World of Color*.

To appeal to children, many of Disney's live-action films prominently featured animals. *A Tiger Walks* is about an escaped circus tiger set loose in a small town and the different reactions the towns-folk have to dealing with the tiger's presence. In the film, Miles stars as the mother of a young girl who advocates against the tiger being shot by local law enforcement. Miles stars opposite her costar from *The Fugitive* pilot episode, Brian Keith, who plays her husband and the town sheriff who is torn between putting the tiger down for the safety of his community or sparing its life to keep his daughter happy. Keith had become a regular in Disney live-action films after starring in the 1960 Disney Western film *Ten Who Dared*, followed by the studio's 1961 hit *The Parent Trap*. Shooting for *A Tiger Walks* began May 13, 1963, at Walt Disney Studios, and it was scheduled to be Disney's Easter 1964 theatrical release. The film was directed by Norman Tokar, a former stage actor who transitioned to directing television episodes, most notably directing nearly one hundred episodes of the sitcom *Leave It to Beaver*. His experience directing young actors brought him to the attention of Walt Disney, and Tokar became the equivalent of a "house director" for Walt Disney Productions and directed many of the studio's films until he died in 1979. *A Tiger Walks* was the third feature he directed for the studio, and he also directed Miles in her next two Disney films, *Those Calloways* and *Follow Me, Boys! A Tiger Walks* was the first of six films that Miles would make for Walt Disney Productions over the next decade.

Shortly after production on *A Tiger Walks* finished, Disney signed Miles for another film, originally titled *Wild Goose Stop*, which was set for an early October start date (the film was renamed *Those Calloways* before release). Miles again stars as a mother—and again opposite a husband played by Brian Keith—though this time of a Vermont family who attempts to establish a sanctuary of wild Canada geese. Originally, the studio planned to film the movie in Maine, but by the end of September 1963, the decision was made to shift production to Vermont. However, most of the filming took place back west at the Disney back lot, where the studio had built a New England town complete with painted autumn leaves.

After more than fifteen years away, Miles returned to Wichita in late March 1964 with Larsen for the first time since she had left for Hollywood for the Kansas premiere of *A Tiger Walks*. To help promote the film, she crowned the winner of the KAKE-TV (the local ABC affiliate station) Miss Kakeland pageant, owing to her roots as a beauty queen. For the three-city midwestern tour for the film, which also included stops in Salt Lake City and Denver, Miles hired Oscar-winning MGM costume designer Helen Rose to create a new wardrobe for her, since it was her first substantial publicity tour since her introduction to the media as Hitchcock's newest protégée. Larsen accompanied Miles on the tour, and the couple treated the trip as a working vacation. At the time, they were considering *Mary and the Fairy*, a surrealist fairy-tale play adapted from a 1940 radio drama by famed writer Norman Corwin, for a production at the Pasadena Playhouse as a follow-up to *Rain*, which would then transfer to the University of Utah. The production never materialized, and Miles and Larsen would instead turn their attention back to developing film projects instead of stage productions. Weeks later, Miles noted that the tour made her realize that she fully intended to work harder on building her career. "After 10 or 12 years in this business I've decided to stay in it," she remarked. "The Disney tour helped clarify the picture for me. I'm not just selling a picture, I'm also selling me, and I don't mind that now because I want to stay in the business."[5]

Luckily, she had plenty of opportunities ahead of her at Disney. Miles very quickly became one of Walt Disney's favorite actresses, and he welcomed her in a more prominent role with the studio. In May 1965, he was already considering Miles for a third film, this time based on the MacKinlay Kantor novel *God and My Country*, a tribute to the Boy Scouts of America. Dick Van Dyke was originally considered for the lead role in the film as a man who becomes an influential scout-master in a small town, but the role ultimately went to another Disney favorite, Fred MacMurray. Though MacMurray might be recognized by film critics and historians for his lead role in Billy Wilder's 1944 film noir masterpiece *Double Indemnity* and supporting role in Wilder's Oscar-winning 1958 film *The Apartment*, he had a parallel career as a "classic dad" in the 1960 to 1972 sitcom *My Three Sons* and the numerous family-friendly films he starred in for Disney from 1959 to 1973. By 1965, MacMurray had already starred in four other films for Walt Disney Productions. MacMurray and Miles first worked together in *My Three Sons* when Miles guest starred in three episodes as a possible love interest of MacMurray's character. The episodes aired on September 16, 23, and 30, 1965, and were the first after the series moved from ABC to CBS and began airing in color.

Miles immensely enjoyed working with Walt Disney, whom she called "an artist in what I consider the true sense of the word," in an interview with the *Salt Lake Tribune* to promote *A Tiger Walks*, adding, "He has a genius for reaching children and adults with just the right taste." In 1984, she told *Disney Channel Magazine*, "When we were doing *Follow Me, Boys!* we filmed outdoors at night on the back lot. It was very cold; we'd sit around salamanders to keep warm. Almost every evening, out of the darkness and the shadows, would come Walt. He'd sit around the salamanders, put his feet up, and just be with us. . . . That was extraordinary for a head of a studio. He *cared*, and his involvement with his studio was total."[6]

Miles enjoyed working with Disney, though she did initially question why the living legend had taken such a shine to her. "Disney is less emotional than most producers," she remarked in a March 1965 interview before the production of *Follow Me, Boys!* "I think he simply hires people he believes have talent. Maybe he does have a type of woman in mind for his heroines—a Walt Disney type. But what, I wonder myself, is that type?"[7]

Her casting opposite MacMurray in *Follow Me, Boys!* gave a clear answer to her question—as much as MacMurray would come to exemplify the "Disney dad" in his seven films for the studio, Miles would exemplify the "Disney mom" in her six movies for the studio. In *Follow Me, Boys!*, the two would embody those roles by starring together as husband and wife, naturally. However, this childless on-screen couple would become "father" and "mother" to dozens of boys through their involvement with the Boys Scouts of America. MacMurray plays Lem Siddons, a former traveling musician who settles in a quaint town in Hickory and becomes the local scoutmaster of the Boy Scout troop. Miles plays a bank clerk who eventually becomes his wife and a strong supporter of his scouting endeavors, though she has a few choice lines where she dresses him down for his bravado. The movie began filming on July 12, 1965, on the Disney back lot as well as the studio's Golden Oak Ranch in Santa Clarita. The studio had purchased the ranch in 1959 after renting it to shoot several films, most notably 1957's *Old Yeller*, and the studio built a covered bridge across a stream for the production of *Follow Me, Boys!* To promote the film, Miles was scheduled to embark on an eight-city screening tour for the film in the latter half of August 1966 in advance of its December release. *Follow Me, Boys!* was the last Disney film released during Walt Disney's lifetime—only the first three of Miles's Disney movies were made while Walt Disney was alive. The film was released throughout the United States on December 1, 1966, just two weeks before Walt Disney passed away.

During this period, Miles became closely associated with the Disney studio. In November 1965, she presented an award to Walt Disney from the Motion Picture and Television Make-Up Artists and Hair Stylists at the 13th Annual Hollywood Deb Star Ball at the Hollywood Palladium in recognition of Disney's "many outstanding contributions to the motion pictures and television industries and in recognition of his wholesome entertainment and artistic excellence." Singer Maurice Chevalier received the award on Disney's behalf. When she participated in KTLA's Arthritis Foundation nineteen-hour telethon in February 1965 along with *Mary Poppins* stars (and fellow Walt Disney favorites) Dick Van Dyke and Julie Andrews, Van Dyke attempted to recruit Miles to costar with him in the film *Divorce American Style*, written by Norman Lear. However, the role was eventually filled by Debbie Reynolds when the movie was released in 1967. In a May 1966 interview with the *Deseret News*, Walt Disney expressed disappointment in Van Dyke's choice to make a film with that title because of his close association with his family-friendly movies. That perhaps explains why Disney was so focused on preserving the image of his preferred "Disney mom." During that same *Deseret News* interview, which was conducted on the Disney studio lot, Miles walked by during the interview (she was on the lot to dub lines for *Follow Me, Boys!*). Disney called her over, calling her his "favorite actress," and asked about a movie she was making with comedian Sid Caesar at Paramount. Disney inquired, "Is it clean?" and Miles responded, "Why Mr. Disney, you know I would never work on a dirty picture." Walt responded with a laugh.[8]

On June 25, 1966, Miles attended the premiere of Disney's Dick Van Dyke film *Lt. Robin Crusoe, U.S.N.* on the navy supercarrier USS *Kitty Hawk* in San Diego, which served as a location for the movie during filming. The premiere raised money for the Navy-Marine Memorial Foundation. Later that year, Miles appeared on the cover of the November issue of the company magazine, the *Disney World*, and in March 1967, she visited Brigham Young University in Salt Lake City to accept the Best Family Film award for *Follow Me, Boys!* on behalf of Walt Disney Studios. Also in 1967, Miles and her family attended the premiere of *The Jungle Book* at Grauman's Chinese Theatre on October 18 as well as the premiere of Disneyland's newest parade, Fantasy on Parade, and the annual Christmas candlelight procession on December 16. Miles, now a mother of four and in her thirties, was comfortably embracing her "Disney mom" persona as a new phase in her film career.

Though Miles was working steadily for Disney, her maternal roles in the films were largely forgettable, and the movies she starred in are not cited among Disney's classic films. Even at the time of their release, the reviews of these movies were largely dismissive. The *Variety* review of *A Tiger Walks* called the movie "synthetic and childish" but noted that kids would enjoy it. The *Los Angeles Times* review of *Those Calloways* called it "plain pleasant entertainment" and noted that Miles is "a beauty even in baggy clothes and no makeup." The *New York Times* review noted that "Mr. Disney has left in nothing that could possibly offend anyone. Everything is innocuous, wholesome, and professional, and entrapped adults may always grab a short nap." The *New York Times* review of *Follow Me, Boys!* called it "a clutter of sentimental blubberings about the brotherhood of the Boy Scouts and indiscriminate ladling of cornball folksy comedy." In his otherwise lukewarm review of the film, which was published just eleven days after Disney's death, *Los Angeles Times* reviewer Philip K. Scheuer said that the film nonetheless "will stand as a monument to the late master of entertainment and, often through the years, of art as well" for Walt Disney. Nonetheless, the film did well at the box office and set the single-day box office record at New York's Radio City Music Hall.[9]

While Miles was undoubtedly appreciative of the work from Disney—or else she wouldn't have kept agreeing to star in so many of the studio's films—she did publicly lament the quality of film roles that she was being offered during this period. While she continued to work steadily on television, as for films, Miles never recovered from the fallout of pulling out of *Vertigo* because of her pregnancy. While actresses just a few years younger, like Elizabeth Taylor, Shirley MacLaine, and Shirley Knight, were starring in Oscar-nominated roles in prestigious films, Miles had rapidly shifted from playing sexy roles in movies like *Beau James* and *A Touch of Larceny* to predominantly playing housewife supporting roles in *A Tiger Walks* and *Those Calloways* in less than a half-dozen years.

As a result, Miles worked on developing her own projects that she hoped would create more satisfactory roles for her. While that would become increasingly common for actors in the following decades, she was one of the few actresses of her era to make the effort on her own. As early as 1957, Miles began developing a biopic of Amelia Earhart that she had hoped to star in (in her April 28, 1958, column, Sheilah Graham reported that Miles "has read everything available about the famous aviatrix"), though the project never came to fruition. While Miles was constantly working in television at this time, in his June 7, 1958, column Mike Connolly reported that Miles was also so dissatisfied with the teleplays offered to her that she was planning on writing her own television project (again, nothing came from that either). Similarly, while promoting Miles's appearance on the television series *The Asphalt Jungle*, the April 23, 1961, issue of the *Washington Evening Star*'s *Sunday Star TV Magazine* noted that Miles "hasn't found the success in the manner predicted for her."[10]

Larsen, too, was also working on potential projects that would feature Miles now that he was no longer regularly acting. In 1962, Larsen worked on a screenplay adaptation of the pulp fiction book *Sin Street* by Bob Bristow with television writer Herman Groves that Larsen and Miles intended to produce, with Miles potentially starring, though that project was never made. On October 17, 1963, *Los Angeles Times* columnist Philip K. Scheuer reported that actress Fay Baker was writing a screenplay, *Idonea Darling's War*, for a movie that Miles and Larsen would star in together. The screenplay was based on a true story about a widow in England who waged a long campaign against the local government to have a bridge built in her community, seemingly perfect material for an artistic melodrama. Baker decided to write the screenplay herself when she couldn't find any writers who were interested in working on it after she came across the story. Larsen paid Baker

$50,000 for her screenplay to produce it himself and reserved a role for Baker in the film, telling Sheilah Graham about Miles, "My wife has never had a chance to show what she can really do." The couple planned to shoot the film in England in the summer of 1964.[11]

Idonea Darling's War was yet another instance of Miles attempting to create an opportunity for herself to have more than a supporting role in a film. She told Don Alpert of the *Los Angeles Times* on March 29, 1964, "Does it seem to you that women don't have an identification? They don't seem to have a vital place in our society. There's such a preponderance of good male stars. Where do you find a good woman's story? If someone does write one they call it a soap opera. There must be a position that women occupy today that isn't soap operish." While Miles was doing what she could to change this, even an actress as headstrong as she was faced challenges with creating female-led projects.[12]

By May 1964, Larsen was scouting Scotland and in talks with veteran English actor Richard Todd (best known for his Oscar-nominated role in 1949's *The Hasty Heart* and Alfred Hitchcock's 1950 film *Stage Fright*) to star with Miles in *Idonea Darling's War*. In June, Hedda Hopper reported that Miles and Larsen "already have most of the financial backing." However, the film was ultimately never made, and Larsen decided to pursue other projects for him and Miles instead. Over a year later, Hedda Hopper reported in her August 23, 1965, column that Miles and Larsen would shoot a movie in Spain "next spring" based on a story written by Larsen and screenwriter Vincent Fotre. Larsen and Fotre both appeared in bit parts in the 1951 John Wayne movie *Operation Pacific*, and Fotre had written episodes of television series like *Alfred Hitchcock Presents*, *Lassie*, and *Target* as well as the screenplay for the low-budget 1958 creature feature *Missile to the Moon*. Miles shed little light on the project, saying, "It's untitled, but I assure you I won't play a female James Bond." This film also never materialized, although Larsen and Fotre cowrote the very low-budget 1970 sexploitation horror film *Night of the Witches*, though Larsen's filmmaking contributions were credited to "Keith Erik Burt" (his real name was Keith Larsen Burt, and Erik is the name of his son with Miles).

Considering the amount of skin shown by the witches in the publicity stills (though not in the actual film, which does not feature nudity), it's extremely unlikely that this was the same project that Miles was meant to star in, nor is it likely to have been a script the duo had been sitting on for five years.[13]

While Miles and Larsen worked to get their own projects going, Miles again spoke out about the lack of strong roles for women, this time on television, in a *Los Angeles Times* article on May 22, 1964, titled "Vera Advises TV to 'Love a Little,'" encouraging television producers to offer more romantic programming. She explained, "I am so sick of playing in these psychological things. I seem to be the cancer type this season, or when they don't have me dying of cancer, then it is some kind of mental derangement." Referencing her role in the pilot of *The Eleventh Hour* as a deranged murderess, she added, "I finally got to do a love story on another *Eleventh Hour* and I'm sure it's the only one they ever did. Wendell Corey and I were in love, but of course I only had six months to live, and died right on schedule." Ostensibly, this interview was promoting Miles's appearance on *Bob Hope Presents the Chrysler Theatre* in an episode titled "The Sojourner," based on a Carson McCullers short story, which aired on May 29, 1964, on NBC. Regarding the episode and the roles offered to her overall, Miles lamented, "We didn't get the script until just a few days before shooting, because I understand the sponsor was worried over the fact that my first husband in the story is impotent. I think it's fear which prevents love stories being done on TV. Of course, when I complain to the producers, they say the writers aren't writing them. Ask the writers, though, and their answer is that the producers don't want love stories." In sum, Miles clearly articulated the frustrating position that actresses had faced in Hollywood for decades before and after her stardom.[14]

At the end of the article, Miles concludes, "If something isn't done about it soon, I am going to write my own love stories." She reaffirmed her position in November 1964, saying that while she was getting bored of playing similar roles (which she referred to as "the lady" and "cool, classy type"), "I have nothing against sex, in its place, but I don't want to be in one of those dirty movies they're making these days," adding, "I've never wanted to become a star. I've just wanted to be an actress. I don't want the limelight," and, in an echo of her response to Hitchcock's criticism of her choosing children over stardom, "I never want my work to overrule my home life. Having children means more to me than anything." Accordingly, in his brief review of "The Sojourner," Cecil Smith of the *Los Angeles Times* praised the episode's color cinematography and noted, "Miss Miles proved again much too beautiful to be so fine an actress." Yet again, Miles's beauty was highlighted by a reviewer over her abilities as an actress.[15]

Even if Miles wasn't satisfied with the quality of her roles, she didn't allow those feelings to pare down her television work schedule over the previous year, including appearing in her first episode of the anthology series *Insight*, titled "The Conspirator." Miles would star in five episodes of the groundbreaking series, which was produced by Paulist Productions, a Los Angeles production company established by a Catholic priest, Father Ellwood Kieser. The syndicated anthology series regularly focused on social issues or societal ills and billed itself as "an exploration in depth of the spiritual conflicts of the twentieth century." Occasionally, the series would delve into historical dramas. In "The Conspirator," which first aired on March 29, 1963, Miles half-heartedly attempts a German accent as the wife of a German officer who plots to kill Adolf Hitler. She would film another episode, "Prometheus Bound," the following year. In "Prometheus Bound," Miles stars as a woman who attempts to save her marriage with her alcoholic, cheating husband by getting pregnant, though her plan takes an unexpected turn when the child is born mentally challenged. That episode first aired in September 1964 (a syndicated series, *Insight* aired at different times in different television markets, though most channels aired the show on Sundays). While filming an episode in October 1965 titled "The World, the Campus and Sister Lucy Ann," in which she starred as a nun going to college, Miles wore her costume off set. She would later tell the Associated Press, "As soon as I stepped off the curb, I knew I should have gone back. All the cars screeched to a stop to let me cross. If I had gone across in civilian clothes, I would have been taking my life in my hands."[16]

On July 26, 1963, Howard Duff and Miles were announced as the guest stars for the "Isn't It a Lovely View?" episode of *Arrest and Trial*, which aired on September 22. Miles also appeared opposite her *The Man Who Shot Liberty Valance* costar Lee Marvin in the two-part episode of *Perry Como's Kraft Music Hall / Suspense Theater*, "The Case against Paul Ryker: Part 1" (aired on October 10) and "The Case against Paul Ryker: Part 2" (aired on October 17). Marvin starred as the title character, an American soldier who is court-martialed for treason, convicted, and sentenced to death. Miles, who plays Marvin's wife, rushes to his side to defend him and protest his treatment.

Writing for UPI, reviewer Rick Du Brow critically ripped the first episode apart, focusing his ire on Miles's character in particular. He called her character's story "an assortment of plot contrivances threatened by a writer," with the piece headlined "Useless Woman Character Mars Otherwise Good TV Drama." In the *Los Angeles Times*, Cecil Smith had much stronger praise for the show but also criticized the inclusion of Miles's character in the narrative by noting that she was "whisked there by magic of the scriptwriter" and that the story was "hokum, but of such hokum have movies ever been made." The review in *Variety* also called it "skillful, if spotty scripting" but noted it had an "all-around excellent cast" and that Miles was "first-rate." The reviews highlighted Miles's complaints about the parts offered to her—that her characters were often superfluous melodramatic additions to productions.[17]

After the massive box office success of Lee Marvin's film *The Dirty Dozen* four years later, Universal reedited the two episodes into a feature and released it to theaters in early 1968 under the title *Sergeant Ryker*. The *Los Angeles Times* review, noting it was an obvious cash-in, declared, "Sergeant Ryker was made for television, and that's where it should have stayed" in its opening sentence.[18]

Still, Miles had her share of far more interesting projects. In early 1964, she costarred with Barbara Rush in the pilot of an anthology science fiction series that was to be titled *The Unknown*, written by *Psycho* screenwriter Joseph Stefano. Instead of launching a new series, the program was repurposed as the final episode of the first season of the science fiction program *The Outer Limits*, which was also produced by Stefano. *The Outer Limits* served as ABC's answer to the success of *The Twilight Zone*, though the series was occasionally marked by much "denser" science fiction episodes than those featured on *The Twilight Zone*.

The episode aired on May 4, 1964, under the title "The Forms of Things Unknown." In the bizarre episode—directed by German filmmaker Gerd Oswald like a European arthouse film and not a weekly episode of television typical of the time—Miles's and Rush's characters poison a man, André Pavan (portrayed by Scott Marlowe), whom they are traveling with. After they drive to a mysterious house with an occupant who claims to have the ability to raise the dead, André, whose body is in the trunk, seemingly comes back to life. While a memorable episode, its numerous twists and turns—for example, the occupant of the house, Tone Hobart (portrayed by David McCallum) is revealed to be a boarder who is experimenting with time travel, and the house's owner, played by Sir Cedric Hardwicke in his final role, is a blind man who is initially presented as a caretaker of the mansion— add layers of curiosity to a far-fetched plot. "It's a mad show," Miles later said regarding the episode's out-there premise. "It's Joe Stefano, a mad man."[19]

The shoot was challenging, and production lasted eighteen days, nine days over schedule. In a March 15, 1964, interview with Hedda Hopper in the *Los Angeles Times*, Rush praised Miles, saying, "It's odd how you never meet people in this business then, all of a sudden, discover them. Vera is such a good sport and has a great sense of humor. We had to go running in a forest in the rain and got wet and muddy; they'd wrap us in blankets after a scene but couldn't give us brandy. I don't drink, neither does Vera who's a Mormon, and it could have been grim; but somehow or other she managed to make it all great fun." Rush also added that Miles remarked, "No matter what happens; if anybody ever runs away from me into a forest and it's raining, they're on their own. Forget it!" The actress's frustration with the scene was not surprising—the exterior rain sequences were shot over five days on the MGM back lot and were so trying that Miles's and Rush's stand-ins quit.[20]

The episode was the only time that Miles and Rush would work together (Rush was previously married to Miles's *The Searchers* costar Jeffrey Hunter). Miles, for her part, appreciated the rare opportunity to star alongside another actress in a television program. "Women never get to work together," she later said. "Now I've known Barbara Rush casually for years, and then we spent those nights under lights in the rain and we discovered we liked each other. We also found out that we would rather work with women than with men. Why is it male actors generally feel they must prove their masculinity? It was nice not to have to deal with that for a change."[21]

The Outer Limits did not have the staying power of *The Twilight Zone*—it was canceled in January 1965 during its second season—but like *The Twilight Zone*, it has continued to have a cult following.

Miles was busy at the end of 1964. On September 14, 1964, she started filming the episode "Portrait of a Widow" of the Western series *The Virginian* alongside fellow guest star (and her *Psycho* costar) John Gavin (the episode aired on December 9). On September 20, she appeared in the eighth season premiere of *Wagon Train*, and on October 7, Miles guest starred in the ABC detective television program *Burke's Law* in the episode "Who Killed the Horne of Plenty?"

Perhaps Miles's most notable project in the fall of 1964 was the television movie *The Hanged Man*, which aired on November 18 on NBC. The month before, NBC launched a series of made-for-television movies with *See How They Run*, starring John Forsythe, Jane Wyatt, Leslie Nielsen, and George Kennedy, which is considered by media historians to be the first-ever made-for-television movie. The crime drama *The Hanged Man* was the second made-for-television movie in the series, though it was released theatrically in the United Kingdom and other international markets. The revenge thriller features Miles as a femme fatale, which at least allowed her to do something other than worry about her on-screen husband and children. Nonetheless, the role still didn't give her much to do. In Paul Gardner's *New York Times* review of *The Hanged Man*, he wrote that Miles "paraded around hotel suites in silky garments that implied that she is too sensual to continue playing intelligent Billie Dawns." The "Billie Dawn" quip is a reference to the 1946 play *Born Yesterday* (and its 1950 film adaptation), whose main character, Billie Dawn, is initially an unintelligent and uncouth showgirl but becomes educated throughout the play. In the *Los Angeles Times*, Cecil Smith said *The Hanged Man* "was stuffed full of costly production values as a Thanksgiving turkey—and the resemblance did not end with the stuffing. The show was two hours of melodramatic claptrap in which stock characters whizzed through stock situations mouthing some of the most banal dialogue I've ever heard," though he listed Miles as one of "talented folk" who "were involved in the mishmash." Last, Miles kicked off 1965 on New Year's Day by guest starring in an episode of the short-lived television series *Slattery's People*.[22]

The premiere of the film *Those Calloways* was held on January 28, 1965, at two brand-new Atlanta theaters, the Westgate Cinema and Eastgate Cinema. Miles skipped out of attending the premiere to film her final episode of *The Alfred Hitchcock Hour*, "Death Scene," which aired on March 8. It was the tenth and final season of Hitchcock's television series. In the episode, Miles stars as the glamorous daughter of a once-prominent, elderly, wheelchair-bound Hollywood director played by John Carradine. She begins dating and later becomes engaged to the auto mechanic who repairs the family's car, though the aging director disapproves of the match when the mechanic says something negative about one of his movies. The episode also marked the final time that Bernard Herrmann scored a Hitchcock production. She continued her regular television appearances throughout 1965, including an episode of *Mr. Novak* that aired on April 6 and an episode of *I Spy* that aired on December 29. That year, Miles also participated in the filming of the first test pilot for the future hit game show *The Hollywood Squares*, and the series would eventually premiere over a year later on NBC (Miles regularly appeared as one of the squares during the show's first season). Miles also appeared in a two-part episode of the spy series *The Man from U.N.C.L.E.*, "The Bridge of Lions Affair" (parts 1 and 2), which aired in February 1966. Later that year, it was edited into the film *One of Our Spies Is Missing*.

Shortly before production began on *A Tiger Walks*, Miles and Larsen moved their family from Malibu back to Miles's house in Sherman Oaks, which had gone unsold after some trouble with an initial buyer. In a March 27, 1964, interview with Hedda Hopper, Miles admitted she hated living on the beach but knew that Larsen had dreamed of raising a family at the former Capra beach house he owned. She told Hopper, "You can't shatter a man's dream. So we were there for two years. I wasn't the one who cried uncle. One day Keith said, 'I can't stand this, I want to go where there's some action.' We moved immediately."[23]

That wasn't the only domestic change in the life of the Larsens. In the fall of 1963, Miles converted to Mormonism, the religion of Salt Lake City native Larsen. Earlier that year in July, Miles and Larsen traveled to the historic Salt Lake City Tabernacle for a four-night performance of a pageant titled Valiantly Onward as part of the Days of '47 celebration of Pioneer Day, an annual Utah holiday commemorating the Mormon pioneers who settled Salt Lake Valley on July 24, 1847. Miles and Larsen served as narrators of the massive production, which featured two thousand cast members, including dancers, musicians, and singers, and a six-level stage with live vegetation. Miles and Larsen arrived with their four children in Salt Lake City on July 20, and both actors were presented with keys to the city during their visit.

Their participation must have left an impression on the couple because in June 1964, the *Salt Lake Tribune* announced that Miles and Larsen would return to narrate the Days of '47 pageant in 1964, this year titled The Seed of a Miracle. Again, it would run for four days, but this year, Miles's three oldest children—Debra, Kelley, and Michael—would join the two-thousand-member cast of the pageant. However, Miles would not be able to participate in the first three performances of the production because she was finishing shooting the NBC television movie *The Hanged Man*, but she arrived in time to star in the final night's performance on July 27.

Though her three oldest children had small parts in the pageant, Miles told columnist Don Alpert a few months earlier that she did not plan on letting her daughters enter the profession. "I will not let them be child actresses," she said. "We do, however, encourage them to study acting in school and look forward to their being actresses, if they want. I think it's a wonderful profession to pass through the family. When you know the pitfalls you're much better equipped than I was coming from Kansas to here, which was like coming from Earth to Mercury." All four of Miles's children mounted careers in entertainment to different levels of success (although Michael went uncredited, columnist Marilyn Beck noted that he worked as a production assistant on at least one of Larsen's films, though that appears to have been his only work in the industry).[24]

The performances marked Miles and Larsen's growing propensity to work together, which would continue over the next few years—until it became obvious that Miles was far more able to get projects off the ground than her husband was.

12

A Disaster in the Philippines

Around the time Miles started working for Disney, she began to speak out more often with her opinions about modern womanhood and Hollywood's role in portraying the image of women of the 1960s on screen. Frequently these discussions would stem from an interviewer pointing out how much Miles worked in film and television while also maintaining a home with four children. Miles would credit the long hours she claimed to work in her Kansas upbringing as her main drive to keep working and spoke frankly about how she felt that the declining number of hours that women devoted to housework and rearing children led to too much idle time for women. "They are lost," Miles theorized. "And so many of them hit the bottle. You'd be surprised how many respectable women today drink the days away."[1]

And yet, despite all her professional activity, Miles still lamented the quality of roles out there for women. "The only things written about today's women are sexy or smutty stories—plays and books and movies. I suppose that reflects the main interest of today's women," Miles remarked. "At any rate, I find that the best stories and the best parts are not contemporary. I rarely play a contemporary woman nowadays. There really isn't anything written about contemporary women that I'd like to play." In another interview, Miles argued, "There was a time when women's stories were all over the place, stories for Joan Crawford, Roz Russell, Bette Davis. It was a woman's era. Now the truth is, there are not enough women's roles to go around."[2]

At the same time, Miles's argument begs the question, if she truly believed there weren't enough good roles for women, why did she act so frequently? Miles admitted one of the reasons she worked so often was to avoid professional jealousy over the few roles she considered desirable: "People say, look you're a movie star, why do you do television? And the answer is pure jealousy. I'm much too jealous to let someone else get an interesting role—there are so few of them today. So when an *Outer Limits* comes along with a real far-out part, I grab it. When they need someone to kick off *Dr. Kildare*, I'm their girl." Despite her prolific career, Miles also reiterated her desire not to be a regular in a series: "That would be death, playing the same character every day. You go to work each morning and say to yourself, 'Well, here I am. Mrs. So and so again.' That's not for me."[3]

There was one type of role—or, more accurately, a role requirement—Miles did not find interesting, which was anything involving nudity or what she considered "smut." Though Miles's *Psycho* has been noted for paving the way for more graphic films of the 1960s, on more than one occasion, she took aim at the 1964 film *The Carpetbaggers*, starring her "Incident at a Corner" costar George Peppard, a sexually charged film that includes a nude scene featuring actress Carroll Baker: "I happen to think movies like *The Carpetbaggers* are just awful and if actresses—not mentioning any names—have a desire to take off their clothes to get an image or out of pure exhibitionism, that's their affair so long as they don't expect me to do the same thing." Miles went into more detail about her opinion of nudity on screen in an interview with Louella Parsons in April 1965. "All this exposure of nudity on the screen today by well-known actresses—and some not as well-known—is a clear sign of emotional and mental immaturity on their part," Miles declared. "A star who shall be nameless made the statement the other day that she only appeared in the nude when it was absolutely necessary to the story. Well, I've never read a script yet in which a naked actress was absolutely essential."[4]

In February 1966, columnist Sidney Skolsky published a reader's letter that spoke enough to Miles that she felt obligated to respond.

The reader wrote, "Why do classy chicks like Vera Miles, Dina Merrill, Diana Hyland, and Lois Nettleton get put out to pasture in television series, when they could grace so many movie casts?"[5]

Whether Merrill, Hyland, or Nettleton ever noticed the question is anyone's guess, but Miles certainly read the query. The following month, Miles responded to the question in a letter to Skolsky that he published in his column. "As a matter of fact," she wrote in part, "I like television. But good roles are few and far between and that seems to be an insurmountable problem. Anyway, it's nice to know the readers are thinking of me."[6]

Though Miles showed her appreciation in her response, she was also focusing intently on the direction of her career. As Larsen kept trying to get more personal projects started for him and Miles, she continued working on nearly whatever opportunity was offered to her. On April 18, 1966, the *Los Angeles Times* announced that Miles would costar with comedian Sid Caesar in the film *The Spirit Is Willing* as a replacement for actress Joanne Dru, who withdrew from the film to have eye surgery. The film began shooting on April 28. Caesar and Miles play a married couple who rent a house in a seaside community in New England that is haunted by three ghosts, who launch all kinds of mischief to get the family to leave their home. The film was directed and produced by William Castle for his independent production company William Castle Productions but was released by Paramount Pictures. By 1967, Castle had become known for churning out gimmicky, low-budget B movies, like *The Tingler* (1959) and *13 Ghosts* (1960), which featured in-theater gizmos like buzzers in the seats to vibrate and cellophane glasses to show "hidden" images. Though *The Spirit Is Willing* did not feature those types of gimmicks, it had the star power of Caesar, who was the popular host of the variety shows *Your Show of Shows* and *Caesar's Hour*, as well as one of the stars of the ensemble comedy hit blockbuster *It's a Mad, Mad, Mad, Mad World* (1963). While shooting *The Spirit Is Willing*, the cast and crew threw a party for Sid Caesar to celebrate his twenty years in show business. Miles later told Dick Kleiner that she was thinking, "Twenty years! My, what a long time. And then, I started figuring up—and I realized that I've been in pictures here for 18 years myself."[7]

Though it wasn't a Disney film, Miles began shooting a film, *Gentle Giant*, on September 6, 1966, that was very much in the Disney vein (and another role featuring her as a mother) for Paramount Pictures. The "gentle giant" of the title is a black bear named Ben, who becomes fast friends with a young boy played by Clint Howard (Howard's father, actor Rance Howard, also appeared in the film). The film was based on the 1965 children's novel *Gentle Ben* by pulp writer Walt Morey. Miles stars as Howard's mother and wife to Dennis Weaver, future president of the Screen Actors Guild and then best known for his starring role on *Gunsmoke* from 1955 to 1964 (and later Miles's costar in the disastrous 1968 film *Mission Batangas*). Filming took place in Palm Beach Gardens, Florida, over thirty-five days.

Gentle Giant was meant to introduce a CBS television series, *Gentle Ben* (the original title of the film), that would follow the film's release. The producer of *Gentle Giant*, Ivan Tors, had done just that with his 1963 dolphin film *Flipper*, which was followed the next year by a popular television series, and his 1965 film *Clarence, the Cross-Eyed Lion*, which launched the 1966–69 African-based television series *Daktari*. Tors, who had previously produced Larsen's short-lived series *The Aquanauts*, had built a studio complex outside Miami, Ivan Tors Studios, for producing his brand of animal-themed entertainment projects for families. The location of the studio shifted the setting of *Gentle Giant* from the novel's setting in Alaska to Florida as well as the species of the bear from an Alaskan brown bear to an American black bear to better fit the Tors Studios location. While in Florida, Miles and Weaver were invited to speak to University of Miami film students who attended classes at Ivan Tors Studios about their experiences in the industry.

However, *Gentle Giant* did not follow the *Flipper* format of using a popular film to launch a television series. Inexplicably, the *Gentle Ben* television series debuted on September 10, 1967—six weeks before the film, which was supposed to launch the series, premiered in theaters. The title of the film was changed to avoid too much confusion with the television series it was supposed to launch. The pilot for the television series retained Weaver and Howard but replaced Miles with actress Beth Brickell. Like most of Tors's animal series, *Gentle Ben* was short-lived and aired for two seasons.

Miles passed on the series because she was reluctant to transplant her children from California to Florida—or, alternatively, be away from them for months—so she could shoot the series. She later said that she was up front with Ivan Tors Productions about not signing to do the television series: "I agreed [to star in the film], but only on the condition I would not be committed to the series. I had nightmares of chasing that damned bear through endless Florida swamps." She made no secret that she had no interest in working with bears regularly after working with the animal in two films. Miles told Dick Kleiner in April 1967, "I've had it with bears. I worked with one in *Those Calloways* and with another in *Gentle Ben* [*sic*]. And I've come to the conclusion that they are the dumbest animals around."[8]

Of course, Miles, as usual, also had too many other television projects in her schedule to accept a role in a series that was filmed in Florida. On November 9, 1966, she starred in the *ABC Stage 67* episode "The People Trap" for the short-lived attempt by the network to revive the anthology series format. The episode was a science fiction program featuring Miles and Stuart Whitman as a wife and husband in the year 2067 who are refused permission by the US government to have a child in the now vastly overpopulated nation (Miles's character is arrested for the crime of "unlicensed pregnancy," which sounds like something Hitchcock might have dreamed up when her third pregnancy was revealed to him). "The People Trap" was later edited into a film titled *The Last Generation* and released in 1971.

In addition, after several years of unsuccessfully trying to launch projects as a producer, Larsen was working on screen again. After a nearly decade-long absence from film, Larsen made his return to the big screen in the 1966 exploitive adventure film *Women of the Prehistoric Planet*, which starred Miles's fellow Actors Theater member Wendell Corey. The low-budget film was created by a short-lived production company with a name that sounded more like an insurance office than a production house: Standard Club of California Productions. The only other film released by the company was 1966's *The Navy vs. the Night Monsters*, which was released with *Women of the Prehistoric Planet* on a double bill in April 1966 by Realart Pictures, a distributor best known for its numerous successful rereleases from the Universal Pictures catalog. Its frequent rereleases of Universal's monster films helped solidify Universal's depictions of Frankenstein's monster, Dracula, the Wolf Man, and others in pop culture. Realart's cofounder Jack Broder was one of the producers of both Standard Club of California Productions films, which reused much of the same production crew. In the early 1950s, Broder began filming low-budget films, including some in which he cast over-the-hill horror icons whose popularity he had helped keep alive in films meant to turn an easy profit, most notably 1951's *Bride of the Gorilla* starring Lon Chaney Jr. and 1952's *Bela Lugosi Meets a Brooklyn Gorilla*, though *Women of the Prehistoric Planet* and *The Navy vs. the Night Monsters* would be the last films he would produce.

Though *Women of the Prehistoric Planet* is undeniably science fiction schlock, it predates the much more successful *Planet of the Apes* that would be released two years later by featuring a similar twist ending—the titular planet that the protagonists land on at the end of the film is a prehistoric Earth. Nonetheless, while *Planet of the Apes* went on to inspire a hugely successful franchise that has spanned decades of cinema history, *Women of the Prehistoric Planet* was quickly forgotten until it was used as a punchline decades later by the comedy film review series *Mystery Science Theater 3000*.

Larsen followed up *Women of the Prehistoric Planet* by starring in another low-budget feature, the thriller *Caxambu!*, named after a Brazilian city. Though set in Brazil, *Caxambu!* was filmed in the Philippines and directed by W. Lee Wilder, the brother of Academy Award–winning director Billy Wilder.

Filming a feature in the Philippines left an impression on Larsen, particularly in the realization of how cheaply a movie could be made there. On December 31, 1966, the *Los Angeles Times* reported that after many unsuccessful attempts, Miles and Larsen finally got one of their own projects off the ground, a war film titled *Batangas* (eventually released as *Mission Batangas*) that would begin shooting in the Philippines on January 15. Larsen would make his directorial debut on the film and had written the original screenplay about the occupation of the island Corregidor during World War II. However, the male lead of the film, Dennis Weaver (Miles's *Gentle Giant* costar) objected to the poor quality of Larsen's script and suggested that his friend, actor and director Lou Antonio, quickly rewrite it based on Larsen's story even though Antonio had never written a screenplay before. In the film, Miles, a nurse and missionary, and Weaver, an unscrupulous pilot, team up to smuggle the Philippine national gold reserves before the arrival of invading Japanese forces. The initially caustic relationship between them develops on their journey, very similar to the classic 1951 Humphrey Bogart and Katharine Hepburn adventure film *The African Queen*. However, while that film was a lush studio production under the direction of the iconic filmmaker John Huston, *Mission Batangas* was shot by a rookie director on a tight budget on an island with a severe lack of production capacity. Larsen ended up investing much of his own money because he could not interest investors in financing the film.

During the first week of 1967, Larsen announced the formation of his new production company, Batangas Productions Inc., to make the film and future projects (Miles later identified herself as the production company's secretary). However, *Mission Batangas* would be the company's only release. Larsen utilized much of the *Caxambu!* crew to shoot *Mission Batangas*, including the same cinematographer (Herbert V. Theis), production manager (Vicente Nayve), script supervisor (Maria Abelardo), and sound recording supervisor (Levy Principe). Theis, Nayve, Abelardo, and Principe would then work on Larsen's third and final film shot in the Philippines, 1968's *The Omegans*, which was also directed by *Caxambu!* director W. Lee Wilder and was the last film Wilder would direct before his death fourteen years later.

Mission Batangas was unlike any other film Miles made in her career and certainly completely different from the family films she had been making since *Psycho*. Because the budget for the film was extremely low, the cast and crew (mostly locals who were hired for little money) braved some challenging conditions to make the movie in a slapdash fashion. For example, Larsen and Miles spent their first two days in the Philippines casting locals in the film, and Weaver was nearly struck by a bullet that was meant to trigger an explosion during the filming of the movie's first battle scene; it took a day for the ringing in his ears to stop. In a letter to entertainment columnist Dick Kleiner after filming started, Miles noted, "I am sunburned, mosquito-bitten, very scratched up, dirty, and tired. Now comes the good part. We all feel so smug and fulfilled because we are getting so many tremendous values. If everything keeps going our way, we're going to have a very fine picture."[9]

After wrapping production in early 1967, it would be two years before *Mission Batangas* would reach the public. However, Larsen had immediate success finding partners for the release to make the film profitable. Not only did he sell the television rights to NBC after CBS passed when the network thought the war film wouldn't program well with Weaver's family-friendly *Gentle Ben* series on CBS, but an independent distributor named Manson Distributing—a company better known for releasing foreign and low-budget films with titillating titles like *Sinderella and the Golden Bra*, *Adulterous Affair*, and *Playgirls of Frankfurt*—acquired the foreign rights to *Mission Batangas*. Long after the film was in the can, the *Los Angeles Times* reported on December 29, 1967, that it was given a new lurid title, . . . *Except People Get Killed*, though it would eventually be released as *Mission Batangas*.

UPI reporter Vernon Scott devoted one of his August 1968 columns to Larsen and Miles's upcoming film, and he wasn't shy about presenting the former *Aquanauts* star as a washed-up has-been, opening by noting that fate had been "dealing him mediocre roles in wretched movies, four abominable television series, and unemployment" and presenting *Mission Batangas* as Larsen's bridge to becoming a notable filmmaker. According to the column, because of the film's low budget, Larsen "already has triple his money back and more" by selling the rights, with Larsen noting that NBC bought the rights to air the film twice after its theatrical run. According to Larsen, the deal with NBC alone made the film profitable. However, the column takes this development to an absurd length even by Hollywood hype standards, claiming that the movie "has catapulted Larsen from the brim of adversity and oblivion to a position of influence and affluence in short-memoried Hollywood."[10]

Yet it wasn't so much Hollywood's short memories as it was the limited interest audiences had in the movie, no matter how much Vernon Scott oversold it in his piece. *Mission Batangas* held press screenings in Los Angeles in November 1968, and *Variety* was one of the few meaningful outlets to publish a review, calling it "a tepid programmer" that "is not helped by lifeless thesping and limp direction." Perhaps because of the negative reviews, Larsen cut the hundred-minute preview version to an eighty-two-minute version for some markets (the original hundred-minute version is the one most widely available on home media). *Mission Batangas* did not begin to roll out in US theaters until January 1969, when it began screening in various midsize and small markets through April 1969, followed by playing the military base circuit in July through the end of the year. Though the film had already been in general release for at least three months, a "world premiere" was advertised for April 4, 1969, in Phoenix, Arizona, at the Indian Drive-in Theater, with Miles to be in attendance. However, Miles called out because of illness (the *Arizona Republic* reported she was sick with "the Hong Kong flu," the 1968 flu pandemic), and Larsen appeared instead of her at the premiere. In fact, it's entirely likely that Miles never intended to attend the Phoenix belated "world premiere" in the first place.[11]

Mission Batangas was still making its way through small markets at the bottom of double features by the end of the year when it aired on *NBC Monday Night at the Movies* on December 15, 1969. NBC then aired it again on May 23, 1970, as the network's Saturday night feature, to fulfill its contract with Larsen. The film would regularly fill holes in TV schedules for the next decade but otherwise dropped into obscurity as quietly as it had arrived.

Mission Batangas remains obscure with good reason—for all of Weaver and Miles's best efforts, it is simply a poorly made film that fails to rise above its meager budget. Both Miles and Weaver make a valiant attempt to turn the material into something compelling, but Miles in particular appears to be pining for a guest spot on any television series in existence instead of performing in this film. Two years later, Weaver would give an interview to the *San Bernardino Sun* to promote his television series *McCloud* and spoke about some of his career mishaps, including *Mission Batangas*, in which he noted the issues with Larsen's script (who is misidentified in the article as "Keith Andres") and called the film a "disaster." He recalled, "So what we did was improvise. If there was an actor down there who didn't mind working for nothing, we'd write him into the script. Would you believe we had a convicted murderer playing a bit part in the movie? I sure wouldn't want to do that again." Yet because it was made so cheaply, *Mission Batangas* was a profitable enterprise for Larsen and would allow him to work as a filmmaker, albeit on the fringes of the industry, for the next fifteen years.[12]

On July 4, 1967, the *Los Angeles Times* announced that Miles signed for her third starring role in a film in the last ten months in *Kona Coast*, which would shoot in Hawaii starting August 1967. Humorously, this came after Miles told Dick Kleiner in December 1966, "Next year I won't do so much." The following week, the *Los Angeles Times* also announced that Miles was replacing Rita Hayworth as the guest star in "The Inhuman Predicament" episode of *Run for Your Life* after Hayworth came down with the flu. The episode aired on September 20, 1967.[13]

In *Kona Coast*, Miles stars as a recovering alcoholic who is the former lover of Sam Moran, a fishing charter boat captain, played by Richard Boone, who is investigating the murder of his daughter in the Hawaiian Islands. Boone, best known for his starring role in the Western television series *Have Gun—Will Travel*, which aired from 1957 to 1963, had moved to Hawaii and established a production company, Pioneer Productions, to develop film and television projects in the Aloha State. Lamont Johnson, Boone's friend and director of several episodes of *Have Gun—Will Travel*, directed and produced the film. Unfortunately for Miles and the rest of the cast and crew, production was marred by a heatwave and rainstorms (Miles later called it "one big steam bath"). *Kona Coast* cost $877,000, largely funded by CBS, and was intended to be a possible pilot for a CBS television series that would shoot in Hawaii, though it did not come to pass, as CBS decided to move forward with another Hawaii-based television series, *Hawaii Five-O*, instead. The network made the right choice, as *Hawaii Five-O* ran for twelve seasons, and Miles guest starred in an episode of the series in 1971. Instead of premiering on television, *Kona Coast* was released theatrically in May 1968. Perhaps Miles's role is best summed up by the *Variety* review, which notes, "Miss Miles, however, is lost in shuffle—although beautifully photographed."[14]

Unfortunately for Miles, occasionally her film parts ended up on the cutting room floor. At the end of 1967, the *Los Angeles Times* announced that Miles would appear as John Wayne's wife in *The Green Berets*, a film codirected by Wayne depicting the Vietnam War from Wayne's conservative, anticommunist perspective. Wayne started shooting the film in Georgia in August 1967, and principal photography had wrapped before Miles was even cast in it. Her brief scene was shot in a Hollywood studio, though it does not appear in the released film. Miles later recalled, "Wayne needed an actress to play his wife, a one-scene role. Since we had worked together on three previous occasions, I was comfortable. As it turned out, the film was overlong, the wife's role unnecessary, and so it was out."[15]

Miles's role in *The Green Berets* consisted of a single precredit scene set in the Main Officers Club in Fort Benning, Georgia, before Colonel Mike Kirby, Wayne's battle-hardened character, departs for Fort Bragg, North Carolina, en route to Vietnam to support South Vietnamese forces. Her character, Lee Kirby, is described in the screenplay as "in her early forties" and "a good-looking woman, a warm-looking woman," which is the full extent of her characterization (Miles, of course, was not yet forty when the film was shot).

The couple meets at the club for a drink before heading to her room at the guest house for some intimate time. The scene establishes Kirby as dedicated to a fault in his life as a soldier, a man who has spent more time away from his family than with them. In fact, Lee even presents Kirby with a photograph of their son, Joe (initially identified as an air cavalry soldier but later referenced in the screenplay as a marine) so that he will recognize him if they bump into each other in Vietnam, implying Kirby is away so often that he doesn't even know what his son looks like. Though Lee is depicted as excited to see her husband in the scene, she still laments the time they don't spend together. "Twenty-three years ago, I thought I was marrying a man named Michael Kirby," she says. "It turned out to be APO San Francisco." Nevertheless, she doesn't hesitate when Kirby suggestively proposes that they go find out if her room key works.

Wayne would later blame Warner Bros. for cutting the scene to keep the focus on the film's action sequences, but it's hard to argue that the scene is not completely superfluous. Not only does Lee immediately disappear from the film, but her existence factors in no other scenes of the movie, which had already been shot, except for a brief mention of her in another scene that was cut, in which Kirby meets up with his son in Vietnam. Wayne's typical on-screen persona for the last few decades was familiar to audiences, and it's doubtful anyone in the audience would have questioned his character's supreme dedication to his duty at the expense of his domestic life, a trait that was frequently baked into Wayne's standard characters. Arguably, the scene doesn't humanize him at all, because the sequence is based on the fact that he neglects his family life for his career.

The extraneous nature of the scene is highlighted by the fact that the shooting script is dated May 15, 1967, and the added pages featuring the scene between Kirby and his wife are dated August 15, 1967. It's possible that *The Green Berets* screenwriter James Lee Barrett did not even write the scene, as he was a marine veteran who would have unlikely made the mistake of identifying Joe as an air cavalry soldier in the added scene instead of the marine he was already established as elsewhere in the script.

The devoted wife character was not atypical for Miles's less prominent roles, and it was almost just as well that the scene was cut—the nearly two-and-a-half-hour film is mostly remembered for being one of the few films about the Vietnam War that is pro–American involvement. Furthermore, Miles turned down the $10,000 fee for the role because she considered the few hours she was on set as a favor to Wayne (who also offered to buy her a car, which she also turned down). The Green Berets was a commercial hit but was critically ridiculed for what was thought by critics to be a simplistic viewpoint of the war.

But perhaps because of the film's financial success—and Miles's refusal to take payment—Wayne felt bad about the studio cutting her part out of The Green Berets. As an attempt to make amends, Wayne cast her in his next film, Hellfighters—a movie about Texas oil well firefighters that stars Wayne as the head of the firefighting company— as his character's ex-wife. Hellfighters, which was loosely based on the life of the renowned oil well firefighter Red Adair (who served as a consultant on the film), was shot on location in Houston and Casper, Wyoming, as well as the Universal back lot. Though the sexagenarian Wayne had previously indicated he felt he was now too old to have love interests in his films, he admitted he made an exception for Miles, telling the Associated Press, "If I turned down a love scene with Vera I'd not only have to be old, but stupid besides." Much like in The Green Berets, Wayne plays a man in Hellfighters so dedicated to his duties as an oil well firefighter that his home life has suffered, though he and his ex-wife reconcile when Wayne's character (briefly) leaves his job for a corporate job. Katharine Ross, fresh off her Oscar-nominated role in 1967's The Graduate, stars as Wayne and Miles's daughter in the film, although she is only ten years younger than Miles, who is yet again playing older in the film. An oft-told tale about the film is that Ross, unhappy that Universal cast her in the film, told a reporter that Hellfighters was "the worst piece of crap I've ever done" in her then ten-year career. When asked to respond to Ross's comment, Miles—who had a long list of credits that weren't banner material—replied, "Well, it's not the worst piece of crap *I've* ever done." The exchange, while possibly apocryphal, is recalled in actress Susan Strasberg's 1980 autobiography *Bittersweet* (Miles and Strasberg would work together shortly after the book's publication in the 1982 television movie *Mazes and Monsters*) and, even if not authentic, does reflect Miles's approach to her career of taking acting seriously while also doing some roles that she would've rather not have had on her résumé.[16]

The premiere of *Hellfighters* was held in Houston at the Majestic Theatre on December 19 with much of the cast, including Miles, in attendance. The very positive *Variety* review said, "Miss Miles as usual is charming," while the also-positive review in *Box Office* said, "The too-rarely seen Vera Miles is especially good." However, the *Box Office* review also points out the film's biggest flaw—its decidedly "old-fashioned approach to story and character," noting that *Hellfighters* "contains all the elements that made the action pictures of the Forties so predictable and pleasant to watch." While the reviewer notes this as a positive thing in their opinion, other reviewers (and most audiences) of 1968 felt otherwise. Wayne would later tell biographer Michael Munn about Miles's role in the film, "When we had to cut her scenes from *The Green Berets*, I told her I'd make up for it by giving her the role of my ex-wife in *Hellfighters*. Since the film was such a bomb, maybe I didn't do her any favors." As Wayne indicated in his quote, *Hellfighters* was not a financial success, though he would bounce back with his next film, *True Grit*, for which he was finally awarded the Academy Award for Best Actor after being the industry's top box office attraction for nearly his entire adult life.[17]

13

Molly and Dinner with Ms. Miles

While Miles's film work began to slow down again by the end of the 1960s—she shot a crime drama, *It Takes All Kinds*, in Australia, and she was supposed to shoot a film titled *A Woman Screams* in Denmark for producer Claude Giroux, former head of Allied Artists, but the project never materialized—she again considerably ramped up her television work to make up for the difference. She appeared as a guest star in many programs, both classic and forgettable, including *Run for Your Life* (September 20, 1967), *Off to See the Wizard* (December 15, 1967), *Judd for the Defense* (December 29, 1967), *Ironside* (February 29, 1968, and September 25, 1969), *Journey to the Unknown* (November 28, 1968), *Mannix* (October 11, 1969), *The F.B.I.* (September 28, 1969), *Marcus Welby, M.D.* (January 7, 1970), and *Gunsmoke* (October 5, 1970). Miles also appeared as a guest star on the wheel television series *The Name of the Game* in an episode titled "The Revolutionary" that aired on December 27, 1968. The producers considered adding her as part of the regular cast, though she would only guest star again in two more episodes, "Keep the Doctor Away," which aired on February 14, 1969, and "Man of the People," which aired March 6, 1970, both as completely different characters. She was also considered to play James Stewart's wife in the short-lived *The Jimmy Stewart Show*, but the role went to Julie Adams, an actress who had previously starred with Stewart in the 1952 Western *Bend of the River*. In many of these roles, Miles portrayed what had now become her stock character—a sophisticated mother or mature professional woman—and her fame as a well-known actress was often expected to elevate the episode.

Miles also continued to make occasional television movies, including two that aired in March 1971, *In Search of America* (aired on March 23) and *Cannon* (aired on March 26). Both were intended to serve as pilots of potential television series, and *Cannon* launched a successful detective television series starring William Conrad, which aired from 1971 to 1976. Miles would guest star as different characters on two episodes of *Cannon* in 1972 and 1975. For *In Search of America*, Miles starred as the mother of a college dropout, played by Jeff Bridges, who convinces his family to embark on a cross-country road trip. Though for once Miles committed to starring in the series if the pilot was successful, it was one of the few pilots she appeared in that did not result in an ongoing series.

Again, despite Miles's constant work on television, she still felt slighted by the industry's lack of compelling parts for women. "Women have no real identity in Hollywood outside the bedroom and kitchen," she told the *Hollywood Citizen-News* in May 1968. "We simply aren't viewed as vital, interesting individualists in our own right. . . . Movies are a man's domain. How many female Doctor Zhivagos, Jonas Cords, or Sammy Fains do you see on the screen? Epic characters simply aren't being written for women."[1]

Despite Miles's preference for movie roles, her constant work in television also taught her it was important to stay busy, and, more importantly, visible on the small screen as the medium continued to gain more viewers. "It's axiomatic in the TV industry these days that when people don't see you too often on nighttime shows they think you're dead or something," she lamented to the *Hollywood Citizen-News*. "Often strangers will come up to me and say, 'Oh, you're Vera Miles, aren't you? I remember seeing you. Have you retired?' When I tell them, well, no, I've done three movies in the past 12 months they often say something like, 'Oh, the wife and me never go to the movies.'"[2]

Worse, in the same interview, Miles expressed that with an increasing number of movies shown on television, fewer TV parts were available to actors, who now had to compete with their old movies for screen time: "The actor not only doesn't get paid for the movie's showing on TV, but with seven movie nights a week now on television there are literally thousands of jobs per season less in regular television shows. Other than a modest payment to their general health and welfare fund actors receive no financial benefit at all from the very thing that has greatly reduced the number of jobs available to them on television." Miles was referring to the 1960 Screen Actors Guild strike over the lack of residuals, in which negotiations led by SAG president Ronald Reagan resulted in actors receiving residuals on all films made in 1960 and afterward. However, films made from 1948 to 1959 were not deemed eligible for actor residuals, and instead, SAG accepted a onetime payment of $2.25 million to help establish the group's health and pension plans. Unfortunately for Miles, that meant whenever *The Searchers*, *The Wrong Man*, or any other film she made in the first decade of her career was aired on television, she would receive no additional financial benefit. To this day, Miles and all other actors (or their estates) do not receive residuals for pre-1960 films when aired on television, which is perhaps a reason she began working even harder in the latter half of her career.

Perhaps to prove her point as much as it was to take another job, three years after the release of *Follow Me, Boys!*, Miles returned to Disney for another "Disney mom" film role. In August 1969, Disney announced that Miles would costar with Steve Forest, a journeyman actor then best known for his role in the 1953 Warner Bros. drama *So Big* (in which Miles had a small role), in the movie *The Newcomers*. The film also reunited Miles with her *Gentle Giant* costar Clint Howard and also starred Howard's older brother, *The Andy Griffith Show* child star (and future Academy Award–winning filmmaker) Ron Howard, who played the children of Miles and Forest (father Rance Howard also appeared in the film in a minor role and served as an uncredited dialogue director). Before its release, the film was retitled *The Wild Country*.

The Wild Country is based on the 1950 autobiographical book *Little Britches: Father and I Were Ranchers* by Ralph Moody, a writer who had grown up on a ranch in Colorado and wrote a series of popular books based on his experiences in the early-twentieth-century American West. Walt Disney acquired the film rights to the book in the late 1950s. The material was an ideal fit for Disney, who had established a successful series of frontier adventure films in the 1950s in the wake of the studio's massive success with its *Davy Crockett* television series. *Little Britches* went through various iterations throughout the 1960s at the studio, including one version that would have gender-swapped the older son's character so the role could be played by studio favorite child actress Hayley Mills. The version of the film that finally made it before cameras was scripted by veteran television writers Calvin Clements Jr. and Paul Savage and directed by Robert Totten. Totten had directed the 1963 war film *The Quick and the Dead* but had a more prolific career in television, having directed over a dozen episodes of *Gunsmoke* as well as episodes of other Western series like *The Virginian* and *Bonanza*. Totten and Miles would work together again when he directed her in a 1970 episode of the drama series *Dan August*—a police drama starring Burt Reynolds—titled "When the Shouting Dies," which was shot after *The Wild Country* but aired three weeks before the film was released. Miles spends a considerable amount of time in the episode in a bikini sipping a cocktail, quite a different depiction when contrasted with yet another Disney mom film role (in August 1970, columnist Marilyn Beck noted that Miles and Totten were in a relationship, but it appears to be the only media reference to their involvement).

Set in the 1880s (twenty years earlier than the period depicted in the novel it was based on), *The Wild Country* is about the Tanners, a Pittsburgh family that moves to Jackson Hole, Wyoming, and quickly learns to adapt to the challenges of the frontier and the threats of an aggressive, powerful rancher. The film was shot on location in Jackson Hole—leading Miles to return to the state where she shot part of *Hellfighters*—from August to October 1969 on a $2.5 million budget. Miles noted to columnist Marilyn Beck that the shoot was the most physically taxing of her career, including dealing with the frequently muddy sets. The period sets were destroyed for the climax of the film, in which the villainous ranchers try to smoke out the homesteading Tanners. Also notable about the movie is that it was the first Disney film to depict a man and woman in bed together—of course, Mr. and Mrs. Tanner were fully clothed in the traditional sleepwear of the 1880s, so not quite as scandalous as one might suspect.

The Wild Country is a fine, though unremarkable, film that probably would have had more success had it been released a decade earlier, perhaps following Disney's 1960 blockbuster family adventure film *Swiss Family Robinson*. Even though, by 1970, the studio's frontier adventure formula had run a bit thin with some audiences, *The Wild Country* received generally positive reviews. The *New York Times* review called it "excellent viewing for children up to about 11 years old" and noted, "All told, the picture is hard to resist on its own plain, simple terms, doggedly concerned with such matters as family love, true grit, and legal justice. The Disney people, like the ones we see here, have something." The *Los Angeles Times* had even higher praise, calling it "one of the best Disney efforts in recent memory and therefore one of the few that can accurately be described as wholesome." The mostly positive review in *Variety* noted that Miles "is up to her usual high standard" in her typical wife-and-mother role.[3]

On November 23, 1969, the *Los Angeles Times* reported that Miles filed for divorce from Larsen on grounds of extreme cruelty in the Los Angeles Superior Court after separating from him earlier that month. Almost immediately afterward, Larsen traveled to Japan to codirect the war film *Aru heishi no kake* (*The Walking Major*). Unlike Miles's quick Mexican divorce from Gordon Scott, the divorce proceedings between Miles and Larsen continued for nearly two years. During that time, Miles moved from her longtime Sherman Oaks home to a townhouse in Calabasas, blaming the San Fernando Valley's smog for the move. Nearly two years later, on October 27, 1971, the *Los Angeles Times* reported that Miles was granted a default divorce in Los Angeles Superior Court from Larsen and granted custody of their son. The couple divided their $231,471 estate. At eleven years, Miles's marriage to Larsen was her longest-lasting one, though they were together for eight years before separating.

While going through the divorce, Larsen, under the name Keith Erik Burt, directed, cowrote, and starred in the bizarre 1970 exploitation film *Night of the Witches*. After their divorce, Larsen's fortunes in the industry did not improve much. As noted, *Mission Batangas* was virtually forgotten before it was even released, though it did teach Larsen that he could make money on a film if he made it cheap enough and sold it for distribution at a higher price. He cowrote, directed, and starred in the 1972 adventure movie *Trap on Cougar Mountain*. The film was cowritten by Larsen with Erik, his then-eleven-year-old son with Miles, who also starred in the film. Afterward, he would write, direct, produce, and star in two more films—1979's *Young and Free* (also featuring Erik) and 1982's *Whitewater Sam* (in which Erik served as a stand-in for his father, his last work in film)—before retiring from the industry, though in an interview to promote *Whitewater Sam*, Larsen stated his intention to keep making films. None of Larsen's later films had any significant impact. He passed away in December 2006.

Despite the failure of—or perhaps because of—*Mission Batangas*, Miles was still actively pursuing her own projects. Among other assets, when Miles and Larsen divorced in 1971, they divided motion picture story rights, which included Miles getting ownership of a Western screenplay titled *Cactus*, which Larsen had acquired in 1968 as a possible follow-up project to *Mission Batangas* for the couple. After considering shooting the film in Europe, Larsen had gotten as far on the project as scouting locations for the film in Peru in 1968 and New Mexico in 1969, while Miles had also scouted locations in Australia while filming *It Takes All Kinds* before their divorce. *Cactus* tells the story of a sheriff's lovelorn wife, Molly Parker, whose loneliness is manipulated by a younger, handsome outlaw in her husband's jail to aid in his escape. It was a genre that Miles had far more experience and success with than war dramas like *Mission Batangas*. The project would also allow her to branch out from the doting wife-and-mother roles that made up the bulk of her film parts even before *Psycho* a decade earlier. In a 1971 interview, Miles relished the opportunity to be able to play the "older woman with young lover" role, saying, "It's marvelous to reach the age where they think of you for that kind of role. When I was younger, I played roles with old lovers" (of course, Miles wasn't very far removed from playing John Wayne's ex-wife in 1968's *Hellfighters*). It also was one of the few Westerns up to that point to have a female protagonist in the leading role.[4]

Cactus, which would later be retitled *Molly and Lawless John*, was written by novice screenwriter Terry Kingsley-Smith, the son of screenwriter Dorothy Kingsley. Kingsley had been nominated for an Oscar for the screenplay for the 1954 hit musical film *Seven Brides for Seven Brothers*. In 1971, Kingsley-Smith cofounded the production company Malibu Productions (not the same company as B-movie king Roger Corman's Malibu Productions) with his brother, Dennis Durney, to produce the film. The production scouted the Las Cruces, New Mexico, area in May 1971 for possible locations for the film shoot after plans to shoot it in Arizona fell through. By the following month, actor Sam Elliott was cast to play the male lead, Johnny Lawler. The tall, thin Elliott, fifteen years Miles's junior, had several bit parts, mostly in television Westerns, in the late 1960s before landing a recurring role on the hit series *Mission: Impossible* as medical doctor Doug Robert. *Molly and Lawless John* was Elliott's first leading role in a film, though he was also second-billed in the 1972 horror film *Frogs*, which was shot after *Molly and Lawless John* but released earlier. Elliott would later become known for his deep voice and bushy mustache, making him a popular go-to character actor for Western films and television series, though he has appeared in acclaimed films across a variety of genres in his five-decade career. *Molly and Lawless John* is the only film in which Miles is top-billed both on the poster and in the trailer, though subsequent home media releases have featured Elliott's image more prominently on the cover art, often using a photo of him with the bushy mustache he would later become known for, although he does not have a mustache in the film.

Playing the film's sheriff, and Molly's neglectful husband, was veteran television actor John Anderson. In the very first scene they shot together, Anderson had to slug Miles. After shooting the scene, Anderson informed Miles that they actually had appeared in the same movie together before: in *Psycho*, Anderson portrays the car salesman California Charlie, who sells Janet Leigh's Marion Crane a new car. However, Miles and Anderson didn't work together on *Psycho*, as they did not appear in any scenes together in the film. Anderson and Miles would later work together a final time in a 1991 episode of *Murder, She Wrote*, "Thursday's Child."

Molly and Lawless John marked the feature film directorial debut of Gary Nelson, a longtime television director who served as second assistant director on *The Searchers*. In fact, while shooting interior scenes in Los Angeles, John Ford visited the set. In 2016, Elliott recalled Ford's set visit to *Cowboys and Indians* magazine, saying, "One day John Ford showed up—he was there to visit Vera. John Ford! That stopped the show for a while. It might as well have been the pope." Perhaps as a favor to Miles, a quote from Ford—"This is my kind of a movie"—appeared prominently in advertising for the film, labeling the four-time Oscar winner as "master movie maker."[5]

Filming on *Molly and Lawless John* began in New Mexico in early June 1971, reusing some locations that were utilized in the 1968 Clint Eastwood Western *Hang 'Em High*. Filming in Las Cruces lasted about a week and included scenes set in a cave, a mining shaft, and along the Rio Grande. Parts of the film were also shot in Santa Fe. The weather was noted to be brutally hot, with Elliott telling columnist Marilyn Beck that Miles passed out from the heat one day when temperatures reached triple digits.

Molly and Lawless John officially premiered in Los Angeles on December 15, 1972, though it had been playing in theaters in New Mexico since October after a premiere screening at the Cinema East Theatre in Albuquerque on October 25 with Miles, Elliott, and Durney in attendance (however, several other theaters in New Mexico, as well as one theater in El Paso, Texas, also advertised the "world premiere" of the movie on their screens on the same date, with all the New Mexico theaters also heavily promoting the film's local origin). Kevin Thomas's review in the *Los Angeles Times* said the film was made "with painstaking craftsmanship" and that "Vera Miles has graced numerous Westerns, including a couple of John Ford's but none of them has offered her so meaty a role." On the other hand, the *Variety* review was far more negative, saying, "The film fails on most levels. Though admirable in its goal of trying to tell an oater story from a femme viewpoint, the momentum of Western cliche will not be mitigated by this fumbling diversionary approach." Most other professional reviews ranged from giving the film faint praise, such as the one in *Box Office*, to dismissing it for its melodramatic elements, like the one in *Independent Film Journal* (unsurprisingly, the review in the local *Albuquerque Tribune* was one of the film's most positive write-ups).[6]

Oddly, Lydia Lane's beauty column in the September 6, 1974, edition of the *Los Angeles Times* refers to *Molly and Lawless John* as if it were an upcoming movie, nearly two years after the release of the film, and says that it is the first film of Miles's own production company. While Miles did have ownership of the screenplay through her divorce from Larsen, she did not produce it (she never served as a producer of any film throughout her career), nor did she have a production company involved with the film. The column's numerous errors were likely the result of it being an inventory story from 1972 that was on file for future use and hadn't been thoroughly edited (or corrected) before publication.

Molly and Lawless John received little attention aside from a Golden Globe nomination for Best Original Song for "Take Me Home," written by Oscar-winning songwriters Johnny Mandel (music) and Alan Bergman and Marilyn Bergman (lyrics). However, because of Miles's prominent role in the film (both as an actress and behind the scenes) and the later success of Sam Elliott, it remains a significant film in her career. Her performance in this mostly pedestrian Western demonstrates that she could carry a film as a lead no matter how many times she played a guest star on television as a concerned mother or a devoted wife. Miles's Molly stands up to Elliott's John after figuring out his cruelty and impressively portrays her character's growing inner strength. With a larger audience, *Molly and Lawless John* would have likely had a bigger impact on Miles's film career, and it was much more appropriate material for her to show off her range than *Mission Batangas*.

Following filming *Molly and Lawless John*, Miles returned to largely appearing in television productions, including a two-part episode of *Medical Center* (airing on December 29, 1971, and January 5, 1972) and television movies like *A Howling in the Woods* (November 5, 1971) and *Jigsaw* (March 26, 1972). However, Miles felt she wasn't being challenged in these roles, remarking, "Here I am in the most interesting and exciting period of my life, and I'm generally given my choice of the humorless, neurotic mother and wife or the sexually frustrated older woman in search of a young stud." The latter type included Peter Bogdanovich's classic 1971 film *The Last Picture Show*, for which Miles was under consideration to play Ruth Popper, a depressed middle-aged woman who starts an affair with a member of the local high school wrestling team, which her husband coaches. Bogdanovich decided to go with a less familiar actress, Cloris Leachman, another former Miss America contestant. The role would win Leachman the Academy Award for Best Supporting Actress and catapult her career, later winning multiple Emmy Awards for her role in the popular television series *Mary Tyler Moore*.[7]

However, Miles regularly received praise for her television work, including in the ABC television movie *A Great American Tragedy*, about a middle-aged couple that faces challenging times when the husband (played by *Cool Hand Luke* Academy Award–winning actor George Kennedy) loses his job, and his wife (played by Miles) goes back to work to support the family. When the movie aired in October 1972, Kevin Thomas of the *Los Angeles Times* said it was Miles at her "best" in one of the "finest roles" she ever had. Similarly, the *New York Times* called it a "first-rate" performance. In 1971, Miles also filmed the television pilot *Baffled!* in England opposite *Star Trek* star Leonard Nimoy. However, the project sat unsold until it played in cinemas in the United Kingdom in December 1972 and in other territories over the next several years before airing as a television movie in the United States on January 30, 1973.[8]

Miles also made a brief return to theater in the summer of 1972, headlining a production of the play *Forty Carats*—about a woman who has an affair with a man half her age, written by playwright and screenwriter Jay Presson Allen, who had written the screenplay for Hitchcock's 1964 film *Marnie*—at the Alhambra Dinner Theatre in Jacksonville, Florida. Her then nineteen-year-old daughter, Kelley Miles, was also part of the cast. "When Kelley got her first role, she asked me some questions about acting," Miles later recalled about working with her daughter. "Since I never had any formal training, I couldn't talk on the subject. Instead, I said, 'We'll go off and do a play together, and after six weeks on a stage you will know what you don't know about acting. So we went to Florida and did *40 Carats*. I had a ball, and Kelley learned so much. We recently repeated the partnership by doing episodes of *Owen Marshall* and *Cannon* together."[9]

Both of Miles's daughters pursued careers in show business. Debra demonstrated some initial interest in acting, though ended up in behind-the-scenes roles. "Debbie went to Pasadena Playhouse and later studied with Lee Strasberg, but she found that if you can't handle rejection, you can't handle this business," Vera Miles later explained to the *Independent Press-Telegram*. She later served as assistant to the producer for the television series *Police Woman*. Debra appeared in small parts in two episodes of *Police Woman*, and her sister, Kelley, and half brother Erik also appeared on the series during its run. Debra also served as an associate producer of the 1979 television movie *Undercover with the KKK* alongside *Police Woman* producer Doug Benton.[10]

Of Miles's four children, Kelley had the most substantial career in entertainment. Kelley, who made her film acting debut in the 1972 disaster film *Skyjacked*, would make several television guest appearances alongside her mother—most notably in the 1973 disaster television movie *Runaway!* and a 1975 episode of *Cannon*—but, soon after a short stint in the soap opera *Days of Our Lives* in 1982, would largely leave acting. She also had a brief music career, including recording songs for two of Keith Larsen's films costarring her half brother Erik, *Young and Free* and *Whitewater Sam*. "I love working with Kelley," Miles told UPI in a joint interview with Kelley after the pair shot an episode of *Owen Marshall* together. "Young people turn away from paternal suggestions most of the time, but Kelley has learned not to be defensive about that. I make a few suggestions about acting and she listens." Kelley would also work as a screenwriter, cowriting the story for a 1993 episode of *Star Trek: Deep Space Nine* (titled "Sanctuary") with her husband, Gabe Essoe, a screenwriter and author who also worked in publicity at Walt Disney Studios. Kelley and Essoe also cowrote the 1995 film *The Adventures of Black Feather* and the 1998 television movie *Out of the Wilderness* (Kelley appears in both films, while Essoe codirected the latter project). She has also pursued many interests outside of Hollywood, including gaining some notoriety as a restorer of classic comic books.[11]

Miles ended 1972 by starring as a last-minute replacement for actress Rosemary Forsyth (who reportedly suffered an accident) in the Disney film *One Little Indian*, which began shooting in September. It marked Miles's fifth film with the studio, and she once again played a mother. Though ostensibly the female lead, Miles's part was small relative to her billing. She portrays a mid-nineteenth-century rancher with a daughter, played by future Academy Award–winning actress Jodie Foster, who encounters a cavalry soldier on the run with a pair of camels (played by veteran actor James Garner). The film began production in Kanab, Utah, but returned to shoot in Los Angeles when poor weather made filming difficult. The shoot was particularly challenging for the studio despite being under the direction of accomplished television director Bernard McEveety, who had previously directed Miles in a 1970 episode of *Gunsmoke*. Miles would later tell Joan Crosby that the only animal she ever worked with that she didn't like was the camel in the film, remarking, "Their disposition is as overwhelming as their smell." On its release in June 1973, the film made little impression on critics but was enough of a hit that Disney signed Garner and Miles for another film together, 1974's *The Castaway Cowboy*.[12]

On January 1, 1973, Miles married director Robert Jones in Mexico and moved to his horse ranch in Malibu Canyon. In her June 10, 1973, column, Joan Crosby called Miles "a modern-day version of those pioneer women she often plays" in her new life on the ranch. Miles's marriage to Jones was her fourth and perhaps shortest (media reports indicate that the couple split in June 1975 after eighteen months of marriage). Jones was an unsuccessful actor who turned to the production side of filmmaking in 1966 when he served as an assistant director of the 1966 Western film *Johnny Reno*. Afterward, he mostly worked as an assistant director in television, in between tending his horse ranch in Agoura Hills. Though Jones mainly worked in television—his early credits include several episodes of the short-lived Western series *Dusty's Trail*, starring *Gilligan's Island* star Bob Denver—he served as assistant director on a few films, including 1974's *Where the Lilies Bloom*, which was shot May–August 1973 in North Carolina. Though Miles did not appear in the film, she was on set with her new husband for part of the filming. In their 2021 memoir *The Boys*, Ron and Clint Howard, who had both starred with Miles in the 1971 film *The Wild Country*, said that when their father, actor Rance Howard, told their mother, Jean Speegle Howard, that production on *Where the Lilies Bloom* ran over schedule and he would need to spend additional days in North Carolina, she accused him of having an affair with Miles. Miles was by that time married to Jones, who happened to be a close friend of Rance Howard, and it was all apparently a misunderstanding.[13]

On March 31, 1973, Miles and Jones attended the inaugural AFI Life Achievement Award ceremony, presented to her *The Searchers* and *The Man Who Shot Liberty Valance* director John Ford. The ceremony, which was hosted by Ford's longtime collaborator John Wayne, was held at the Beverly Hilton Hotel in Beverly Hills and also featured US president Richard Nixon, who, in a surprising move, presented Ford with the Presidential Medal of Freedom (Nixon also humorously announced that he was temporarily promoting Ford, who rose to the rank of rear admiral in the US Navy Reserve, to the rank of full admiral for the duration of the ceremony). The guest list was so preeminent—including then California governor Ronald Reagan and wife, Nancy Reagan; then AFI Board chairman Charlton Heston; Maureen O'Hara; James Stewart; Cary Grant; Gregory Peck; Kirk Douglas; and many other top stars—that Miles's name does not appear in media reports about the event. However, she is listed as an attendee on the guest list archived at the Richard Nixon Presidential Library.

Miles continued working steadily, mainly on television, through the remainder of the decade, though she did have one last notable film role when she made her sixth, and final, film for Disney. The studio reteamed Miles with James Garner for a film initially titled *Hawaiian Paniolo* or just *Paniolo*, which would later be retitled *The Castaway Cowboy*. It marked Miles's second movie filmed in Hawaii. Garner portrays a cowboy who is shanghaied in San Francisco and washes ashore on the Hawaiian island of Kaua'i. He meets Miles's character, a widow (and, of course, because this is a Disney film, she is also a mother) who is unsuccessfully managing a farm. Garner's cowboy suggests that the family starts ranching the wild cattle that live on the island. The film's story had been floating around the studio since before Walt Disney's death in December 1966 and had been worked on by numerous writers. Like *One Little Indian*, the film was directed by a longtime veteran of television, Vincent McEveety, who would go on to direct Miles in several television projects (including her second-to-last appearance on television in a 1990 episode of *Murder, She Wrote*). Prerelease coverage said that the reigning Miss Hawaii, Kanoe Kaumeheiwa, would make her acting debut in the film alongside the one-time Miss Kansas, though Kaumeheiwa does not appear in the film. The on-location shoot mobilized much of the studio's resources, and unlike *One Little Indian*, this second teaming of Garner and Miles was well received. On its August 1974 release, the *Los Angeles Times* review called *The Castaway Cowboy* "a lovely summer daydream for kids and a nostalgic idyll for their parents" and remarked that Miles "projects a pretty, plucky quality." Similarly, the *New York Times* review said it was "a new Disney live-action movie that won't, for a change, make parents wince." The review in *Variety* said the "fun-fest" film "hit the bull's-eye" and called Miles "pleasantly effective." Though Disney would continue to regularly release similar family-friendly live-action fare in theaters, the then-forty-five-year-old Miles appeared to have aged out of the Disney mom age range after ten years and six films with the studio.[14]

Her six films with Disney—as well as other Disney-related projects dating back to her first television appearance, *One Hour in Wonderland*—have made Miles something of an unsung star in the history of Walt Disney Studios. Likely because she never appeared in one of the Disney live-action films that became popular classics, like *The Parent Trap*, *Mary Poppins*, or *The Love Bug*, Miles's significant contribution to the studio's films has largely gone unrecognized. Most notably, she has gone unrecognized by the company's Disney Legend program, which honors individuals who have made significant contributions to the studio (the first-ever honoree was Fred MacMurray, her *Follow Me, Boys!* costar), despite Miles having more credits with the studio than many others already recognized by the honor.

But similar thoughts about Miles being an unrecognized star could be expressed about her career for the next decade. As she had noted for at least a decade by then, while she was a constant presence on television because of both new projects and repeats of her dozens of notable film and television roles, more dynamic projects simply didn't come her way. She more often than not appeared in television pilot movies that were intended to launch television series, such as *The Underground Man* (aired on May 6, 1974), *State Fair* (February 13, 1976), and *Our Family Business* (September 20, 1981), as well as several stand-alone television movies, including *Live Again, Die Again* (February 16, 1974, which was adapted by *Psycho* screenwriter Joseph Stefano), *The Strange and Deadly Occurrence* (September 24, 1974), *Judge Horton and the Scottsboro Boys* (April 22, 1976), *Fire* (May 8, 1977), *Roughnecks* (July 14, 1980), *Mazes and Monsters* (December 28, 1982, also featuring a young Tom Hanks), and *Travis McGee* (May 18, 1983, which reunited her with *Molly and Lawless John* costar Sam

Elliott, who played the title role, as well as *Hellfighters* director Andrew V. McLaglen). She also appeared as a guest star on several successful series, such as *Columbo* (September 23, 1973), *The Streets of San Francisco* (October 2, 1975), *Barnaby Jones* (November 17, 1977), *How the West Was Won* (two episodes, March 5, 1978, and March 12, 1978), *Buck Rogers in the 25th Century* (March 27, 1980), *Magnum, P.I.* (November 26, 1981), *The Love Boat* (three episodes that aired from 1982 to 1984), *Little House on the Prairie* (February 21, 1983), and *Trapper John, M.D.* (March 20, 1983). A number of those series aired as reruns on television and streaming services for decades afterward, making Miles a nearly ever-present face on television for the last sixty years. Regarding her frequent appearances on television in films and programs that stretched from the late 1940s to the then-present day, Miles said in 1976, "I sometimes feel a little overexposed, except that I'm always seen at a different age. That's okay, it keeps 'em guessing."[15]

More often than not, Miles spoke much more passionately in her increasingly rare interviews about her stage work, which she was now doing with much more regularity, and particularly dinner theater, a "dinner and a show" presentation that began growing in popularity in the 1970s. Dinner theater was becoming a favored circuit for aging film and television stars who struggled to find work in Hollywood as the number of dinner theaters rapidly increased across the United States, often featuring productions of plays that had recently left Broadway. From January 29 to February 24, 1974, Miles performed in Neil Simon's play *The Gingerbread Lady* at the Cirque Dinner Theatre in Seattle. The play, one of Simon's bleaker pieces, about an aging cabaret singer whose addiction to alcohol and nymphomaniac tendencies derailed her career, became a favorite of Miles's, and she appeared in it several more times over the next decade. She first reprised the role in February 1981 at the Beverly Dinner Playhouse in New Orleans, directed by Ross Hunter (who directed her in 1961's *Back Street*). In an interview to promote the play, Hunter said of Miles, "I think she has an ability few people have touched yet. She has a charisma that embraces the audience, and the audience embraces her back. She started with us in *Back Street* and she's such a disciplined actress. She gets under the character and this role is the most difficult she's done." In December 1981, Miles reprised the role in Chicago, replacing Shelley Winters after she had a back injury, and was scheduled to do the play again in Manassas, Virginia, at the Hayloft Dinner Theatre in 1983.[16]

Miles would then make her Chicago stage debut starring in *Finishing Touches*, a play by Jean Kerr, at the Drury Lane Theater in Evergreen Park, Chicago, and scheduled to run nine weeks, through January 12, 1975. Miles played the same role as her *Five Branded Women* costar Barbara Bel Geddes did in the short-lived 1972 Broadway production. When speaking to the Chicago local papers, Miles remarked that her kids "fussed a lot when they found out mother would not be home to cook their Thanksgiving turkey this year, but the girls are old enough and they can manage. Anyway, they are all out doing their thing so I felt I would do mine." Miles said she instead had Thanksgiving dinner with one of her brothers, who was a dean of students at a college in Kansas City, Missouri, and his family, "who she hasn't seen for about 15 years." Miles would return to the Drury Lane Theater four years later to star in *Turn of the Worm*, a comedy by George Tibbles, from August through December 1979. Tibbles was a multitalented and prolific writer who, among other credits, was nominated for an Oscar for cocomposing "The Woody Woodpecker Song." Tibbles had also written over eighty episodes of *My Three Sons*, including the three 1965 episodes that featured Vera Miles as a guest star.[17]

Starting in October 1978, Miles starred in *Same Time, Next Year*, a play by Bernard Slade. The comedy is about a married man and a married woman who have a sexual encounter after staying at the same inn in Northern California together and how they proceed to meet once a year at the inn over the next twenty-four years. Actress Ellen Burstyn won a Tony Award for her performance as the female lead during its 1975 Broadway run. The production began at Sebastian's West Dinner Playhouse in San Clemente, California, and played through November 26. It then switched to Sebastian's Dinner Playhouse at the Grand Hotel in Anaheim, California, from November 28 through January 28.

Likely because of its proximity to Los Angeles, this production gar-
nered more attention from the press than Miles's other roles in dinner theater. A review in *Tustin News* said that Miles's "excellent acting
ability attests to why she is constantly sought after for guest appearances on television dramas." On December 30, the *Los Angeles Times*
reported that the play had "a slow start" in San Clemente, but "enthusiastic word-of-mouth has made it one of the most successful hits in
Sebastian's history. It has just been extended for three weeks through
January 28 at Sebastian's Dinner Playhouse at the Grand Hotel in Anaheim." The article noted that Miles "gives a performance radiant in its
scope and precise in its variable focus." Next, *Texas Monthly* magazine
reported that Miles would star in the musical *Divorce Me, Darling!* at
the Windmill Dinner Theater in Houston, Texas, from late January
through March 14, 1979. The musical was written by Sandy Wilson,
who is best known for his 1953 play *The Boy Friend*, of which *Divorce
Me, Darling!* is a sequel. The musical is set in 1936 and debuted in
December 1964 at the Players' Theatre in London, later moving to the
West End. However, perhaps because of Miles's extended commitment
to *Same Time, Next Year* in California, it is not clear if the production
moved forward.[18]

Two years later, Miles starred in an original "adult sex comedy," *Ping
Pong*, written by Rick Talcove, the drama critic for the *Valley News*, in a
limited six-week engagement at Scott Hardy's Dinner Theatre in Glen-
dale, California, just the second production at the venue. It marked
the second time Miles acted on stage with her daughter Kelley. Again,
Miles received strong praise for her performance, which was often
missed in reviews of her screen and television work. The *Los Angeles
Times* review praised Miles's "shrewd instincts" and noted that she "is
a luminous and commanding stage presence." *Hollywood Reporter* also
gave the play an extremely positive review and called Miles "a marvelous stage actress."[19]

Miles continued to periodically act in theater throughout the
1980s, including in the US premiere of the play *Children of the Wolf* by
Irish playwright John Peacock at the California Repertory Theater in

Monterey, California, in 1984; a production of Thomas Babe's *Taken by Marriage* at the Burt Reynolds Theatre in Jupiter, Florida, in 1986; and a production of Mark Harelik's *The Immigrant* at the La Mirada Civic Theatre in La Mirada, California, in 1989. Each production ran just a few weeks or about a month while Miles was between television roles.

The few film roles that Miles had in the late 1970s and early 1980s were forgettable. For starters, she was cut out of director Robert Aldrich's 1977 political thriller *Twilight's Last Gleaming* so late in the editing process that her character, the first lady of the United States, appeared in the sneak previews, and her name was included in prerelease advertising (Miles still attended the world premiere in Washington, DC). Aldrich, who had previously directed Miles in 1956's *Autumn Leaves*, was coming off a series of films that featured few or no female characters, including *The Flight of the Phoenix* (1965), *The Dirty Dozen* (1967), *Too Late the Hero* (1970), *Ulzana's Raid* (1972), *Emperor of the North* (1973), and *The Longest Yard* (1974). He was disappointed that cutting Miles out of *Twilight's Last Gleaming* resulted in another one of his male-heavy films, telling *Film Comment* in 1977, "We actually shot two scenes for *Twilight* with Vera Miles as the First Lady, and she was very very good. We did a domestic scene in which she realized that being the wife of the President was no fun at all. And we did a scene in which he says goodbye. I cut the first scene out because the picture was too long, and it didn't move the story. And I cut the goodbye scene out because it tipped the scales too much in terms of 'Is he going to get killed?' I was very proud of both scenes. Now another Aldrich picture comes out and there are no ladies in it!"[20]

Miles also replaced Ida Lupino in a horseracing film titled *The Thoroughbreds* a few weeks into shooting, when Lupino had "artistic differences" with the project. The film was renamed *Run for the Roses* when it was released in theaters in November 1978, before being quickly forgotten. The same can be said about her 1982 film *BrainWaves*, a failed science fiction thriller starring Tony Curtis that somehow manages to run out of interesting things to do in its brief seventy-seven-minute runtime. In both of these films, Miles has fairly insignificant parts, and she likely saw them as similar fare to her regular guest-starring roles on television—small jobs that she would quickly move on from.

Though seemingly as busy as ever in Hollywood and regional theater, by the mid-1970s, Miles had moved from the Los Angeles area—her home since arriving in Hollywood in 1948—to Big Bear Lake, a resort community in the San Bernardino Mountains about one hundred miles east of her former home in Sherman Oaks. Miles spoke warmly about her life in Big Bear Lake, remarking, "I like changes in weather. We get snow and springtime and all those wonderful things, yet it's only two hours from the city. I don't like to travel that much, but making films now means going on location. I've just finished pictures in London and Texas, I'm home again, and Big Bear looks heavenly to me."[21]

14

The Return of Lila Crane

After releasing *Psycho* in 1960, Hitchcock directed six more films from 1963 to 1976, all of which were distributed by Universal Pictures. Hitchcock's long-term partnership with Universal in his final years was equally beneficial, as the director amassed a sizable ownership stake in Universal in 1964 and became one of the studio's largest shareholders. The studio secured a stronger footing with the director's catalog when it acquired the rights to *Psycho* in 1968 from Hitchcock (in 1983, four years after Hitchcock's death, his daughter, Patricia, sold the rights to the five additional films that Hitchcock had full ownership of, including *Vertigo*, to Universal). Even before Universal owned the rights to *Psycho*, the studio had been featuring the Bates mansion as one of the centerpieces of the Universal Tram Tour on its back lot since its debut in 1964. On acquiring the rights to the film, Universal almost immediately started to receive revenue generated from *Psycho*; the studio rereleased the film to theaters in 1969 behind a big "the version they can't show on television" promotional push in reference to the cuts made to the film during television airings. But those frequent television airings, as well as midnight screenings in theaters, kept the film in the public eye, and offbeat merchandise like Norman Bates greeting cards and Bates Motel bath towels continued to generate revenue for the property long after its blockbuster original theatrical release, during an era when merchandising for classic films was otherwise virtually nonexistent.

Though Hitchcock never showed any interest in making a sequel to *Psycho*, Universal couldn't ignore the potential of turning one of its most popular catalog films into a lucrative franchise, particularly after Universal's horror film hit *Jaws*, which was briefly the highest-grossing film of all time after its release in 1975, spawned a sequel, *Jaws 2*, in 1979. While not as critically acclaimed as its predecessor, *Jaws 2* was still a massive box office hit and, also for a short time, became the highest-grossing sequel in film history.

What also helped make a case for a sequel to *Psycho* was the rapidly growing popularity of a new genre of horror films that had been directly inspired by *Psycho*: the slasher film. Led by the success of the low-budget box office hits *The Texas Chain Saw Massacre* in 1974 and *Halloween* in 1978—which coincidentally starred Janet Leigh's daughter, Jamie Lee Curtis, in her first major film role—a legion of horror movies featuring deranged knife-wielding killers followed. In addition to casting Curtis, *Halloween* director and cowriter John Carpenter paid further homage to *Psycho* by naming the psychiatrist of the killer in his film Sam Loomis, which is the same name as John Gavin's character in *Psycho*. Universal acquired the distribution rights to the *Halloween* franchise in 1981, which has included more than a dozen sequels over the next forty years, and its masked killer Michael Myers has since become one of the most recognizable characters in horror cinema.

Despite those trends, Universal executives weren't fully sold on the idea of making a *Psycho* sequel, perhaps wary that an extension of Norman Bates's story would hurt the continued impact of the original film and the reverence that the public had for Hitchcock as a filmmaker. But others felt differently, and a pair of rookie screenwriters named Gary Travis and Michael January determined if Universal wasn't going to make a sequel to *Psycho*, they would.

On August 31, 1981, the *Los Angeles Times* made the exciting announcement that Perkins, Miles, and Martin Balsam would be returning in *Psycho II, the Return of Norman Bates*, written by Gary Travis and Michael January (Balsam was noted as playing the brother of his *Psycho* character, since Dr. Arbogast had been murdered by Bates in the original). Perkins was also noted as having "agreed to direct" the film. The article describes this version of the film as focusing on

Miles's Lila gaining ownership of the Bates Motel and reopening it. It also noted that producers "intend to approach Jamie Lee Curtis for the role of Miles' daughter," in what would've amounted to another strong connection to the original film. However, Gavin was noted as not participating in the film. Earlier that year, Gavin retired from acting after he had been appointed as the US ambassador to Mexico by his former Hollywood colleague president Ronald Reagan, a post that Gavin would hold until 1986. The film was to be produced by C. O. "Doc" Erickson, noted as an "executive producer" of films like *Urban Cowboy* and *Blade Runner* (though he was actually a production manager on both films), for a company named Picture Striking Company. Curiously, the article didn't bother to mention that Erickson had worked as a unit production manager on five Hitchcock films, including *Vertigo*, which would otherwise seem like an important detail to connect this project to the Master of Suspense himself.[1]

Not mentioning the connection between Erickson and Hitchcock was the least of what is wrong with the article, which is, at best, misleading Hollywood hype, if not outright false. Attentive readers would notice that Universal Pictures is not mentioned at all in the article and with good reason—the studio had nothing to do with this project. More brazenly, none of the actors mentioned in the article as "convinced" to return was signed to work on the film. In short, *Psycho II, the Return of Norman Bates* was little more than an unauthorized spec script continuing the *Psycho* story written by two fans of the original film who had no legal standing to produce a sequel film.

Several months later, the genre film magazine *Cinefantastique* reported on the project in its February 1982 issue. By that time, much of the reporting in the *Los Angeles Times* article proved to be inaccurate. While Universal declined to comment for the *Cinefantastique* article, *Psycho* author Robert Bloch dressed down the myriad of legal issues with the project quite thoroughly, stating, "These gentlemen who represent themselves as screenwriters are not members of the writers guild. The man who is alleged to be producer of this project [Doc Erickson of *Blade Runner*] disclaims any knowledge of it whatsoever.

Nobody has been cast or signed and apparently these gentlemen have no realization that there are such things as copyright laws and screen-rights. I'm further advised that Universal Pictures have sent these gentlemen a very firm letter telling them to cease and desist."[2]

Nonetheless, the article states that Travis and January intended to press on with their project, now titled *The Return of Norman*, and stressed that it was "not a sequel . . . but a completely new story drawing upon Hitchcock's *Psycho*." January explained that the project originated as an unrelated story that the duo then retooled into a *Psycho* follow-up story and that their legal advisers gave them the impression that it was perfectly legal to use the characters. Perhaps the whole enterprise was best summed up by Jamie Lee Curtis; the article notes that the actress reportedly thought the role intended for her was "dumb" and turned it down. In short, the article's subheading—"Two Hollywood neophytes ask the question, 'Do you need to buy the rights to film a sequel?'"—can be answered with a three-letter response: yes. A few months later, Travis and January were planning to rewrite the film as a stand-alone story with the title *The Return of the Psycho*, though no version of this project was ever made. The entire situation may have prompted little more than a November 1982 follow-up article in the *Los Angeles Times* titled "Shadow of a Doubt over Hitchcock Film Rights," which investigated exactly which studios held remake and sequel rights to each of Hitchcock's films now that Hollywood had begun to fully embrace the idea of creating franchises out of its popular film properties.

But curiously, this rogue project was the impetus for the creation of two very different versions of *Psycho II*. After word of Travis and January's project first came out, Bloch's agent proposed that he capitalize on the news and obvious public interest in the original film by channeling his annoyance at the unauthorized project into finally writing a sequel to his 1959 novel. Published in 1982, the novel *Psycho II* depicts Bates escaping the asylum that he has been committed to for over twenty years. While Bates is on the run, his story is intertwined with the bloody ongoings of the production of a film in Hollywood based on the original Bates murders. The novel is full of metacommentary on the production of the real-life *Psycho* and other slasher films. "*Psycho II* was written to convey my feelings of disgust at the way in which Hollywood now treats such subject matter," Bloch told *Cinefantastique* in March 1986. "Movies have turned to explicit violence, gratuitous gore, and shock-for-shock's sake, often without rhyme or reason." Unsurprisingly, Universal passed on using Bloch's *Psycho II* as the basis of a film sequel, as the novel was a little too "inside baseball" for Universal to entrust its valuable property.[3]

However, both the planned unauthorized film and novel sequel demonstrated to Universal executives that the public did have an appetite for the return of Norman Bates. "Universal didn't want to do a film at all until my advance publicity on the book alerted them to the fact that people were interested in a sequel," said Bloch.[4]

That changed when, in early 1982, Universal entered an agreement with a San Diego–based production company named Oak Media Development Corporation to make four films that would air on one of the burgeoning premium cable television networks, ON TV, which existed between 1977 and 1985 and at the time was seeking to expand its share of the premium cable market. One of the project ideas that Universal offered Oak was a sequel to *Psycho*. Oak hoped the project with name recognition like *Psycho II* would be enough of a draw to get audiences to take the plunge to subscribe to the premium cable network. Executive producer Bernard Schwartz was put in charge of the project. "We had to make movies that people would first pay money to see in theaters," Schwartz said about the project. "They couldn't look like television movies of the week about athletes who overcome cancer. . . . We wanted to kick off with something special. *Psycho* had a marvelous pre-sell. We knew people would go to the theaters to see *Psycho II*."[5]

Schwartz was a recent Best Picture Academy Award nominee for *Coal Miner's Daughter*, Universal's 1980 biopic of country singer Loretta Lynn. Before that, Schwartz had moderate success as the producer of several low-budget genre films, including the blaxploitation films *Hammer* (1972), *That Man Bolt* (1973), and *Bucktown*

(1975), starring former professional football defensive back Fred Williamson.

Universal may have thought of *Psycho II* as a cheap cable movie—the project was budgeted at just $4 million, less than a fourth of the budget *Jaws 2* had five years earlier—that would inexpensively establish a franchise, but the talent behind it thought otherwise. To serve as producer, Schwartz turned to Hilton Green. Though *Psycho II* would be Green's first film as a producer, he brought with him an important pedigree. Green had a long professional relationship with Hitchcock, having served as assistant director on over forty episodes of *Alfred Hitchcock Presents* from 1956 to 1962 and as director of one episode, 1960's "Party Line." Most importantly, that experience led to Green working as the assistant director of *Psycho* when Hitchcock utilized much of his television crew to shoot the film. He would later continue to work with Hitchcock as assistant director of *Marnie* and production manager of *Family Plot* and, off-screen, as Hitchcock's "minder" on the Universal lot, where he had gotten to know Hitchcock on a personal level. Green brought an immeasurable amount of Hitchcockian authenticity to the project.

Schwartz had recently served as executive producer of an Australian thriller, titled *Road Games*, about a truck driver tailing a driver he suspects had murdered a young woman, one of several Australian road movies released in the wake of the massive box office success of 1979's *Mad Max*. Though *Road Games* fared poorly at the box office both in its native Australia and in the United States, the movie did receive several positive reviews that noted its clear Hitchcockian influences (incidentally, the film costarred Jamie Lee Curtis, who plays a young woman called Hitch, an obvious nod to Hitchcock).

To call *Road Games* director Richard Franklin a "student" of Hitchcock was not just a turn of phrase. When the Australian-born director was just twelve years old, *Psycho* made such an impression on him that he saw it five times. Deciding to become a filmmaker, he moved to the United States to attend the University of Southern California Film School, where he had the extraordinary opportunity to meet Hitchcock when he helped arrange a three-week retrospective of the director's films at USC. Hitchcock invited Franklin to the set of two of his later films, 1968's *Topaz* and 1976's *Family Plot*. A few years later, Franklin intended to film the voyeuresque *Road Games* as a version of *Rear Window* in a moving vehicle. As a devotee of the Master of Suspense, Franklin was Schwartz's first choice to pitch a concept for *Psycho II*. "I took the view that if I didn't do it, someone else would," Franklin told *Cinefantastique* in 1986. "I thought I could do justice to Hitchcock's memory better than most directors. I honestly felt that he would be well remembered by the film."[6]

At a meeting of Schwartz, Green, and Franklin, the group discussed Bloch's sequel novel. "I told them that from my understanding of Bloch's novel it was completely wrong in the first place, because Norman would never have to *escape* from an institution nowadays," Franklin recalled in a 1986 interview with *Cinefantastique*. "They would let him out. And they said, 'Wow, what a great idea. Don't read the Bloch novel, go off, get a writer and come up with a story.'"[7]

Franklin's take on the circumstances of Bates's release was certainly timely. Since the release of *Psycho* in 1960, the prevailing consensus on mental health treatment had gradually turned against institutionalizing those deemed mentally unwell except in the most extreme cases. In the United States, the Mental Health Systems Act of 1980, signed into law by President Jimmy Carter in October 1980, sought to replace institutions nationwide with mental health support systems that focused more on rehabilitation. However, the act was virtually dismantled by Congress for budgetary reasons the following year. Reports of patients with severe mental illness simply being let out into the streets with little to no treatment provisions in place, whether based on truth or the fodder of urban legends, became a growing concern throughout the early 1980s. Norman Bates being let out of mental health treatment was a scenario that tapped into a public fear that was making headlines at precisely the time the movie was being developed.

Screenwriter Tom Holland, who had written the screenplays for the 1978 television film *The Initiation of Sarah* and two 1982 films,

The Beast Within and *Class of 1984*, was hired to write the *Psycho II* screenplay after meeting with Franklin. Holland and Franklin resisted the urge to easily turn Norman, already well known for brandishing a knife, into a then-popular run-of-the-mill slasher villain not unlike Michael Myers in *Halloween* or Jason Voorhees in *Friday the 13th Part 2* and *Friday the 13th Part III*. "I didn't want to do a slasher film," Holland told *Cinefantastique* in 1986. "At the same time, as you can tell from parts of the film, there was a feeling from the studio that there should be enough shock moments to satisfy the slice-and-dice crowd out there. Given today's market, I couldn't really disagree with them a lot. If you think about it, it was *Psycho* that opened up that whole genre."[8]

The production team also incorporated other Hitchcock veterans into the production. Albert Whitlock, a member of the Visual Effects Society Hall of Fame, who had worked on the visual effects of a dozen Hitchcock films dating back to the original version of *The Man Who Knew Too Much* in 1932, was the matte artist on *Psycho II*. Peter V. Saldutti, who was the costume supervisor on *Topaz*, was the costume designer on *Psycho II*. The Directors Guild of America trainee on *Family Plot*, Don Zepfel, was the first assistant director on *Psycho II*. James R. Alexander worked on the sound mixing of both *Family Plot* and *Psycho II*. Finally, actress Virginia Gregg returned as the voice of Mother in the film. "It was the last gathering of people who worked with Alfred Hitchcock, so as a fan, it was fascinating to me," remembers Holland.[9]

Among the Hitchcock newcomers to the production team was cinematographer Dean Cundey, who had been behind the camera for several films directed or produced by John Carpenter, including 1978's *Halloween*, 1980's *The Fog*, 1981's *Escape from New York*, 1981's *Halloween II*, and 1982's *Halloween III: Season of the Witch*. Cundey would go on to film some of the most iconic special effects films of the next decade, including *Back to the Future* and its two sequels (1985–90), *Who Framed Roger Rabbit* (1988), *Jurassic Park* (1993), and *Apollo 13* (1995). Of the new cast members, the most notable was actor Robert Loggia, who plays Bates's psychiatrist, Dr. Bill Raymond. Like Miles,

Loggia was known for his extensive work in television as well as some film roles. In the 1960s, Loggia appeared in two episodes of *Alfred Hitchcock Presents* and two episodes of *The Alfred Hitchcock Hour*, though none of those four episodes had been directed by Hitchcock himself or featured Miles.

But for *Psycho II* to become a success, the film would need its most important pieces to succeed with audiences—actors from the original. The most important, of course, was Perkins, who had spent the last two decades mostly avoiding playing characters like Norman Bates. "It was frustrating," Perkins told *People* magazine in June 1983. "I had plenty of offers, but not for the lighter roles, the comedy roles I had always felt would be the main strength of my career. Even today I don't get as many of those offers as I'd like." The production team considered other choices for Bates in the instance that Perkins refused to reprise the role, with rumors claiming that Academy Award–winning actor Christopher Walken was a top choice. "Universal didn't know what they had," remembers Holland. "Richard Franklin and I knew that there was huge interest in a sequel, especially if it was any good. But we also knew that we couldn't convince Universal of that. The key to it was getting Tony Perkins to say 'Yes.' So I had to write *Psycho II* in a way that was actor's bait to get Tony. I wrote a script that had a hell of an arc for an actor. It was a standalone story with a very strong acting piece." (Holland, who began his career in the industry as an actor, also appears in the film in the small role of one of the sheriff's deputies.)[10]

Holland's screenplay toes the line between a psychological thriller and a slasher film. Two decades after the *Psycho* murders, Norman Bates is declared mentally sound and released from a mental institution, to the dismay of Lila Crane, now Lila Loomis, who loudly protests his release. Though advised against it by his therapist, Dr. Bill Raymond (played by Robert Loggia), Bates returns to his family home and motel, with the latter now run as a vice-filled flophouse by the current manager, Warren Toomey (played in the film by actor Dennis Franz, several years before achieving fame in the television show *NYPD Blue*). Bates fires Toomey, who is later murdered by a mysterious assailant, and also begins working as a short-order cook at a local diner when an older waitress, Emma Spool (played by Claudia Bryar), takes pity on his circumstances. There he begins to receive notes from Mother, and he later receives calls from "her" in the mansion. He strikes up a friendship with a waitress at the diner, Mary (played by Meg Tilly), and after inviting her to live in the mansion, he confesses that he believes he is losing his sanity or suspects that his mother is still alive. A pair of teenagers sneak into the Bates mansion to have sex (which Holland notes is his nod to the sex-filled slasher genre), and the same mysterious figure from earlier murders the male trespasser. Bates suspects that he murdered the boy after falling under the influence of Mother again. However, it is revealed that "Mother" is actually Lila Loomis, who has taken on the role of Mother in an attempt to drive Bates insane again and send him back to the asylum, and that Mary is her daughter and part of the elaborate plot. However, Lila is killed, seemingly by Bates, and Mary accidentally kills Dr. Raymond when she dresses up as Mother in an attempt to reveal to Bates that it was all a vengeance-filled lie. Mary is arrested by police and incorrectly charged with committing all the murders, leaving Bates a free man. In the film's final twist, Emma Spool visits Bates and reveals to him that she is his actual mother and that Mrs. Bates, her sister, adopted him when she was institutionalized after his birth. She claims to be the true culprit behind all the murders in the film, which she committed to protect him. Bates, now truly without his sanity, murders her and brings her body upstairs as Mother again takes over his mind. As a result, the end of *Psycho II* resets the story to put Bates back in the same situation he was in when Marion Crane arrives at the Bates Motel in the original *Psycho*—the caretaker of the motel under the influence of a dead "Mother."

Holland's script was strong enough that Perkins agreed to return as Norman Bates after reading it. "For years I'd resisted the whole idea of *Psycho* exposure," said Perkins in the *Psycho II* press kit. "I felt *Psycho* had been sufficient in itself. It was a well-constructed story. It never occurred to me there would be more juice in those characters. When I received Tom Holland's script I liked it very much. It is a well-crafted narrative which is a logical extension of the first story. It is really Norman's story."[11]

Perkins's agreement to star in the film to reprise his most famous role immediately raised the profile of the entire project. "Once Tony said yes, everything fell into place," Holland remembers. "Universal put out a press release saying that Tony Perkins was coming back to play Norman Bates in *Psycho II* and the entire world went crazy. Then Universal said, 'Whoops, wait a minute, we may have more than a cable movie here!'" (Holland is quick to add that despite the new excitement for the project, Universal "didn't give us any more money.")[12]

Shortly afterward, Miles also agreed to return for the sequel. "I had seen several scripts on a sequel to *Psycho* before, but when I read this one, I thought it was quite good," Miles was quoted in the film's press kit, possibly referring to the earlier unauthorized *Return of Norman* screenplay. "When Tony said he would do it, it made it a legitimate *Psycho II*. With Hilton as the producer, it was like coming home. The timing was right." Though Miles's Lila Loomis is revealed to have married John Gavin's Sam Loomis between the two films, as previously noted, Gavin had retired from film and was still serving as the US ambassador to Mexico (his character is depicted as having passed away before the events of *Psycho II*). Both Perkins and Miles were announced publicly as heading the cast in early July 1982, after the sequel started filming. Regarding working with Perkins again in a *Psycho* sequel, Miles said in her interview for the press kit, "22 years have gone by, and when you reach a certain age your guard goes down and you say, 'Oh well, what the hell.'"[13]

Though Miles referred to *Psycho II* as "Norman's story," Holland's script also offered Miles her most prominent film role since *Molly and Lawless John* a decade earlier and, more sensationally, her most villainous role to date. While Lila was not particularly fleshed out in the original *Psycho*, in *Psycho II*, she is driven mad from the grief of her sister's murder, exacerbated by Bates's release, which she staunchly opposes. In truth, Miles's role in *Psycho II* is far more complex than any Hitchcock himself would have likely cast her in even if she had fulfilled his vision of her becoming the successor to Grace Kelly's "quiet sex" roles in his films. The screenplay also offered an intriguing twist on the original—for much of the sequel's runtime, Norman is the timid hero, while Lila is the calculating villain. At the same time, the role is a worthy natural extension of Lila's characterization in the original film as a driven woman who refuses to take no for an answer when searching for her sister's whereabouts. The Lila of *Psycho II* is similarly driven to see Norman back in an institution by any means necessary, even putting the health and safety of her daughter on the line to exacerbate Norman's suffering. Masterfully, the story and Miles's performance help make Norman, depicted as an unsettling psychotic killer in the original film, a sympathetic character in the sequel.

Legendary art director and production designer Robert F. Boyle, another frequent Hitchcock collaborator—who worked on *Saboteur, Shadow of a Doubt, North by Northwest, The Birds,* and *Marnie*—and a longtime employee of Universal, was able to supply the production team with the architectural drawings of the house in the original *Psycho*. In addition to using the original house on the Universal Studios lot (which was moved from its location on the studio tour to a place on the lot that was a better visual match for the surrounding landscape depicted in the original film), the props department was able to find many of the props used in the original film. The Bates Motel had to be rebuilt and furnished from scratch, particularly challenging because there were no color photographs from the original set. Miles was particularly impressed by this attention to detail. "When I walked on the set, it was eerie—and miraculous," she said. "It looked like they had found 100 percent of the props from the original movie, even the pictures on the walls."[14]

Filming on the sequel began on June 30, 1982, and wrapped by late August. "We shot it in the same way that Hitchcock had shot the original," explains Holland. "Everything was done on the back lot except for the one shot at the cemetery."[15]

On May 31, 1983, Universal held a packed media screening of *Psycho II* at the Rivoli Theatre in New York City. *Variety* reported that about 150 people, including some angry critics, had to be turned away. The screening was followed by an afterparty at the infamous Studio 54 (including numerous working, but bloody, shower stalls as decorations). Perkins, Miles, and Franklin were in attendance, along with Hitchcock's daughter, Patricia Hitchcock O'Connell. Initially, Patricia Hitchcock (who herself appeared in *Psycho*), seemed cautiously positive about the potential of *Psycho II*. "I don't see why they shouldn't make a *Psycho* sequel," she told the *Los Angeles Times* after filming had wrapped on the movie but before its release. "I'm sure they're trying to be faithful. Anyway, I can't stop them." She later added, "It's too bad there isn't more imagination. On the other hand, copying is the greatest form of flattery. No material is sacred. It's what you do that's important." However, Patricia Hitchcock was undoubtedly a fan after she saw the film; in 1986, Franklin shared with *Cinefantastique* that she thanked him at the New York City screening of *Psycho II*.[16]

Another way in which the film followed its predecessor closely was in its box office success. *Psycho II* grossed $8.3 million in its opening weekend—ranking number two behind *Return of the Jedi* in its second week of release—and grossed nearly $35 million at the US box office, seven times its small budget. Executives at Universal were shocked at the success of the film. They had expected the film to put up similar numbers to 1981's *Friday the 13th Part 2* ($21.7 million) or *Halloween II* ($25.5 million), so the box office performance of *Psycho II* exceeded their expectations. "I remember Tony Perkins had a piece of the film's profits, and Universal buried it with their bookkeeping," Holland recalls. "Because Tony threatened to sue them, I got my deferment, which otherwise they never would've paid. Universal threatened Tony, saying, 'If you do this, you'll never work in Hollywood again.' Tony broke down laughing and said, 'Sure, until you need me the next time.'" Perkins was right—two years later, Universal began production on *Psycho III*, with Perkins both returning as Bates and directing the film. Though *Psycho III* was not as successful at the box office as *Psycho II*, Perkins starred in a final sequel (which also features a flashback to Norman's youth, making it also a prequel), 1990's *Psycho IV:*

The Beginning, a made-for-television movie for the premium channel Showtime that was written by original *Psycho* screenwriter Joseph Stefano. Unlike the previous three *Psycho* films, *Psycho IV: The Beginning* was shot at Universal Studios Florida in a recreated Bates Motel and house set that would, like the California originals, become part of that theme park's studio tour.[17]

Decades later, Hitchcock's *Psycho* has created a continuing franchise legacy that includes additional novels, a 1998 remake of the original film, a 2013–17 television series titled *Bates Motel*, and all manner of merchandise, fully solidifying the film as Hitchcock's most financially successful one by nearly any measure. Miles's return as Lila Crane played an important role in laying the groundwork for the franchise's continued success and serves as one of the final highlights of her acting career. While her partnership with Hitchcock may have ended disappointingly for both of them, with *Psycho II*, Miles was able to play a substantial part in a tribute to a filmmaker who once enthusiastically believed in and supported her and helped make her an in-demand actress in the late 1950s and early 1960s.

15

Vera Miles's Priority List

In hindsight, *Psycho II* probably should have been Miles's final film, as it revisited her character in her biggest box office hit and served as a tribute to Hitchcock, who gave her career a substantial boost. After *Psycho II*, Miles appeared in just three more theatrically released films—1984's *The Initiation*, 1985's *Into the Night*, and 1995's *Separate Lives*. Miles was also supposed to appear in a film titled *Fast Eddie*, but the production shut down in August 1983 after only one day of filming in Detroit because a major investor in the production pulled out. The film never restarted, and luckily Miles hadn't left for the Motor City before the shutdown. The project is representative of the less-than-stellar film projects she appeared in the final years of her career.

Of the three completed films, Miles has the most prominent role in *The Initiation*, a low-budget, independently produced slasher horror film made to cash in on the growing popularity of the horror genre at the beginning of the 1980s, the same popularity that Universal successfully tapped into with *Psycho II*. *The Initiation* is about a college student, Kelly, played by actress Daphne Zuniga, and her fellow sorority pledges who are being murdered one by one as they participate in an initiation ritual in a department store overnight. Miles plays Kelly's mother, who is hiding a deadly secret from her daughter: the murderer is Kelly's insane twin sister, who was institutionalized as an infant and whom Kelly never knew was alive. Though first-billed in the credits, Miles has a minimal role in the final product.

Miles initially agreed to do the film after meeting with the project's original director, Peter Crane, who, like Miles, had experience in television, though they had not previously worked together. However, she had worked with the film's two executive producers, actor-turned-producer Jock Gaynor and Bruce Lansbury, who had served in production roles on "Flight of the War Witch," Miles's 1980 episode of *Buck Rogers in the 25th Century*. After directing a few scenes of *The Initiation*, Crane was fired by the production team and replaced by Larry Stewart, who had directed Miles's episode of *Buck Rogers in the 25th Century*. Much of the film was shot in Dallas, and shooting finished in July 1983.

While Miles continued acting on television—most notably in three episodes of the mystery series *Murder, She Wrote*, which aired from 1985 to 1991 and starred Bruce Lansbury's sister, Angela Lansbury—her appearances became few and far between, with roles that generally typecast her as little more than a mature, sophisticated woman. It was almost sadly appropriate that her career was used as a punchline in the 1986 mystery drama film *The Morning After* starring Jane Fonda—daughter of Miles's *The Wrong Man* costar Henry Fonda—as a has-been, alcoholic actress suspected of murder and Jeff Bridges as a former policeman who believes she is innocent. At one point in the film, Fonda's character, reflecting on her lack of success in Hollywood, exclaims, "I was being groomed to be the new Vera Miles." Bridges's character replies, "Who?" with Fonda responding, "See! I was getting ready to replace somebody the public didn't even know was missing!" Bridges's character not knowing who Miles is has an additional level of irony because he is the son of Lloyd Bridges (who starred with Miles in *Pride of the Blue Grass* and *Wichita*), and he also played her son in the 1971 television movie *In Search of America*.

Unfair remark or not, Miles's career was winding down on all fronts by the 1986 release of *The Morning After*. Her April 7, 1991, appearance on *Murder, She Wrote* was her final television role. A year later, she made her final appearance on the stage, in *Driving Miss Daisy*—the

Pulitzer Prize–winning play about the relationship between an elderly Southern woman and her Black chauffeur over twenty-five years— opposite *The Love Boat* star Ted Lange at the California Theatre of the Performing Arts in San Bernardino in ten performances in April and May 1992. Speaking about the play at the California Theatre before opening night, Miles shared her thoughts about her character in words that seem to reference her own longevity and retirement: "What it is about the play that drew my interest is how true it is to the dilemma of the aging person. It's so indicative of what's going on in the world today. People are living longer, and when they reach a certain age, they become susceptible to losing an inch a day in power, in independence, in their own self-determination." The *San Bernardino County Sun* gave the production a rave review after its opening-night performance, writing, "Miles wonderfully captures the cantankerous and feisty spirit of Miss Daisy, a woman who finds herself losing her independence to age. In a multilayered performance, Miles takes full advantage of every precious moment on stage."[1]

Miles's final acting appearance essentially amounted to an extended cameo in the thriller film *Separate Lives* three years later. Though Miles is third-billed after stars James Belushi and Linda Hamilton, the part was so small that *Baltimore Sun* critic Stephen Hunter said her scenes were "obviously all shot in a single day, possibly even a single morning, before the first doughnut break."[2]

Afterward, she retired from acting and public life. Miles has since turned down all public opportunities to discuss her work as an actress after moving to Palm Desert, California, shortly before the production of *Separate Lives*, though she has privately corresponded with fans. Unfortunately, this is likely why she has since received very little recognition for her extraordinary career. Miles's accomplishments, along with her sheer longevity, would have made her an obvious honoree at any number of film festivals for retrospectives, lifetime achievement awards, and similar celebrations of her career at any point over the past three decades, if she were seeking that sort of recognition. Aside from being honored with one of the first stars on the Hollywood Walk of Fame (as such, there was no individual ceremony like those that often happen today), a Golden Boot Award by the Motion Picture and Television Fund for achievements in Western films in 1989, and the Glenn Strange Honorary Award from the New Mexico Film Critics Association in 2021 (perhaps awarded in part to recognize her for *Molly and Lawless John*, which was filmed in the state), Miles has not received the customary lifetime achievement awards and film festival honors frequently bestowed on actors and filmmakers in their later years. Similarly, Miles could have easily been a major figure on the fan convention circuit at any point over the last four decades alongside many of her contemporaries. As one of the last living actors to have worked with John Ford, Alfred Hitchcock, and Walt Disney—three of the most prominent names in twentieth-century Hollywood whose collective work continues to be widely viewed—Miles has likely had no shortage of invitations to share her memories of working during Hollywood's golden age.

Over the last few decades, Miles is most often referenced for her missed opportunity of starring in *Vertigo*, particularly as the acclaim and reverence for that film have grown. Her dozens of notable roles that she actually appeared in—most particularly, her frequent television roles that made her a near-weekly presence on the airwaves in the 1960s and 1970s—are less familiar to modern audiences. The fact that she is possibly best known for a role she didn't play has typically cast her in narratives as a tragic figure, one whose career in Hollywood was derailed by the timing of her third pregnancy. Yet Miles continued to act for thirty-five years after the release of *Vertigo* and, while she had ample opportunities to do so, has spoken very little about the missed opportunity and never expressed regret. In fact, it was Hitchcock who spoke more about Miles's "lost opportunity" far more than she ever did.

For an actress who worked constantly for several decades, even while speaking negatively about the quality of roles she was being offered in her later years, Miles deciding to retire from acting still comes as a surprise. Her children, whom she spoke so supportively about in interviews throughout her career, had long been adults by the time she began scaling back her roles. Her exit from the screen and stage was quite contrary to a remark she made in 1971 in an interview with Joan Crosby, declaring, "I figure I could go on indefinitely. They will carry me off feet first."[3]

Yet nearly two decades after Miles made that statement, she was much more reflective on her career, in an interview to promote her role in a stage production of *The Immigrant*, when the major roles in her career were long past. Reiterating that family was far more important to her than any star-making project she may have missed out on, Miles explained,

> At this stage of my life, I don't want to work as hard as I used to. I'm not endowed with any great ambition, and the good scripts are few and far between. I never wanted to be a star, anyway. And I certainly never wanted to be an aging star who is all alone because she made the wrong choices. I feel responsible for everything that has happened to me, and I'm totally happy with the decisions I've made. I've managed my life the way I've wanted and, if a few great roles were lost along the way, it was because there was something higher on the priority list.[4]

In an industry that historically is full of cautionary tales of stars who suffered from addictions, mental health issues, and other tragedies, Miles's overall outlook on stardom is refreshing. The fact that she has chosen to move on from her history and not dwell on her professional glory years as is standard in Hollywood is equally admirable. Yet it is also important not to forget just how truly remarkable Miles's career was just because she has not been vocal about her place in Hollywood history. It could not be a coincidence that so many great artists in the industry looked at her as a gifted, talented, intelligent, and beautiful actress who was constantly in demand for film and television work for nearly five decades.

While Miles may have had a stronger career and legacy if she were more of a self-promoter, especially in her later career, her place in Hollywood history is assured by her work with some of the industry's giants. If opportunities like that of *Vertigo* passed her by because she chose other, more personally fulfilling paths for her life, those were decisions she was happy to make and has continued to stand by in her retirement.

Acknowledgments

I must first acknowledge Lee Sobel, who said to me during one of our long telephone calls, "You know, nobody has ever written a book about Vera Miles."

Thank you to the staff members of the Atlantic City Free Public Library, the Academy Film Archive, the National Archives and Records Administration, and the Lilly Library at Indiana University (and Dan Ford).

This book owes a debt to three men who were extremely generous with their time and memories: David Boushey, Tom Holland, and Patrick Wayne. Special thanks also to Joel Gunz, Rebecca McCallum, and Andrew Ramage for also sharing their insight.

Last, cheers to Erin for all her support.

Notes

Preface

1. Dick Williams, "Vera Miles Star and Mother," *Los Angeles Mirror* (Los Angeles: October 11, 1958), 27.

2. Hedda Hopper, "Acting's Natural to Vera," *Los Angeles Times* (Los Angeles: November 11, 1956), F1.

3. John L. Scott, "Vera Steps Up to Stardom," *Los Angeles Times* (Los Angeles: May 27, 1956), E5; Walter Ames, "Magnetic Video Tape Gets Tryout; Vera Okays Reruns," *Los Angeles Times* (Los Angeles: October 25, 1956), A12.

4. Hedda Hopper, "Vera Miles' Screen Career Skyrockets," *Los Angeles Times* (Los Angeles: September 15, 1956), B8; Hedda Hopper, "Adler Seeks Monroe for Axelrod Movie," *Los Angeles Times* (Los Angeles: September 10, 1956), C12; Ames, "Magnetic Video Tape," A12.

5. Hopper, "Acting's Natural to Vera," F1.

6. Rebecca McCallum (writer, speaker, editor, and creator/host of the *Talking Hitchcock* podcast), interview with the author, November 2, 2023.

7. McCallum, interview.

1. From Boise City to Atlantic City

1. Barry Koltnow, "Searching for Stardom Wasn't a Priority for Proper Vera Miles," *Orange County Register* (Irvine, CA: January 10, 1989), F01.

2. Jack Edmund Nolan, "Films on TV," *Films in Review* (New York: October 1971), 498.

3. Lydia Lane, "Actress Gives Up Smoking," *Los Angeles Times* (Los Angeles: January 4, 1970), H13.

4. Lloyd Shearer, "Vera Miles: She's Alfred Hitchcock's Newest Acting Find," *Parade* (San Bernardino, CA: Sun-Telegram, January 3, 1957), 16.

5. Amy Francis, "Vera Miles Says: 'I'm Glad I Was Poor,'" *Screenland* (New York: Affiliated Magazines, Inc., May 1955), 57; Shearer, "Vera Miles," 16.

6. Shearer, "Vera Miles," 17; Vera Miles, "Future Actresses Given Advice: Stay Away from Beauty Pageants," *Madera Tribune* (Madera, CA: June 27, 1958), 5.

7. Lydia Lane, "Judging Vera by Her Inner Strength," *Los Angeles Times* (Los Angeles: September 6, 1974), F12.

8. Joe Grossman, "Models Are Models but—Their Techniques Differ," *Atlantic City Press* (Atlantic City, NJ: September 11, 1948), 7.

9. Grossman, "Models Are Models," 7.

10. Carl Clement, "I Walked Away from Fear," *Photoplay* (New York: September 1957), 111; Ellin Thompson, "The Dream That Lasts a Lifetime," *Photoplay* (New York: June 1957), 114.

11. David Boushey (founder, Society of American Fight Directors), interview with the author, March 2, 2022.

12. Miles, "Future Actresses Given Advice," 5.

13. Don Alpert, "Vera Miles—Corn-Fed Beauty Who Knows Her Oats," *Los Angeles Times* (Los Angeles: March 29, 1964), E9.

2. Vera Miles on TV and in 3D

1. John K. Newnham, "She's the Girl Who Doesn't Know," *Picturegoer* (London: December 19, 1959), 4.

2. "'Miss Kansas,' Vera Ralston, Works in Film," *Wichita Eagle* (Wichita, KS: August 26, 1951), 28.

3. "'Miss Kansas,' 28.

4. Shearer, "Vera Miles," 17.

5. Clement, "I Walked Away from Fear," 112.

6. "Fraternity Problems Are Reviewed," *New York Times* (New York: January 16, 1952), 21; Howard McClay, "Film Review: 'For Men Only,'" *Los Angeles Daily News* (Los Angeles: January 17, 1952), 25; "Henreid Scores in Three-Way Credit," *Hollywood Reporter* (Los Angeles: January 14, 1952), 3; Edwin Schallert, "'For Men Only' Exposes Hazing Sensationally," *Los Angeles Times* (Los Angeles: January 17, 1952), B9; "For Men Only," *Modern Screen* (New York: March 1952), 22.

7. Edwin Schallert, "Quinn to Portray Ryan Rival; 'Rose Bowl Story' Fetes Marshall Thompson," *Los Angeles Times* (Los Angeles: March 22, 1952), 13.

8. Steve Kahn, "Built-in Happiness," *Radio and TV Mirror* (New York: February 1961), 14.

9. "The Rose Bowl Story," *Exhibitor* (Philadelphia: August 27, 1952), 2; "'Rose Bowl Story' Lively; 'Secret People' for Arties," *Hollywood Reporter* (Los Angeles: August 22, 1952), 3.

10. "Choose Your Star," *Photoplay* (New York: August 1952), 94.

11. Howard McClay, "Everything Is Real Chummy on the Set of New 'Kettle' Film; Vera Miles in 3-Der," *Los Angeles Daily News* (Los Angeles: April 13, 1953), 19.

12. "The Charge at Feather River," *Motion Picture Daily* (New York: June 30, 1953), 6; William Brogdon, "The Charge at Feather River," *Variety* (Los Angeles: July 1, 1953), 6; Edwin Schallert, "3D Western Gets Showmanship Okay," *Los Angeles Times* (Los Angeles: July 17, 1953), 17.

13. Vernon Scott, "Hollywood Report," *Oxnard Press Courier* (Oxnard, CA: October 28, 1953), 31.

14. "What's on the Air," *Los Angeles Daily News* (Los Angeles: October 30, 1953), 51; Shearer, "Vera Miles," 17.

15. Mike Connolly, "Rambling Reporter," *Hollywood Reporter* (Los Angeles: August 7, 1953), 2.

16. Mike Connolly, "Rambling Reporter," *Hollywood Reporter* (Los Angeles: October 20, 1953), 2; "Rambling Reporter," *Hollywood Reporter* (Los Angeles: April 15, 1954), 2.

17. Hopper, "Acting's Natural to Vera," F1.

18. Hedda Hopper, "Vera's Film Career Had a Hitch in It," *Los Angeles Times* (Los Angeles: June 24, 1962), A5.

19. Clement, "I Walked Away from Fear," 112.

3. Up the Tree with Tarzan

1. "Pride of the Blue Grass," *Variety* (Los Angeles: March 24, 1954), 6; Milton Lubin, "'Blue Grass' Mild Hoss Racing Film," *Hollywood Reporter* (Los Angeles: March 22, 1954), 3.

2. Frank Scully, "Scully's Scrapbook," *Variety* (Los Angeles: October 6, 1954), 73.

3. John L. Scott, "Vera Leaps to Jungle," *Los Angeles Times* (Los Angeles: September 19, 1954), D1.

4. Clement, "I Walked Away from Fear," 112; Sheilah Graham, "Hollywood: Everybody Sings, Even Stewart," *Washington Post* (Washington, DC: July 20, 1955), B-23.

5. Boushey, interview.

6. Boushey, interview.

7. Walter Ames, "Amos Will Explain Lord's Prayer on Annual Yule Show," *Los Angeles Times* (Los Angeles: December 19, 1954), D11.

8. Ken Wayneman, "Wichitan Gains Stature as Movie Star," *Wichita Eagle* (Wichita, KS: January 23, 1955), 3.

9. "Tarzan's Hidden Jungle," *Variety* (Los Angeles: February 16, 1955), 16; "Tarzan's Hidden Jungle," *Harrison's Reports* (New York: February 19, 1955), 32.

10. "Tarzan's Hidden Jungle," *Film Bulletin* (Philadelphia: March 21, 1955), 17; "Independent Trade Reviews: 'Tarzan's Hidden Jungle,'" *Independent Film Journal* (New York: March 5, 1955), 22.

11. Desi Arnaz, "Desi Arnaz Chooses This Year's TOPS (Television's Own Promising Starlets)," *TV Guide* (Philadelphia: July 14, 1955), 6.

4. Tea in Monument Valley

1. Patrick Wayne (actor, son of John Wayne), interview with the author, September 28, 2022.

2. Wayne, interview.

3. Shearer, "Vera Miles," 17; Francis, "Vera Miles Says," 64.

4. Wayne, interview.

5. Wayne, interview.

6. Dorothy Manners, "Around Hollywood," *Middletown Times Herald* (Middletown, NY: August 15, 1955), 14.

7. Mark Hemeter, "'Fighting Trim' Vera Miles Still a Doer," *New Orleans Times-Picayune* (New Orleans: February 20, 1981), 6; "Vera Miles 'Psycho II,'" Universal News Press Department Release (Universal City, CA: April 8, 1983), 2–3.

8. Koltnow, "Searching for Stardom Wasn't a Priority for Proper Vera Miles," F01.

9. Wayne, interview.

10. Sheilah Graham, "Hollywood: Zanuck Turns to Hemingway," *Washington Evening Star* (Washington, DC: May 19, 1956), B-16; Edwin Schallert, "Kennedy, Field 'Peyton' Favorites; Big Global Group to Honor Disney," *Los Angeles Times* (Los Angeles: May 3, 1957).

11. Sheilah Graham, "Hollywood: Sheree Had to Tell," *Washington Evening Star* (Washington, DC: August 13, 1955), A-11; Sheilah Graham, "Hollywood: Gloria Has Friend, Can Wait," *Washington Evening Star* (Washington, DC: August 26, 1955), C-4; Mike Connolly, "'Emperor Jones' Remake Set," *Desert Sun* (Palm Springs, CA: February 24, 1956), 4.

12. Wayne, interview.

13. "Wichita," *Independent Film Journal* (New York: June 25, 1955), 20; Samuel D. Berns, "Wichita," *Motion Picture Daily* (New York: June 27, 1955), 6; William Brogdon, "Wichita," *Variety* (Los Angeles: June 29, 1955), 6.

14. Louella Parsons, "Hollywood: Buster Keaton's Life Due for Filming," *Philadelphia Inquirer* (Philadelphia: August 31, 1955), 22.

15. Bosley Crowther, "Screen: A New Agonizer," *New York Times* (New York: August 2, 1956), 21; "Autumn Leaves," *Picturegoer* (London: December 1, 1956), 17; Mike Connolly, "Rambling Reporter," *Hollywood Reporter* (Los Angeles: June 4, 1956), 2.

5. The New Grace Kelly

1. James Bacon, "In Hollywood . . .," *Napa Register* (Napa, CA: August 16, 1956), 18.

2. Mike Connolly, "Rambling Reporter," *Hollywood Reporter* (Los Angeles: July 1, 1954), 2; Mike Connolly, "Rambling Reporter," *Hollywood Reporter* (Los Angeles: March 28, 1955), 2.

3. Bob Thomas, "Hollywood," *Santa Cruz Sentinel* (Santa Cruz, CA: November 2, 1956), 21.

4. Herbert Coleman, *The Man Who Knew Hitchcock: A Hollywood Memoir* (Lanham, MD: Scarecrow Press, Inc., 2007), 198.

5. Joel Gunz (president of HitchCon International Alfred Hitchcock Conference and editor of *The Hitchcockian Quarterly*), interview with the author, October 26, 2023.

6. "In Review," *Motion Picture Daily* (New York: October 10, 1955), 9; Leo Guild, "Alfred Hitchcock Presents," *Hollywood Reporter* (Los Angeles: October 4, 1955), 13.

7. Shearer, "Vera Miles," 16.

8. McCallum, interview.

9. Jack Edmund Nolan, "Vera Miles," *Films in Review* (New York: May 1973), 283.

10. Erskine Johnson, "Studio Worried about Grace Being Too Nice," *Miami Daily News-Record* (Miami, OK: January 10, 1956), 8; Sheilah Graham, "Hollywood: The Aga Still Likes Rita," *Washington Evening Star* (Washington, DC: January 21, 1956), A-12.

11. Sheilah Graham, "Power Pays and Pays," *Washington Evening Star* (Washington, DC: December 7, 1955), C-6; William Brogdon, "23 Paces to Baker Street," *Variety* (Los Angeles: May 16, 1956), 18; "'23 Paces to Baker Street' with Van Johnson and Vera Miles," *Harrison's Reports* (New York: May 19, 1956), 79; "23 Paces to Baker Street," *Independent Film Journal* (New York: May 26, 1956), 45.

12. "The Searchers," *Motion Picture Daily* (New York: March 13, 1956), 4; Edwin Schallert, "Frontier Life Powerfully Depicted in 'Searchers,'" *Los Angeles Times* (Los Angeles: May 31, 1956), A6.

13. "Fonda Admires Vera Miles at Distance," *Wichita Eagle* (Wichita, KS: February 24, 1957), 23.

14. "Innocent as Charged," *Wichita Eagle* (Wichita, KS: December 30, 1956), 18.

15. Scott, "Vera Steps Up to Stardom," E1; Bob Thomas, "In Hollywood," *Napa Valley Register* (Napa, CA: May 29, 1956), 10; Erskine Johnson, "Hollywood," *Daily Ardmoreite* (Ardmore, OK: May 30, 1956), 8; Dorothy O'Leary, "Hollywood Love Life," *Screenland* (New York: November 1956), 16.

16. Coleman, *The Man Who Knew Hitchcock*, 169–70, 227.

17. Richard Freedman, "Actress Miles Dispels 'Gossip' about Hitchcock," *Syracuse Herald American Stars Magazine* (Syracuse, NY: June 26, 1983), 8.

18. McCallum, interview.

19. McCallum, interview.

20. Richard Gertner, "Review: *The Wrong Man*," *Motion Picture Daily* (New York: December 21, 1956), 4; "'The Wrong Man' with Henry Fonda and Vera Miles," *Harrison's Reports* (New York: December 22, 1956), 204; A. H. Weiler, "Screen: New Format for Hitchcock," *New York Times* (New York: December 24, 1956), 8; "The Wrong Man," *Variety* (Los Angeles: January 2, 1957), 8; "The Wrong Man," *Film Bulletin* (Philadelphia: January 7, 1957), 10; "The Wrong Man," *Motion Picture Exhibitor* (Philadelphia: January 9, 1957), 3.

21. François Truffaut, *Hitchcock* (New York: Simon & Schuster, 1967), 243.

22. Ernie Player, "The Wrong Man for Vera Miles," *Picturegoer* (London: March 9, 1957), 11.

23. Gunz, interview.

24. McCallum, interview.

6. Singing, Dancing, Scandal

1. "Hitchcock's Latest Discovery Described 'Earthy Grace Kelly,'" *Daily Blade Tribune* (Oceanside, CA: April 27, 1956), 3.

2. Bob Thomas, "In Hollywood," *Napa Valley Register* (Napa, CA: May 29, 1956), 10; Sheilah Graham, "Hollywood: A Sizzling Combination," *Washington Evening Star* (Washington, DC: February 16, 1956), C-7; Harry MacArthur, "The Passing Show: Mindy's Voice Is Ready Whenever the Show Is," *Washington Evening Star* (Washington, DC: April 9, 1956), B-10; Hedda Hopper, "Hope Signs Catlett to Portray Al Smith," *Los Angeles Times* (Los Angeles: July 21, 1956), 12.

3. "The WW Variety Show," *Desert Sun* (Palm Springs, CA: January 10, 1957), 4; "Announcing PHOTOPLAY'S Award Winners of 1956–'57," *Photoplay* (New York: March 1957), 84; Sheilah Graham, "Hollywood: Jerry Lewis Pens Life Story," *Washington Evening Star* (Washington, DC: August 10, 1956), A-18; "Hollywood Lowdown," *Screenland Plus TV-Land* (Dunellen, NJ: September 1956), 8; Sheilah Graham, "Hollywood: 'Good Earth' for Frankie?," *Washington Evening Star* (Washington, DC: October 3, 1956), D-8.

4. Bob Thomas, "Color-Conscious Actresses Sometimes Dress in Extreme," *San Bernardino Sun* (San Bernardino, CA: July 17, 1956), 5; James Bacon, "Photographing Vera Miles Brings Film Controversy," *Santa Cruz Sentinel* (Santa Cruz, CA: March 17, 1957), 24.

5. "For Wichita's Vera Miles, Moviedom Has Spent $42,000 in Full Starmaking Effort," *Wichita Eagle* (Wichita, KS: April 30, 1957), 6A.

6. Gunz, interview.

7. Bacon, "Photographing Vera Miles," 24.

8. Bacon, "In Hollywood . . . ," 18; Ron Burton, "Hollywood Film Shop," *Daily Blade Tribune* (Oceanside, CA: November 28, 1956), 3.

9. Thomas M. Pryor, "Hollywood Film Shop," *New York Times* (New York: July 29, 1956), 5.

10. Mel Shavelson and Jack Rose, "On Hailing His Honor," *New York Times* (New York: June 16, 1957), 7.

11. Sherwin Kane, "Beau James," *Motion Picture Daily* (New York: June 7, 1957), 3; "Beau James," *Motion Picture Exhibitor* (Philadelphia: June 12, 1957), 2; "'Beau James' with Bob Hope, Vera Miles, Paul Douglas and Alexis Smith," *Harrison's Reports* (New York: June 8, 1957), 92; "Beau James," *Variety* (Los Angeles: June 12, 1957), 6; Philip K. Scheuer, "'Beau James' Brings Back 20s," *Los Angeles Times* (Los Angeles: June 9, 1957), F1; "Beau James," *Film Bulletin* (Philadelphia: June 24, 1957), 12; Howard Thompson, "'Beau James' Stars Bob Hope at the Astor," *New York Times* (New York: June 27, 1957), 21.

7. The Woman in the Gray Suit

1. Mike Connolly, "Rambling Reporter," *Hollywood Reporter* (Los Angeles: November 26, 1956), 2; Mike Connolly, "Rambling Reporter," *Hollywood Reporter* (Los Angeles: November 27, 1956), 2.

2. Shearer, "Vera Miles," 16.

3. Shearer, "Vera Miles," 16.

4. "Hollywood Goes to a Ball," *Photoplay* (New York: May 1957), 90.

5. Clement, "I Walked Away from Fear," 110.

6. Sheilah Graham, "Yul Almost Missed the Oscar," *Washington Evening Star* (Washington, DC: March 30, 1957), B-10; Jay Carmody, "The Dingle Bay Irish Got Lindbergh There," *Washington Evening Star* (Washington, DC: April 4, 1957), C-6.

7. Gunz, interview.

8. Bill Davidson, "Alfred Hitchcock Resents," *Saturday Evening Post* (Philadelphia: December 15, 1962), 63; Mike Connolly, "Rambling Reporter," *Hollywood Reporter* (Los Angeles: September 17, 1958), 2.

9. Gunz, interview.

10. Sheilah Graham, "Hollywood: A Moral Somewhere," *Washington Evening Star* (Washington, DC: April 21, 1961), B-7.

11. Sidney Gottlieb, ed., *Alfred Hitchcock: Interviews* (Jackson: University Press of Mississippi, 2003), 65; "The Inside Story," *Modern Screen* (New York: August 1957), 4.

12. Alpert, "Vera Miles—Corn-Fed Beauty," E9; "Vera Miles Airs Dislike of Hollywood 'Barrier,'" *Hollywood Citizen-News* (Los Angeles, May 16, 1968), A-7.

13. Coleman, *The Man Who Knew Hitchcock*, 256–57.

14. Gunz, interview.

15. Thomas M. Pryor, "$200,000,000 Tag Put on New Stars," *New York Times* (New York: April 24, 1957), 27.

16. Lydia Lane, "Vera Miles Loses 10 Pounds Quickly by Avoiding Overprocessed Foods," *Los Angeles Times* (Los Angeles: April 28, 1957), E13.

17. "Gordon Scotts Change Name Legally to—Scott," *Los Angeles Times* (Los Angeles: July 12, 1957), 2; Carl Clement, "Vera Miles' Nine-Month Beauty Course," *Photoplay* (New York: November 1957), 110.

18. Clement, "Vera Miles' Nine-Month Beauty Course," 77; Hedda Hopper, "Borgnine Fee Now $125,000 per Film," *Los Angeles Times* (Los Angeles: January 11, 1958), B2.

19. "Hollywood Fatal to Live Television," *Wichita Eagle* (Wichita, KS: July 11, 1958), 17.

20. "TV Review," *New York Times* (New York: November 29, 1957), 49; "Playhouse 90," *Variety* (Los Angeles: December 4, 1957), 34.

21. Ernie Player, "The Hitch in Her Career," *Picturegoer* (London: February 21, 1959), 4.

8. Bald in Italy

1. Hedda Hopper, "Vera Raps Big Pay of Stars," *Los Angeles Times* (Los Angeles: March 1, 1959), F1.

2. Hedda Hopper, "Linda Christian Predicts Marriage," *Los Angeles Times* (Los Angeles: June 20, 1959), A5.

3. "The FBI Story," *Variety* (Los Angeles: August 19, 1959), 6; "'The FBI Story' with James Stewart, Vera Miles," *Harrison's Reports* (New York: August 22, 1959), 134; "The FBI Story," *Film Bulletin* (Philadelphia: August 17, 1959), 10; Bosley Crowther, "Screen: 'F.B.I. Story,'" *New York Times* (New York: September 25, 1959), 23; Hedda Hopper, "Robson Seeks Five Names for 'Terrace,'" *Los Angeles Times* (Los Angeles: September 14, 1959), C10.

4. Bob Thomas. "In Hollywood . . .," *Napa Register* (Napa, CA: September 29, 1960), 6.

5. Sheilah Graham, "Jungle's Not So Rugged the Way Tarzan Lives," *Washington Evening Star* (Washington, DC: March 1, 1959), C-8.

6. Sheilah Graham, "Hollywood," *Washington Evening Star* (Washington, DC: December 12, 1958), A40; "Beyond This Place," *Variety* (Los Angeles: May 6, 1959), 6; "Web of Evidence," *Harrison's Reports* (New York: September 19, 1959), 150.

7. Hopper, "Vera Raps Big Pay of Stars," F5.

8. Hedda Hopper, "Hawks Will Film Adventure Story," *Los Angeles Times* (Los Angeles: June 30, 1959), C8.

9. Peer J. Oppenheimer, "Shear Madness," *Lawton Constitution and Morning Press* (Lawton, OK: November 15, 1959), 39; James Bacon, "Inside Hollywood," *Independent Star-News* (Pasadena, CA: December 20, 1959), 59.

10. Hopper, "Vera's Film Career Had a Hitch in It," A5.

11. Bacon, "Inside Hollywood," 59.

12. Andrew Ramage (editor of *Forgotten Gems from the Twilight Zone, Vol. 1* and webmaster of *The Twilight Zone Museum* website), interview with the author, March 20, 2023.

13. Ramage, interview.

14. Mike Connolly, "Rambling Reporter," *Hollywood Reporter* (Los Angeles: August 19, 1958), 2; Dorothy Manners, "Hollywood Talk," *Sarasota News* (Sarasota, FL: July14, 1959), 16.

15. Erskine Johnson, "Hollywood Glances!," *Miami Daily News Record* (Miami, OK: July 29, 1959), 8; Sidney Skolsky, "Hollywood Is My Beat," *Los Angeles Evening Citizen News* (Los Angeles: July 29, 1959), 18; Mike Connolly, "Rambling Reporter," *Hollywood Reporter* (Los Angeles: August 11, 1959), 2; Mike Connolly, "Rambling Reporter," *Hollywood Reporter* (Los Angeles: August 26, 1959), 2.

16. "No Vine, No Car, Tarzan Has to Walk," *Van Nuys News* (Van Nuys, CA: October 8, 1959), 54; Sheilah Graham, "Vegas Calls Joan Crawford," *Washington Evening Star* (Washington, DC: October 30, 1959), B-7.

17. "Vera Miles Sheds Screen's Tarzan," *Los Angeles Times* (Los Angeles: March 3, 1960), B1; Louella O. Parsons, "Tarzan Is Left in Tree by Jane, but Vera Not Sour on Marriage," *Sarasota News* (Sarasota, FL: March 20, 1960), 8; Harrison Carroll, "Behind the Scenes in Hollywood," *Brazil Daily Times* (Brazil, IN: August 16, 1960), 7.

18. Richard Lamparski, *Whatever Became Of? Tenth Series* (New York: Crown, 1986), 160.

19. Mitchell Smyth, "Tarzan the Ape Man Is Still Swinging," *Toronto Star* (Toronto: May 3, 1987), D4.

9. Scream Queen

1. Jim Steranko, "A Nice Quiet Evening with Robert Bloch," *Halls of Horror* (London: 1982), 6.

2. Stephen Rebello, *Alfred Hitchcock and the Making of "Psycho"* (New York: Dembner Books, 1990), 65.

3. McCallum, interview.

4. Coleman, *The Man Who Knew Hitchcock*, 290.

5. Marc Shapiro, "Hitchcock's Throwaway Masterpiece," *Los Angeles Times* (Los Angeles: May 27, 1990), 6.

6. Sheilah Graham, "Hollywood Lowdown," *Screenland Plus TV-Land* (New York: May 1960), 59.

7. Hedda Hopper, "Juliette Greco Set in Adler Film," *Los Angeles Times* (Los Angeles: October 10, 1959), 8; Parsons, "Tarzan Is Left in Tree," 8.

8. McCallum, interview.

9. James W. Merrick, "Hitchcock Regimen for a 'Psycho,'" *New York Times* (New York: December 27, 1959), X7.

10. Parsons, "Tarzan Is Left in Tree," 8.

11. Jack Harrison, "Alfred Hitchcock's 'Psycho' Is a Top Mystery Thriller," *Hollywood Reporter* (Los Angeles: June 17, 1960), 3; Gene Arneel, "Psycho," *Variety* (Los Angeles: June 22, 1960), 6; "Psycho," *Film Bulletin* (Philadelphia: June 27, 1960), 45; Dwight MacDonald, "Films," *Esquire* (New York: October 1960), 42; Bosley Crowther, "Screen: Sudden Shocks," *New York Times* (New York: June 17, 1960), 37; Bosley Crowther, "The Year's Best Films," *New York Times* (New York: December 25, 1960), X3.

12. Shapiro, "Hitchcock's Throwaway Masterpiece," 6.

13. Gene Arneel, "Passed Up Wages, Alfred Hitchcock's Before-Takes 'Psycho' Take of $5-Mil.," *Variety* (Los Angeles: September 21, 1960), 1.

14. Cecil Smith, "Hitchcock's 'Incident' Adds Luster to NBC's Startime," *Los Angeles Times* (Los Angeles: April 6, 1960), A13; "TV in Review," the *Logan Herald Journal* (Logan, UT: April 6, 1960), 15.

15. Parsons, "Tarzan Is Left in Tree," 8.

16. Cecil Smith, "Hitch Turns Off Relieving Humor," *Los Angeles Times* (Los Angeles: April 5, 1960), A10.

17. Earl Wilson, "Real Gent," *Desert Sun* (Palm Springs, CA: February 11, 1960), 4.

18. "A Touch of Larceny," *Film Bulletin* (Philadelphia: January 18, 1960), 13; John L. Scott, "'A Touch of Larceny' Droll Story of Hoax," *Los Angeles Times* (Los Angeles: January 28, 1960), B7; A. H. Weiler, "'A Touch of Larceny' at the Normandie," *New York Times* (New York: March 17, 1960), 28; James Meade, "Great Film Scenes Recalled," *Desert Sun* (Palm Springs, CA: August 21, 1974), B12.

19. James Powers, "'Pollyanna' Pure Delight; '5 Branded Women' Jumbled," *Hollywood Reporter* (Los Angeles: April 6, 1960), 3; Hopper, "Vera's Film Career Had a Hitch in It," A5.

20. Sheilah Graham, "Hollywood," *Washington Evening Star* (Washington, DC: July 14, 1960), C16.

21. Hopper, "Vera's Film Career Had a Hitch in It," A5; Donald Freeman, "She Likes Not Having 'Image,'" *Fort Worth Star-Telegram* (Fort Worth, TX: March 21, 1965), 38.

22. Rebello, *Alfred Hitchcock and the Making of "Psycho,"* 91.

23. Richard T. Cloonan, "Hitchcock Uses Simple Formula to Win Success," *Washington Evening Star* (Washington, DC: December 30, 1962), 4.

24. Nolan, "Vera Miles," 283; Gabe Essoe, *The Book of Movie Lists* (Westport, CT: Arlington House, 1981), 150.

25. Hemeter, "'Fighting Trim,'" 6.

26. Karen Butler, "'Hitchcock' Star Jessica Biel Says It's Hard to Balance Fame, Privacy," UPI Entertainment, November 25, 2012, https://www.upi.com/Enter tainment_News/Movies/2012/11/25/Hitchcock-star-Jessica-Biel-says-its-hard-to -balance-fame-privacy/52141353821040/ (accessed October 12, 2022).

10. Print the Legend

1. "Vera Miles Weds Television Actor," *Ada Evening News* (Ada, OK: July 20, 1960), 8.

2. Hedda Hopper, "Vera Miles, Actress, Wed in Vegas," *Los Angeles Times* (Los Angeles: July 20, 1960), 21.

3. Kahn, "Built-in Happiness," 72; Hopper, "Vera's Film Career Had a Hitch in It," A5.

4. Sheilah Graham, "How Scattered the Stars," *Washington Evening Star* (Washington, DC: September 7, 1960), D-11; Sheilah Graham, "Relaxed in Manhattan," *Washington Evening Star* (Washington, DC: September 26, 1960), D-10; Ruth Waterbury, "Hollywood Tie-Line," *Los Angeles Times* (Los Angeles: October 2, 1960), A3.

5. Kahn, "Built-in Happiness," 71–72.

6. Coleman, *The Man Who Knew Hitchcock*, 356.

7. "Hollywood Roundup," *Weekly Television Digest* (Radnor, PA: December 12, 1960), 8.

8. Nolan, "Vera Miles," 286; John L. Scott, "Shirley Plays All Types," *Los Angeles Times* (Los Angeles: December 18, 1960), B4.

9. Hedda Hopper, "Vera Miles Stars in 'Back Street,'" *Los Angeles Times* (Los Angeles: September 2, 1960), 26.

10. "Only Hunter Made the Most of Vera's Looks," *Washington Evening Star* (Washington, DC: August 4, 1963), E10.

11. "Back Street," *Variety* (Los Angeles: October 11, 1961), 6; "Back Street," *Harrison's Reports* (New York: October 7, 1961), 158; John L. Scott, "Romantic Troubles Glamour-Wrapped," *Los Angeles Times* (Los Angeles: October 27, 1961), B8.

12. Eleni Sakes Epstein, "Fashion Is Making Great Comeback in Hollywood," *Washington Evening Star* (Washington, DC: November 18, 1960), C5.

13. Hemeter, "'Fighting Trim,'" 6; Geoffrey M. Warren, "'The Country Girl' Revival Disappoints," *Los Angeles Times* (Los Angeles: February 22, 1961), C11; "Vera Miles Shines as 'Country Girl,'" *Hollywood Citizen-News* (Los Angeles: February 17, 1961), 16.

14. Mad Sylos, "Tarzana-Woodland Hills Mad Chatter," *Van Nuys Valley News* (Van Nuys, CA: August 27, 1961), 16.

15. James Powers, "The Deadly," *Hollywood Reporter* (Los Angeles: November 6, 1961), 3; Philip K. Scheuer, "Stevens Film Goes to United Artists," *Los Angeles Times* (Los Angeles: November 7, 1961), C9; "The Deadly," *Variety* (Los Angeles: November 11, 1961), 64; Mad Sylos, "Tarzana-Woodland Hills Mad Chatter," *Van Nuys Valley News* (Van Nuys, CA: November 21, 1961), 14.

16. Hedda Hopper, "Jerry Wald Signs Susan Strasberg," *Los Angeles Times* (Los Angeles: August 24, 1961), B12.

17. Wayne, interview.

18. Hopper, "Vera's Film Career Had a Hitch in It," A5.

19. "The Man Who Shot Liberty Valance," *Variety* (Los Angeles: April 11, 1962), 6; "The Man Who Shot Liberty Valance," *Film Bulletin* (Philadelphia: April 14, 1962), 12; "The Man Who Shot Liberty Valance," *Box Office* (Kansas City, MO: April 16, 1962), 12; "The Man Who Shot Liberty Valance," *Harrison's Reports* (New York: April 21, 1962), 58.

20. Lane Crockett, "Veteran Actress Vera Miles Says the Hardest Thing about Making 'Hijacking of the Achille Lauro,'" *USA Today* (Arlington, VA: January 26, 1989).

11. The Disney Mom

1. Cecil Smith, "So Now Back to Normalcy, Maybe," *Los Angeles Times* (Los Angeles: October 5, 1962), C12; Sidney Skolsky, "Out of the Mouths of Celebrities," *Hollywood Citizen News* (Los Angeles: December 7, 1962), 9.

2. Cecil Smith, "'The Disenchanted' Uneven, but Shows Some Promise," *Los Angeles Times* (Los Angeles: May 10, 1965), C17.

3. Robert Osborne, "Rambling Reporter," *Hollywood Reporter* (Los Angeles: August 18, 1993), 5.

4. Margaret Harford, "'Rain' Revived on Pasadena Stage," *Los Angeles Times* (Los Angeles: March 9, 1963), B7; "'Rain,' 41 Yrs. Old, Still Good Drama," *Hollywood Citizen-News* (Los Angeles: March 8, 1963), A-6; Bill De Muth, "Talent Pours at Playhouse," *Arcadia Tribune* (Temple City, CA: March 10, 1963), 4.

5. Charles Witbeck, "Unites Career, Family," *Record* (Hackensack, NJ: May 4, 1964), 22.

6. "'Tiger Walks' for Miles Around," *Salt Lake Tribune* (Salt Lake City, UT: March 23, 1964), 24. "Three Disney Channel Stars Remember Walt," *Disney Channel Magazine* (Burbank, CA: February 1984), inside front cover.

7. Freeman, "She Likes Not Having 'Image,'" 38.

8. Howard Pearson, "All for the Best," *Deseret News* (Salt Lake City, UT: May 19, 1966), 29.

9. "A Tiger Walks," *Variety* (Los Angeles: March 18, 1964), 7; Margaret Harford, "'Calloways' Pleasant Family Screen Fare," *Los Angeles Times* (Los Angeles: February 12, 1965), C12; Eugene Archer, "'Calloways' at Forum," *New York Times* (New York: April 15, 1965), 38; Bosley Crowther, "The Screen: 'Follow Me, Boys!' Opens," *New York Times* (New York: December 2, 1966), 45; Philip K. Scheuer, "'Follow Me Boys' Out of the Past," *Los Angeles Times* (Los Angeles: December 26, 1966), D27.

10. Sheilah Graham, "Hollywood," *Washington Evening Star* (Washington, DC: April 28, 1958), A-13; John Finlayson, "Hitchcock Had Plans for Her," *Washington Evening Star Sunday Star TV Magazine* (Washington, DC: April 23, 1961), 4.

11. Sheilah Graham, "Liz, Dick Seek New York Abode," *Washington Evening Star* (Washington, DC: April 15, 1965), 38.

12. Alpert, "Vera Miles—Corn-Fed Beauty," E9.

13. Hedda Hopper, "Walter O'Malley on Melchior's Safari," *Los Angeles Times* (Los Angeles: June 2, 1964), C8; Hedda Hopper, "Hope's Tour May Include Son's Base," *Los Angeles Times* (Los Angeles: August 23, 1965), C23.

14. Hal Humphrey, "Vera Advises TV to 'Love a Little,'" *Los Angeles Times* (Los Angeles: May 22, 1964), C17.

15. "No Sex Movies, Says Vera Miles," *Oxnard Press Courier* (Oxnard, CA: November 14, 1964), 39; Cecil Smith, "Specials Brighten Pattern of Reruns," *Los Angeles Times* (Los Angeles: June 3, 1964), C14.

16. Ernest Thompson, "One for the Show," *Ada Evening News* (Ada, OK: October 17, 1965), 10.

17. Rick Du Brow, "Useless Woman Character Mars Otherwise Good TV Drama," *Lawton Constitution* (Lawton, OK: October 11, 1963), 6; Cecil Smith, "Two-Part Shows Just 7-Day Wait," *Los Angeles Times* (Los Angeles: October 11, 1963), D14; "Kraft Suspense Theatre (The Case Against Paul Ryker)," *Variety* (Los Angeles: October 16, 1963), 31.

18. Kevin Thomas, "'Sergeant Ryker' in Multiple Release," *Los Angeles Times* (Los Angeles: May 24, 1968), C12.

19. Witbeck, "Unites Career, Family," 22.

20. Hedda Hopper, "Barbara: Everything's Coming Up Black, Blue," *Los Angeles Times* (Los Angeles: March 15, 1964), D11.

21. Witbeck, "Unites Career, Family," 22.

22. Cecil Smith, "Amateur Night at the Movies," *Los Angeles Times* (Los Angeles: May 24, 1968), C12; Paul Gardner, "TV: New Film of 'Ride the Pink Horse,'" *New York Times* (New York: November 19, 1964), 79.

23. Hedda Hopper, "Vera Miles Seeks Cosmopolitan Life: She, Husband Keith Larsen Quit Barefoot-Jeans Routine," *Los Angeles Times* (Los Angeles: March 27, 1964), C10.

24. Alpert, "Vera Miles—Corn-Fed Beauty," E9.

12. A Disaster in the Philippines

1. Dick Kleiner, "Women 'Lost' Claims Actress," *Pittsburgh Press Sun* (Pittsburgh: August 30, 1964), 9.

2. Kleiner, "Women 'Lost,'" 9; Freeman, "She Likes Not Having 'Image,'" 35.

3. Freeman, "She Likes Not Having 'Image,'" 35–36.

4. Freeman, "She Likes Not Having 'Image,'" 35; Louella O. Parsons, "Louella's Hollywood," *Tyler Courier-Times* (Tyler, TX: April 4, 1965), 2.

5. Sidney Skolsky, "The Mail Bag: Your Column," *Hollywood Citizen-News* (Los Angeles: February 4, 1966), A-6.

6. Sidney Skolsky, "The Mail Bag: Your Column," *Hollywood Citizen-News* (Los Angeles: March 4, 1966), B-6.

7. Dick Kleiner, "Christine Kaufmann Un-Retires," *Santa Cruz Sentinel* (Santa Cruz, CA: December 11, 1966), 33.

8. Dick Kleiner, "Show Boat: The Vietnam War Affects Sounds of Tijuana Brass," *Santa Cruz Sentinel* (Santa Cruz, CA: April 18, 1967), 8; Nolan, "Vera Miles," 286.

9. Dick Kleiner, "If Robin Is Drafted, Batman Will Get Girl," *Santa Cruz Sentinel* (Santa Cruz, CA: February 26, 1967), 38.

10. Vernon Scott, "Vernon Scott's Hollywood," *Cumberland News* (Cumberland, MD: August 9, 1968), 5.

11. Arthur D. Murphy, "Mission Batangas," *Variety* (Los Angeles: November 13, 1968), 6; Vic Wilmot, "Vic Wilmot," *Arizona Republic* (Phoenix, AZ: April 4, 1969), 42.

12. Jimmy Johnson, "Marshal Wants to Live," *San Bernardino Sun* (San Bernardino, CA: December 27, 1972), C-3.

13. Kleiner, "Christine Kaufmann Un-Retires," 33.

14. George H. Jackson, "Behind the Scenes in Hollywood," *Sidney Telegraph* (Sidney, NE: August 7, 1967), 4; Whitney Williams, "Kona Coast," *Variety* (Los Angeles: May 8, 1968), 6.

15. Nolan, "Vera Miles," 288.

16. Susan Strasberg, *Bittersweet* (New York: Signet, 1981) 222; Michael Munn, *John Wayne: The Man behind the Myth* (New York: New American Library, 2004), 284; "An Eye on Hollywood," *Van Nuys News* (Van Nuys, CA: March 29, 1968), 25.

17. Whitney Williams, "Hellfighters," *Variety* (Los Angeles: November 27, 1968), 6; "Hellfighters," *Box Office* (Kansas City, MO: December 2, 1968), A11.

13. *Molly* and Dinner with Ms. Miles

1. "Vera Miles Airs Dislike," A-7.

2. Allen Rich, "An Actress with Something to Say," *Hollywood Citizen-News* (Los Angeles: January 29, 1969), B-8.

3. Howard Thompson, "'Wild Country' and Western Pioneers," *New York Times* (New York: February 11, 1971), 55; Kevin Thomas, "'Wild Country' Opens Multiple Engagements," *Los Angeles Times* (Los Angeles: February 12, 1971), E20; Whitney Williams, "The Wild Country," *Variety* (Los Angeles: January 13, 1971), 24.

4. Joan Crosby, "No Complaints for Vera Miles," *Ardmore Daily Ardmoreite* (Ardmore, OK: August 8, 1971), 8.

5. Joe Leydon, "Sam Elliott," *Cowboys and Indians*, October 15, 2013, https:// www.cowboysindians.com/2013/10/sam-elliott-1/ (accessed October 12, 2022).

6. Kevin Thomas, "Movie Review: 'Molly,'" *Los Angeles Times* (Los Angeles: December 15, 1972), F26; Arthur D. Murphy, "Molly and Lawless John," *Variety* (Los Angeles: December 27, 1972), 20.

7. Nolan, "Vera Miles," 287.

8. Kevin Thomas, "A Tragedy to Identify With," *Los Angeles Times* (Los Angeles: October 18, 1972), E22; Howard Thompson, "A.B.C. Recounts 'Great American Tragedy,'" *New York Times* (New York: October 18, 1972), 95.

9. Tom Jones, "Vivacious Actress Vera Miles Had Planned to Be a Teacher," *Robesonian* (Lumberton, NC: September 22, 1976), 6.

10. "Stars and Their Daughters," *Independent Press-Telegram* (Long Beach, CA: November 5, 1972), 20.

11. "Mother, Daughter Share Showbiz," *Marshall Evening Chronicle* (Marshall, MI: September 8, 1973), 4.

12. Joan Crosby, "Label Vera Miles a Top Animal Lover," *Ardmore Daily Ardmoreite* (Ardmore, OK: June 10, 1973), 10.

13. Crosby, "Label Vera Miles a Top Animal Lover," 10.

14. Linda Gross, "'Castaway Cowboy' in Hawaii," *Los Angeles Times* (Los Angeles: August 7, 1974), F12; Howard Thompson, "Film: 'Castaway Cowboy,'" *New York Times* (New York: August 15, 1974), 25; Whitney Williams, "The Castaway Cowboy," *Variety* (Los Angeles: July 24, 1974), 20.

15. Jones, "Vivacious Actress Vera Miles," 6.

16. Ron Pennington, "Curtain Calls," *Hollywood Reporter* (Los Angeles: February 12, 1981), 24.

17. Joyce Macey, "Our Cook Likes to Add Her Own 'Finishing Touches,'" *Suburbanite Economist* (Chicago: November 13, 1974), 143.

18. Peggy Blizzard, "'Same Time' Funny, Touching, Tender," *Tustin News* (Tustin, CA: October 26, 1978), 4; John C. Mahoney, "Fine Touch of Dinner-Theater," *Los Angeles Times* (Los Angeles: December 30, 1978), B8.

19. John C. Mahoney, "Vera Miles Gives 'Ping Pong' Bounce,'" *Los Angeles Times* (Los Angeles: November 5, 1980), 16; Ron Pennington, "Ping Pong," *Hollywood Reporter* (Los Angeles: November 7, 1980), 14.

20. Stuart Byron, "I Can't Get Jimmy Carter to See My Movie," *Film Comment* (New York: March–April 1977), 46.

21. "Three Disney Channel Stars Remember Walt."

14. The Return of Lila Crane

1. Eric Kasum, "Just When the Gore Was Getting Thick, 'Psycho II,'" *Los Angeles Times* (Los Angeles: August 31, 1981), M7.

2. Kyle Counts, "Psycho II—The Return of Norman," *Cinefantastique* (Oak Park, IL: February 1982), 4.

3. Edward Gross, "*Psycho II*," *Cinefantastique* (Oak Park, IL: March 1986), 31.

4. Gross, "*Psycho II*," 31.

5. Aljean Harmetz, "After 22 Years, 'Psycho' Sequel," *New York Times* (New York: August 11, 1982), C17.

6. Gross, "*Psycho II*," 53.

7. Gross, "*Psycho II*," 31.

8. Gross, "*Psycho II*," 53.

9. Tom Holland (filmmaker, screenwriter of *Psycho II*), interview with the author, March 9, 2022.

10. Brad Darrach, "Return of *Psycho*," *PEOPLE* (New York: June 13, 1983). Holland, interview.

11. "*Psycho II* Press Information," (Universal City, CA: Universal News Press Department Release, April 8, 1983), 3–4.

12. Holland, interview.

13. "Vera Miles 'Psycho II,'" Universal News Press Department Release (Universal City, CA: April 8, 1983), 1.

14. Harmetz, "After 22 Years," C17.

15. Holland, interview.

16. Nancy Mills, "Shadow of a Doubt over Hitchcock Film Rights," *Los Angeles Times* (Los Angeles: November 21, 1982), P25.

17. Holland, interview.

15. Vera Miles's Priority List

1. Owen Sheeran, "'Miss Daisy' Drives into Town Tonight," *San Bernardino County Sun* (San Bernardino, CA: April 23, 1992), 105; Owen Sheeran, "'Daisy' a Joy, Beginning to End," *San Bernardino County Sun* (San Bernardino, CA: April 24, 1992), 2.

2. Stephen Hunter, "'Separate Lives' Plods Through a Predictable Mystery Formula, and Yet . . .," *Baltimore Sun* (Baltimore, MD: September 11, 1995), https://www.baltimoresun.com/news/bs-xpm-1995-09-11-1995254118-story.html (accessed October 12, 2022).

3. Crosby, "No Complaints for Vera Miles," 8.

4. Koltnow, "Searching for Stardom Wasn't a Priority for Proper Vera Miles," F01.

Index

Index

Index

Index

Index

Index

Index

Index

Index

Index